MENTAL CAUSATION

Our minds have physical effects. This happens, for instance, when we move our bodies when we act. How is this possible? Thomas Kroedel defends an account of mental causation in terms of difference-making: if our minds had been different, the physical world would have been different; therefore, the mind causes events in the physical world. His account not only explains how the mind has physical effects at all, but solves the exclusion problem – the problem of how those effects can have both mental and physical causes. It is also unprecedented in scope, because it is available to dualists about the mind as well as physicalists, drawing on traditional views of causation as well as on the latest developments in the field of causal modelling. It will be of interest to a range of readers in philosophy of mind and philosophy of science. This book is also available as Open Access on Cambridge Core.

THOMAS KROEDEL is Professor of Philosophy of Science at the University of Hamburg. He has published articles in journals including *Analysis, Noûs* and *The British Journal for the Philosophy of Science*.

MENTAL CAUSATION

A Counterfactual Theory

THOMAS KROEDEL

University of Hamburg

CAMBRIDGE
UNIVERSITY PRESS

University Printing House, Cambridge CB2 8BS, United Kingdom

One Liberty Plaza, 20th Floor, New York, NY 10006, USA

477 Williamstown Road, Port Melbourne, VIC 3207, Australia

314–321, 3rd Floor, Plot 3, Splendor Forum, Jasola District Centre,
New Delhi – 110025, India

79 Anson Road, #06–04/06, Singapore 079906

Cambridge University Press is part of the University of Cambridge.

It furthers the University's mission by disseminating knowledge in the pursuit of
education, learning, and research at the highest international levels of excellence.

www.cambridge.org
Information on this title: www.cambridge.org/9781108487146
DOI: 10.1017/9781108762717

© Thomas Kroedel 2020

This work is in copyright. It is subject to statutory exceptions and to the provisions of relevant
licensing agreements; with the exception of the Creative Commons version the link for which
is provided below, no reproduction of any part of this work may take place without the written
permission of Cambridge University Press.

An online version of this work is published at doi.org/10.1017/9781108762717 under a Creative
Commons Open Access license CC-BY-NC-ND 4.0 which permits re-use, distribution and
reproduction in any medium for non-commercial purposes providing appropriate credit to
the original work is given. You may not distribute derivative works without permission. To
view a copy of this license, visit https://creativecommons.org/licenses/by-nc-nd/4.0

All versions of this work may contain content reproduced under license from
third parties.

Permission to reproduce this third-party content must be obtained from these
third-parties directly.

When citing this work, please include a reference to the DOI 10.1017/9781108762717

First published 2020

A catalogue record for this publication is available from the British Library.

ISBN 978-1-108-48714-6 Hardback

Cambridge University Press has no responsibility for the persistence or accuracy of
URLs for external or third-party internet websites referred to in this publication
and does not guarantee that any content on such websites is, or will remain,
accurate or appropriate.

Contents

List of Figures		*page* vi
Preface		ix
	Introduction	1
1	Theories of the Mind and Theories of Causation	13
2	Mental Causation by Counterfactual Dependence	60
3	Mental Causation by Causal Modelling	98
4	The Exclusion Problem	152
5	Conclusion	202
Appendix 1	*Counterfactuals and Spheres*	204
Appendix 2	*Valid and Invalid Inference Rules for Counterfactuals*	207
References		208
Index		221

Figures

0.1	A collision with different possible outcomes despite conservation of momentum and kinetic energy	*page* 9
1.1	A neuron case of double prevention	51
1.2	A neuron case of double prevention with a counterfactual supposition	51
1.3	A real-life case of double prevention	52
1.4	A real-life case of double prevention with a counterfactual supposition	52
1.5	An intrinsic duplicate of the neuron double-prevention case	54
1.6	An intrinsic duplicate of the neuron double-prevention case with a counterfactual supposition	54
2.1	Lei Zhong's argument for downward causation vs my argument	79
2.2	Two types of worlds with violations of (psycho-)physical laws	85
2.3	A geometrical illustration of a true counterfactual	89
2.4	A geometrical illustration of a true counterfactual about physical events and properties	89
2.5	A geometrical illustration of counterfactuals and spheres	89
2.6	A misleading picture of super-nomological necessity	90
2.7	Double prevention in muscle contraction	93
2.8	Double prevention in muscle contraction with a counterfactual supposition	93
3.1	The causal graph of the *Lightning Strike* example	107
3.2	The causal graph of an early pre-emption example	109
3.3	The causal graph of a model for mental causation	115
3.4	The causal graph of a model relevant for evaluating mental-to-physical counterfactuals	116
3.5	The causal graph of an omission example	120
3.6	The causal graph of a double-prevention example	123
3.7	The causal graph of the electrocution example	132

List of Figures

3.8	An alternative causal graph of the electrocution example	136
3.9	Another alternative causal graph of the electrocution example	137
3.10	Yet another alternative causal graph of the electrocution example	137
3.11	The causal graph of an alternative model for mental causation	145
3.12	The causal graph of another alternative model for mental causation	146
3.13	The causal graph of yet another alternative model for mental causation	147
4.1	A geometrical illustration of overdetermination with counterfactual dependence	171
4.2	A neuron case of overdetermination	174
4.3	A neuron case of overdetermination with a counterfactual supposition	174
A.1	A geometrical illustration of counterfactuals and spheres	205

Preface

The mind makes a difference to the physical world. Therefore, the mind causes things to happen in the physical world. You opened this book because you found it interesting (I assume with a bit of self-flattery). When you opened the book, your fingers moved in a certain way. If you had not been interested, your fingers would not have moved in this way. Thus, your interest caused your fingers to move the way they did. Your mind had a physical effect because it made a difference to what was going on in the physical world.

If we think about the relation between the mind and the physical world in this way, we can solve a number of difficult problems. We can explain how the mind and the physical world can interact in principle. We can explain how certain physical effects can have both physical causes (such as certain events in your brain when you opened the book) and mental causes. Moreover, we can explain these things even if the mind is not itself physical. Or so I argue in this book.

A number of people's minds have made a difference to the book. I am indebted to Sebastian Bender, Ralf Busse, Jeremy Butterfield, Catharine Diehl, Daniel Dohrn, Antony Eagle, Luke Fenton-Glynn, Wolfgang Freitag, Jan Gertken, Nick Haverkamp, Christopher Hitchcock, Vera Hoffmann-Kolss, Franz Huber, Andreas Hüttemann, Romy Jaster, Geert Keil, Beate Krickel, Rory Madden, Erasmus Mayr, Beau Madison Mount, Christian Nimtz, Tobias Rosefeldt, Paolo Rubini, Thomas Sattig, Jonathan Schaffer, Stephan Schmid, Markus Schrenk, Moritz Schulz, Wolfgang Schwarz, Barbara Vetter, Lisa Vogt, Ralph Wedgwood, Timothy Williamson, to two anonymous readers for Cambridge University Press, to various further anonymous referees, and to audience members at talks where I presented materials from this book for helpful comments and suggestions. Thanks also to Hilary Gaskin, my editor at Cambridge University Press, for her help and support, and to Mairi Sutherland for her astute copy-editing. I am grateful to the Humboldt University of Berlin, where an earlier incarnation of this book served as my *Habilitationsschrift*, for teaching leave during the winter term of 2013–14.

Chapters 1, 2, and 3 draw on my 'A Simple Argument for Downward Causation', *Synthese* 192 (2015), and Chapters 1, 2, and 4 draw on my 'Dualist Mental Causation and the Exclusion Problem', *Noûs* 49 (2015). Thanks to Springer and Wiley-Blackwell for permission to use this material.

Introduction

> I am not really convinced that it matters very much whether the mental
> is physical; still less that it matters very much whether we can prove that
> it is. Whereas, if it is not literally true that my wanting is causally
> responsible for my reaching, and my itching is causally responsible for
> my scratching, and my believing is causally responsible for my saying . . .
> if none of that is literally true, then practically everything I believe about
> anything is false and it's the end of the world.[1]
>
> Jerry A. Fodor (1989: 77)

0.1   The Problems of Mental Causation

Mental causation is causation by mental causes. More specifically, it is the
causation of physical effects by mental causes. In this book, I will use
'mental causation' in this specific sense. Nothing as fanciful as causing
a spoon to bend through sheer force of will is required for mental causation. Rather, there is mental causation whenever what is going on in our
minds causes our bodies to move. This, it seems, happens all the time.
I have a headache and take an aspirin. In a typical case, my headache causes
my hand to move towards the aspirin. If an argument for the causal claim is
needed, here is one: in a typical case, my hand moves towards the aspirin
because I have a headache. Whatever 'because' means precisely in this
context, it at least implies that my headache causes my hand to move. More
generally, it seems that there is mental causation whenever we act intentionally. Whatever it means precisely to act intentionally, it at least implies
that some of our mental states cause our bodies to move.[2]

---

[1] Jerry Fodor, excerpt from 'Making Mind Matter More', *Philosophical Topics* 17, no. 1 (1989).
Copyright © 1989 by the Board of Trustees of the University of Arkansas. Reprinted with the
permission of The Permissions Company, LLC on behalf of the University of Arkansas Press.
[2] If there are purely mental intentional actions, at least the causation of mental effects by mental causes
is implied.

2   *Introduction*

Thus, both common sense and philosophical theorizing have it that what is going on in our minds at least sometimes causes things to happen in the physical world. All the same, there are philosophical problems about mental causation. This book deals with the two most serious ones: the interaction problem and the exclusion problem. The interaction problem is the problem of how there can be mental causation at all. How, in principle, can the mental causally interact with the physical? If we think of the causing of physical effects as a job, is the mental qualified to do this job?[3] The exclusion problem is the problem of how there can be mental causation given that all physical effects already have physical causes. How could physical effects have additional mental causes? Even if the mental is qualified to cause physical effects, how can it do this job if the physical is already doing all the work? Perhaps there could be some kind of job-sharing between mental and physical causes, such that some physical effects have physical and mental causes that somehow act in tandem. But then, it seems, the situation would be similar to a firing squad[4] where the victim's death is overdetermined by the firings of two shooters, and it seems implausible that physical effects are thus overdetermined whenever there is mental causation. The interaction problem and the exclusion problem are connected. The exclusion problem arises only if the interaction problem has been solved. The mental can compete with the physical for the job of causing mental events or share this job with the physical only if the mental is qualified to do the job.

How serious the interaction and exclusion problems are depends on the nature of mind. The more intimate the relation between mind and body, the less pressing both problems become. The most intimate relation is that of identity. Reductive physicalists claim that the mental is identical to the physical. If reductive physicalism is true, then the interaction problem disappears. If the mental is identical to the physical, then the mental causes of physical effects are *ipso facto* physical causes, and no one doubts that physical effects can have physical causes.[5] The exclusion problem disappears too. If the mental is identical to the physical, there are no additional mental causes, since any mental causes simply *are* physical causes. Physical effects of mental causes are not caused twice over, leading to cases of

---

[3] My presentation of the relation between the interaction and exclusion problems and my use of the job metaphor loosely follows Karen Bennett's (2007: 325, 2008: 281 n. 4).

[4] I shall follow the established tradition of using the somewhat macabre example of the firing squad. In the philosophy of causation, this tradition goes back at least to Mackie (1965).

[5] Almost no one: if one doubts that there is causation at all, as Russell (1912) does, *a fortiori* one doubts that physical effects can have physical causes.

Introduction 3

overdetermination that resemble firing squads; rather, they have a single cause that is both mental and physical.

Non-reductive physicalists claim that the mental is distinct from the physical, while it is still metaphysically dependent on the physical. Metaphysical dependence can in turn be spelled out in different ways; most commonly, it is read as supervenience or asymmetric metaphysical necessitation. The relation of distinctness-cum-metaphysical-dependence is less intimate than the relation of identity. This opens a gap between the mental and the physical through which the interaction problem might enter. It does not, however, seem particularly problematic to see how physical effects could in principle have mental causes given that the mental metaphysically depends on the physical. The exclusion problem, on the other hand, looks serious. If the mental is distinct from the physical, any mental causes of physical effects that already have physical causes are additional causes of those effects. How can there be such additional mental causes without the physical effects' being overdetermined?

Dualists claim that the mental is distinct from the physical and does not even metaphysically depend on the physical. This relation is sufficiently loose to make the interaction problem pressing; it is also sufficiently loose to make the exclusion problem pressing if the interaction problem can somehow be solved. If the mental does not even metaphysically depend on the physical, how do the mental and physical realms interact causally at all? Even if they can interact in principle, how can mental and physical causes of physical effects coexist without yielding cases of overdetermination? The looser the connection between the mental and the physical, it seems, the more the case of a physical effect that has both a mental and a physical cause looks like a firing squad case.

While the severity of the interaction and exclusion problems depends on the nature of mind, it also depends on the nature of causation. The problems are severe if causation requires the transfer of some conserved quantity, such as energy, from the cause to the effect. If this is the case, then, in order to solve the interaction problem, dualists have to explain how something that does not metaphysically depend on the physical can transmit something to something physical. In order to solve the exclusion problem, dualists and non-reductive physicalists have to explain how both a physical cause and a distinct mental cause can transmit something to the same physical effect. These tasks seem hard, if not impossible.

By contrast, if it suffices for causation that one event makes a difference to another – in the sense that the second event would not have occurred had the first event not occurred – then the interaction problem and the

4   *Introduction*

exclusion problem are manageable. In that case, in order to solve the interaction problem, dualists have to explain how the mental can make a difference to the physical. In order to solve the exclusion problem, dualists and non-reductive physicalists have to explain how both a physical cause and a distinct mental cause can make a difference to a physical effect without yielding a case of overdetermination or, at any rate, without yielding a case of overdetermination that is objectionable.

This book pursues the strategy of solving the interaction and exclusion problems through a difference-making account of causation. It argues that, given a difference-making approach to causation, dualists as well as non-reductive physicalists can solve the problems of mental causation. We do not even need a full-blown theory of causation that states necessary and sufficient conditions for causation in terms of difference-making in order to solve the problems for dualism and non-reductive physicalism. It suffices to assume that difference-making is sufficient for causation. This assumption is very plausible. Since it does not amount to a full-blown theory of causation, it is also relatively metaphysically weak. As we shall see, the minimal assumptions about the nature of mind that need to be made in order to solve the problems of mental causation through the strategy advocated here are also relatively weak metaphysically. They are compatible with a dualist position about the mind provided some fine-tuning is made about how easily mental phenomena and their physical bases could have come apart. Thus, the strategy pursued in this book uses weak assumptions both about the metaphysics of causation and about the metaphysics of mind. The metaphysical slack is picked up by the logic of the statements that express difference-making claims. These statements, counterfactual conditionals, obey distinctive logical principles that allow us to derive claims about how the mental makes a difference to the physical from claims about how the physical makes a difference to the physical, together with claims about the nature of mind. The derived claims about how the mental makes a difference to the physical can in turn be combined with the assumption about causation to derive claims about how mental events can have physical effects. In the debate about mental causation, the power of the logic of counterfactual conditionals has been overlooked so far. Instead, theories about the nature of mind have borne the weight of solving the problems of mental causation. Once the power of this logic is utilized, however, weak assumptions about causation as well as about the nature of mind suffice, and even dualists can account for mental causation.

The plan of this book is as follows. Chapter 1 lays the groundwork about the mind and about causation. It characterizes the different theories about

Introduction 5

the nature of mind in more detail. It then turns to causation, its relata, and counterfactual conditionals. Counterfactual conditionals, their general truth-conditions and logical relations are introduced, as are more specific issues about how to evaluate them. The chapter defends a principle about causation in terms of counterfactual conditionals that will be crucial for later arguments. According to this principle, an event causes another (roughly) if the second event would not have occurred had the first event not occurred. While it is very plausible, the principle needs some refinement in order to deal with a number of *prima facie* difficulties. In particular, certain assumptions need to be made about how to evaluate counterfactual conditionals like 'If the first event had not occurred, then the second event would not have occurred.'

Chapter 2 uses the principle about causation to show that there are physical effects of mental causes. If non-reductive physicalism is true, applying the principle is straightforward. Indeed, it might seem that applying the principle is almost too straightforward, for the principle also yields non-mental higher-level causes that might be considered problematic. These causes are best diagnosed as causes that have little explanatory relevance. If dualism is true, applying the principle about causation in order to show the existence of mental causation is less straightforward, but still possible. In order to avail themselves of the principle, dualists need to assume that the laws that connect the mental and physical realms have a special status. In sum, both non-reductive physicalists and dualists can solve the interaction problem.

Chapter 3 shows that more sophisticated difference-making theories of causation that draw on so-called causal models can accommodate mental causation too. Causal modelling theories invoke more complex relations of difference-making than the simple principle about causation does. These relations are represented by causal models. Accommodating mental causation – either in the non-reductive physicalist case or in the dualist case – calls for some heterodoxy in model-building. If the heterodox models are allowed, however, they prove useful not merely for explaining mental causation, but also for capturing the distinction between higher-level causes that are explanatorily relevant and higher-level causes that are not.

Chapter 4 deals with the exclusion problem. If a difference-making approach to causation is adopted, the exclusion problem can be solved. Although mental and physical causes might nominally overdetermine their physical effects, these cases are sufficiently dissimilar to standard cases of overdetermination not to be problematic. Unlike in cases of mental

6 *Introduction*

causation (on the account offered here), in standard cases of overdetermination, the individual causes do *not* make a difference to the effect.

The resulting picture of mental causation, summarized in Chapter 5, has repercussions for debates about the nature of mind. If virtually all theories about the nature of mind can solve the problems of mental causation, then arguments from mental causation against certain theories become irrelevant.

0.2   A Brief History of the Problems

The interaction problem took centre stage in the context of Descartes' view of the nature of mind.[6] Descartes held that human minds are souls and that souls and bodies are radically different – and hence distinct – substances, the soul being thinking and not spatially extended, the body being spatially extended and not thinking. Princess Elisabeth of Bohemia criticized Descartes for being unable to account for how the soul can initiate bodily movements. In a letter to Descartes, she wrote:

> So I ask you please to tell me how the soul of a human being (it being only a thinking substance) can determine the bodily spirits, in order to bring about voluntary actions. For it seems that all determination of movement happens through the impulsion of the thing moved, by the manner in which it is pushed by that which moves it, or else by the particular qualities and shape of the surface of the latter. Physical contact is required for the first two conditions, extension for the third. You entirely exclude the one [extension] from the notion you have of the soul, and the other [physical contact] appears to me incompatible with an immaterial thing.[7]

Descartes replied that we had a primitive notion of the union of the soul with the body, 'on which depends that of the power the soul has to move the body and the body to act on the soul, in causing its sensations and passions'.[8] Since the notion was primitive, it defied further explanation and could be 'understood only through itself'.[9] Elisabeth was not convinced. In her reply, she advanced what might be one of the earliest arguments from mental causation for the claim that the mind is material: 'I admit that it would be easier for me to concede matter and extension to the soul than to

---

[6] Debates about mental causation in antiquity are discussed in Caston 1997.

[7] Elisabeth to Descartes, 6 May 1643, AT 3:661, Princess Elisabeth and Descartes 2007: 62 (parentheses original). (Citations of the form 'AT x:y' refer to p. y of vol. x of Descartes 1996.)

[8] Descartes to Elisabeth, 21 May 1643, AT 3:665, Princess Elisabeth and Descartes 2007: 65.

[9] Descartes to Elisabeth, 21 May 1643, AT 3:666, Princess Elisabeth and Descartes 2007: 65.

Introduction 7

concede the capacity to move a body and to be moved by it to an immaterial thing.'[10]

While he failed to attenuate Elisabeth's doubts, elsewhere Descartes elaborated on the locus of the interaction between soul and body.[11] Vital spirits swirled around the pineal gland, Descartes held, and could move limbs in a quasi-hydraulic manner. By moving the pineal gland, the soul could deflect the motions of the vital spirits and thus initiate bodily movements.[12]

Leibniz read Descartes as saying that the soul never changes the speed of anything, but causes bodily movements by changing the *direction* of the vital spirits. Thus, the soul can influence movements in the body 'much as a rider, though giving no force to the horse he mounts, nevertheless controls it by guiding that force in any direction he pleases'.[13] This account, Leibniz held, was consistent with Descartes' physics, which required merely that the 'quantity of motion' be conserved, where a body's quantity of motion is, roughly, the product of its mass and speed.[14] Leibniz held that his own physics ruled out that the soul could change the direction of a body's motion. He required not the conservation of quantity of motion, but the conservation of what is nowadays called momentum, where a body's momentum is the product of its mass and its velocity, velocity being a vector quantity. The soul's changing a body's direction of motion in the way Descartes – at least Leibniz's Descartes – envisaged would require changing the body's velocity vector and hence would violate the conservation of momentum.[15]

In addition to the conservation of momentum, Leibniz endorsed what is nowadays called the conservation of kinetic energy, where a body's kinetic energy is the product of its mass and the square of its speed. The conservation of momentum rules out that the soul changes the direction of motion

---

[10] Elisabeth to Descartes, 10 June 1643, AT 3:685, Princess Elisabeth and Descartes 2007: 68.

[11] For further discussion of the correspondence between Elisabeth and Descartes, see Garber 1983b and Perler 1996: 123–160.

[12] See Descartes, *Passions of the Soul*, §§34, 41; AT 11:354–11:355, 11:359–11:360; CSM 1:341, 1:343. (Citations of the form 'CSM x:y' refer to p. y of vol. x of Descartes 1984–1991.)

[13] *Theodicy*, §60 (Leibniz 1985: 156).

[14] In fact, Descartes defined a body's quantity of motion as the product of the body's speed and its *size*, which in turn is closely related to, but not identical with, its volume; see Slowik 2014, §4. On the face of it, Leibniz's reading of Descartes seems charitable, but Descartes may not have intended his physical laws to hold without exception. For instance, in the *Principles of Philosophy* he explicitly restricts his third law of motion to causes of corporeal changes that are themselves corporeal and brackets human and angelic minds as possible causes (see AT 8:65, CSM 1:242). See Garber 1983a for further discussion.

[15] See *First Explanation of the New System*, §20 (Leibniz 1898: 327–328).

8 *Introduction*

of a single particle. In principle, it leaves open that the soul interacts with bodies in a different way. For instance, when bodies collide, the conservation of momentum by itself leaves open different post-collision situations, depending on whether the collision is elastic or inelastic. (In the inelastic case, it leaves open different post-collision situations in turn, depending on how inelastic the collision is.) In elastic collisions, kinetic energy is conserved; in inelastic collisions, it is not. One might hypothesize that the soul changes the motion of bodies by causing certain collisions to be elastic and others to be inelastic. If we stipulate that kinetic energy as well as momentum be conserved, that option is ruled out. Indeed, Leibniz thought that once both the conservation of energy and the conservation of momentum are in place, the soul cannot interact with bodies at all: 'without a complete derangement of the laws of Nature the soul could not act physically upon the body'.[16] In contemporary terminology, Leibniz accuses Descartes of falling prey to the exclusion problem: given the nature of the physical world, there is no room left for anything non-physical to bring about physical changes.

Some modern commentators (e.g., Papineau (2001: 15)) have concurred with Leibniz's claim that the two conservation laws fully fix the future position and velocity of bodies and thus rule out any non-physical influence on the motion of bodies. Strictly speaking, this claim is not true, however. Take two point-size particles of equal mass and speed that are about to collide head-on. We would expect their post-collision velocity vectors to be the negatives of the pre-collision velocity vectors. But even if we assume that kinetic energy and momentum are conserved, any rotation of the expected post-collision situation is likewise possible (see Figure 0.1).[17]

Thus, Leibniz's conservation laws leave a loophole that Cartesians could try to exploit. This is not to say that the loophole cannot be closed by supposing further physical principles to hold, although finding suitable principles turns out to be surprisingly tricky.[18] (In order not to raise false

---

[16] *Theodicy*, §61 (Leibniz 1985: 156).

[17] In the example from the figure, the conserved momentum is $m\vec{v}_1 + m\vec{v}_2 = \vec{0}$, and the conserved kinetic energy is $\frac{1}{2}m|\vec{v}_1|^2 + \frac{1}{2}m|\vec{v}_2|^2 = m|\vec{v}_1|^2 = m|\vec{v}_2|^2$.

[18] See Gibb 2010 for discussion. Gibb holds that the classical conservation laws leave it open that momentum and energy be 'redistributed'. It is not clear whether the case illustrated in Figure 0.1 qualifies as a case of redistribution of momentum in her sense, for it is unclear whether there is any more 'redistribution' going on between $\vec{v}_1/\vec{v}_2$ and $\vec{v}_1'/\vec{v}_2'$ than between $\vec{v}_1/\vec{v}_2$ and $\vec{v}_1''/\vec{v}_2''$. For further discussion of the role of energy conservation in arguments against interactive dualism, see Averill and Keating 1981, Montero 2006, and Koksvik 2007. Presumably, Leibniz would have responded to the collision example that the $\vec{v}_1'/\vec{v}_2'$ and $\vec{v}_1''/\vec{v}_2''$ situations are identical because space is not absolute. This response could be blocked by adding another particle that is not involved in the collision. In the new scenario, an alternative response would still have been available to

Introduction 9

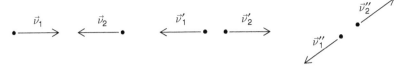

Figure 0.1. A collision ($\vec{v}_1/\vec{v}_2$) with different possible outcomes ($\vec{v}_1'/\vec{v}_2'$ vs $\vec{v}_1''/\vec{v}_2''$) despite conservation of momentum and kinetic energy

expectations, I should say that the account of mental causation I am going to recommend to dualists does *not* exploit any such loopholes.)

One way of sidestepping Elisabethian worries about the interaction between soul and body is to deny that this interaction is direct. One can hold that, instead, God acts as an intermediary whenever there seems to be a direct interaction between soul and body; in particular, God perceives our acts of will and brings it about that our bodies move accordingly. God is not subject to whatever limits there are on the direct interaction between soul and body and brings about their indirect interaction. This is the doctrine of occasionalism, which was held by Malebranche and other followers of Descartes.[19]

Leibniz rejected occasionalism just as he rejected Descartes' interactionism. His reasons for rejecting the two positions overlapped. Leibniz held that, similarly to Descartes' interactionism, the indirect interaction that occasionalism posits would violate the laws of nature. Moreover, occasionalism denigrated God to something like a theatrical *deus ex machina* who has to constantly interfere with his own creation.[20]

Leibniz's own answer to the question of how mind and body interact was that they did not interact at all, directly or indirectly. With interactionism and occasionalism ruled out, he wrote,

> there remains only my hypothesis, that is to say, *the way of the harmony pre-established* by a contrivance of the Divine foresight, which has from the beginning formed each of these substances in so perfect, so regular and accurate a manner that by merely following its own laws which were given to it when it came into being, each substance is yet in harmony with the other,

---

Leibniz. He could have claimed that there is no sufficient reason for the particles to assume the $\vec{v}_1''/\vec{v}_2''$ velocities, while there is a sufficient reason for them to assume the $\vec{v}_1'/\vec{v}_2'$ velocities, namely that the latter are parallel to the initial velocities.

[19] See Malebranche, Dialogue VII from *Dialogues on Metaphysics and on Religion* (Malebranche 1997: 104–126). Nadler (1997) argues that, contrary to the received view, Cartesians did not adopt occasionalism primarily in response to problems about mind–body interaction.

[20] See *Theodicy*, §61 (Leibniz 1985: 156). For further discussion of Leibniz's criticism of occasionalism, see Sleigh 1990 and Rutherford 1993.

just as if there were a mutual influence between them, or as if God were continually putting His hand upon them, in addition to His general support.[21]

According to Leibniz, mind and body are like two clocks that are in perfect agreement with each other because they are made 'with such skill and accuracy that we can be sure that they will always afterwards keep time together'.[22]

Both occasionalism and the doctrine of pre-established harmony assign an indispensable role to God, as a constant causal mediator and meticulous creator, respectively. Once appealing to God in order to solve philosophical problems started to be considered problematic, new approaches to the interaction of soul and body were needed.

One approach was to deny that soul and body are distinct. Julien Offray de La Mettrie endorsed such a materialist view.[23] In his 1748 book *Man a Machine*, he defended the view that 'man is but an animal, or a collection of springs which wind each other up' (La Mettrie 1912: 135). In this machinery,

> the soul is but a principle of motion or a material and sensible part of the brain, which can be regarded, without fear of error, as the mainspring of the whole machine, having a visible influence on all the parts. (La Mettrie 1912: 135)

If the soul is nothing but a part of the physical machinery of our body, there is no problem of explaining how the soul can cause bodily movements.

Another approach was to accept that mind and body are distinct and that there is a causal relation between them, albeit a causal relation that goes merely one way, from body to mind. This is the doctrine of epiphenomenalism, whose chief proponent was Thomas Huxley (1874).[24] Huxley's epiphenomenalism incorporates an aspect of La Mettrie's view, viz. that the body is a complex machine that does not allow, or at least does not require, any non-physical influence. Indeed, Huxley's argument for epiphenomenalism rests mainly on empirical examples of complex bodily goings-on in the absence of consciousness. While there is a causal relation between body and mind according to epiphenomenalism, it is not in the direction from mind to body, which has generally been considered the

---

[21] *Third Explanation of the New System*, Leibniz 1898: 333–334.   [22] Leibniz 1898: 333.

[23] Hobbes was an early materialist too, but, unlike La Mettrie, he was also a theist. See Springborg 2012 and Gorham 2013 for discussion.

[24] Other early proponents of epiphenomenalism include Clifford (1874) and Spalding (1877).

Introduction II

more troublesome direction. Thus, unlike occasionalism, epiphenomenalism need not posit any divine assistance for the causal relation.

Epiphenomenalism never became popular, either in the nineteenth or in the twentieth century; the materialist approach (which today is more commonly called 'physicalism') attracted more followers. Talk of the soul fell out of fashion, but identity theorists like Ullin Place (1956) and Herbert Feigl (1958) instead identified (types of) mental states with (types of) brain states. In the terminology of the previous section, these theorists qualified as reductive physicalists, although they did not apply this label to themselves. Like earlier materialist theories, the identity theory faces no problems from mental causation, for there are no problems with brain states causing bodily effects.

The success of the identity theory did not last long, however. Hilary Putnam (1967) pointed out that different physical states can underlie one and the same mental state, which rules out an identity between the mental state and any of those physical states. With the growing acceptance of this multiple realizability of mental states, which led to non-reductive physicalist theories of the mind, problems of mental causation re-emerged. Jaegwon Kim (1989), building on an argument by Norman Malcolm (1968), challenged advocates of non-reductive physicalism with a version of the exclusion problem. Physical effects already have physical causes. If they have additional mental causes – even mental causes that are tied to the physical causes by a relation of metaphysical dependence – then they are overdetermined; but a widespread overdetermination of the (putative) physical effects of mental causes was unacceptable, Kim held.

Besides arguments from multiple realizability, the identity theory faced an influential modal objection that was advanced by Saul Kripke (1980). Psychophysical identities had to be necessary if they obtained at all, Kripke held, but it seemed possible to be in the mental state without being in the (allegedly) identical physical state, and vice versa. It turned out that similar modal arguments could be advanced against non-reductive physicalism too (see Block 1978, Chalmers 1996). This led to a revival of dualism, although contemporary dualists, unlike their early modern predecessors, tend to hold that mental states or properties are distinct from physical states or properties, without going so far as to say that there are Cartesian souls.[25] Thus, the interaction problem is not

---

[25] According to a survey by Bourget and Chalmers (2014: 476–477), 27.1 per cent of professional philosophers believe in non-physicalism about the mind, and 23.3 per cent believe in the metaphysical possibility of zombies (that is, beings like us physically but without consciousness), which is standardly taken to entail dualism.

quite as severe for contemporary dualists as it was for Descartes, but it still seems hard to explain how mental states and properties, being neither identical to nor metaphysically dependent on physical states and properties, can have physical effects in principle. And even if this problem can be solved, Kim's exclusion problem stands in the way of a complete dualist account of mental causation.

CHAPTER I

Theories of the Mind and Theories of Causation

1.1 Introduction

Explaining how various theories about the nature of mind can accommodate mental causation requires some groundwork. It requires formulating these theories about the nature of mind more precisely. It also requires getting clearer about the nature of causation, which in turn has two aspects: the nature of the relata of causation and the nature of the relation itself. These are the tasks of this chapter.

The aims of the chapter are modest in several ways. I will not attempt to give a complete taxonomy of views about the nature of mind. Instead, I will confine myself to views that are both common and that stand a *prima facie* chance of accommodating mental causation. I will not say much about the comparative advantages and disadvantages of these positions, not least because I do not wish to commit myself to any of them in this book. I will not try to defend a full-blown theory of causation that states necessary as well as sufficient conditions for causation. For one thing, giving such a full-blown theory of causation may well be impossible. For another, it is not necessary for our purposes. Giving a sufficient condition for causation is enough, at least if this condition can be applied in sufficiently many cases of (putative) mental causation. Fortunately, sufficient conditions for causation are easier to find than necessary ones.

The plan for the chapter is as follows. Section 1.2 formulates different theories about the nature of mind. In particular, it defines reductive physicalism, non-reductive physicalism, and dualism. It also defines a version of dualism, naturalistic dualism. Sections 1.3–1.5 discuss the nature of the causal relata and the causal relation. In the context of mental causation, the causal relata are best conceived of as particular or token events, and particular events are best conceived of as being constituted by, and having their identity determined by, triples of an object, a property, and a time (see Section 1.3).

13

As for the causal relation, we can give a sufficient condition for causation in terms of difference-making or counterfactual dependence: one event causes another if (roughly) the second event would not have occurred had the first event not occurred. The counterfactual conditionals that are used to formulate claims about counterfactual dependence exhibit some logical peculiarities (see Section 1.4). The sufficient condition for causation in terms of counterfactual dependence is subject to a few *prima facie* problems, but they can be overcome by making certain assumptions about how the relevant counterfactual conditionals should be evaluated and by restricting the sufficient condition to suitable kinds of causal relata (see Section 1.5). The sufficient condition for causation in terms of counterfactuals conflicts with the view that causation requires the transfer of a physical quantity from cause to effect. Section 1.6 argues that this conflict should be resolved in favour of the counterfactual condition. It also discusses the requirement that causation should involve an intrinsic connection between cause and effect.

1.2 Varieties of Physicalism and Dualism

Generally, physicalists with respect to X hold that X is physical.[1] Cartesians deny that mental substances are physical and thus fail to be physicalists about mental substances. This view has few adherents today;[2] I shall follow the mainstream view and assume that all substances are physical. Instead of focusing on substances, I shall focus on mental and physical properties. Physicalists about mental properties hold that mental properties are physical. This claim can be formulated in different ways. The most straightforward reading is that mental properties are identical to physical properties. This is the position called reductive physicalism, defined as follows:

Reductive physicalism: Each mental property is identical to a physical property.

According to reductive physicalism, the property of having a headache is identical to, say, the property of having firing c-fibres:[3] to have a headache is one and the same thing as to have firing c-fibres.[4]

---

[1] Characterizing the physical raises some problems of its own, which I will ignore here. See Crane and Mellor 1990 and Crook and Gillet 2001 for discussion.

[2] Hart (1988) is an exception. Lowe (1996) endorses a more attenuated substance dualism.

[3] Associating pains with c-fibre-firings is empirically questionable, but has a longstanding philosophical tradition, which I follow here. Indeed, I take the liberty of associating c-fibre firings not with pains *per se*, but with headaches.

[4] As was mentioned in Section 0.2, reductive physicalism was originally called the identity theory and was pioneered by Place (1956) and Feigl (1958). For a recent defence, see Polger 2004.

Theories of the Mind and Theories of Causation

Since identity entails mutual necessitation, reductive physicalism makes it impossible to have a headache without having firing c-fibres and impossible to have firing c-fibres without having a headache.[5] Some physicalists wish to accept the latter impossibility claim while rejecting the former. They hold that mental properties are physical in the sense that mental properties are necessitated by physical properties and necessitate the instantiation of physical properties, but they also hold that the relation between physical and mental properties is many–one, not one–one, as reductive physicalism has it.[6] Thus, there can be different physical properties besides having firing c-fibres that necessitate pain. This yields a form of physicalism that is weaker than reductive physicalism and hence non-reductive.

We can make non-reductive physicalism more precise by using the notion of strong supervenience, which is defined as follows:

Strong supervenience: A set of properties **A** *strongly supervenes* on a set of properties **B** if and only if, necessarily, if anything instantiates some property F in **A** at a given time, then there is a property G in **B** such that that thing instantiates G at that time, and, necessarily, everything that instantiates G at a given time also instantiates F at that time.[7]

Here and throughout, 'necessarily', unless qualified further, expresses metaphysical necessity, that is, truth in all possible worlds or, somewhat more informatively, truth come what may: if pigs were to fly, donkeys were to talk, and particles were to travel faster than light, what is metaphysically necessary would still have been the case. The definition of strong supervenience is a bit cumbersome, but the underlying idea is simple. As an illustration of the definition, consider dot-matrix pictures and their symmetry properties.[8] The symmetry properties of a dot-matrix picture strongly supervene on the arrangement of dots in the picture's matrix. According to the definition, this means that, necessarily, if a picture instantiates a symmetry property at a given time, the dots in the picture's matrix are arranged in a certain way and that this arrangement necessitates the symmetry property whenever

---

[5] See Kripke 1980. I assume, with Kripke, that the names for mental and physical properties are rigid designators, that is, that they name the same property at every possible world. Lewis, by contrast, takes the names of mental properties to be non-rigid designators, which opens up the possibility of contingent psychophysical identities (see Lewis 1980).

[6] Alternatively, we could characterize the position as saying that mental properties are identical to *higher-order* physical properties, which are distinct from, but stand in the necessitation relation to, sufficiently *fundamental* physical properties. For further discussion of this strategy, see Pauen 2002.

[7] My formulation of the definition follows what McLaughlin calls 'Modal-Operator Strong Supervenience' (1995: 95). For further discussion, see Kim 1984 and McLaughlin 1995.

[8] This kind of example is due to Lewis 1986c: 14.

a picture has it. For instance, a 3×3 dot-matrix picture that is point-symmetric has to have the dot arrangement ∴ or ∵ or ⋮ ⋮, etc., and any picture that has the arrangement ∴ has to be point-symmetric, any picture that has the arrangement ∵ has to be point-symmetric, any picture that has the arrangement ⋮ ⋮ has to be point-symmetric, etc. More generally, strong supervenience says that a supervenient property has to be accompanied by some subvening property (that is, by a **B**-property), which in turn necessitates the supervenient property whenever it is instantiated.

If we combine the claim that mental properties strongly supervene on physical properties with the claim that mental properties are distinct from physical properties, we get a version of non-reductive physicalism. Generally, non-reductive physicalists claim that mental properties are distinct from physical properties but maintain that mental properties stand in a relation of metaphysical dependence to physical properties (see Baker 2009). The canonical way of spelling out this notion of metaphysical dependence is to read it as strong supervenience (see Kim 1993). For the purposes of this book, I shall identify non-reductive physicalism with the combination of the distinctness claim and the strong supervenience claim. (I do this mainly because it yields a clear-cut terminology, but nothing hinges on it; alternatively, one could use a different label, say 'strong supervenience physicalism', for the position thus characterized.) Thus, we get the following definition:

Non-reductive physicalism: Each mental property is distinct from all physical properties, but mental properties strongly supervene on physical properties.

According to non-reductive physicalism, the property of having a headache is distinct from the property of having firing c-fibres and from all other physical properties. But, owing to the strong supervenience of mental properties on physical properties, it is impossible for someone to have a headache without instantiating some physical property that in turn necessitates having a headache.[9] In my case, that physical property is the property of having firing c-fibres, but in other cases (actual or merely possible), it might be the property of having firing x-fibres (which, let us assume, are actually present not in humans but merely in octopuses), the property of having an active semiconductor network of a certain kind in

---

[9] It seems that this necessitation relation holds only if the relevant physical properties include properties to the effect that certain background conditions obtain and that certain laws of nature hold. This issue will be taken up again in Section 4.4.

one's head, etc.[10] Thus, non-reductive physicalism allows for the multiple realizability of mental properties by physical properties.

Some theorists reject not only that mental properties are identical to physical properties, but also that they strongly supervene on physical properties. The view they advocate is dualism, defined as follows:

Dualism: Each mental property is distinct from all physical properties, and no subset of mental properties strongly supervenes on physical properties.

According to dualism, the property of having a headache is not merely distinct from all physical properties, but can be instantiated without a physical property that would in turn necessitate the property of having a headache. In my case, having a headache is accompanied by having firing c-fibres, but, according to dualism, it is possible for there to be someone with firing c-fibres who does not have a headache. Likewise, according to dualism, it is possible in principle for someone to have a headache without being in any physical state whatsoever.

Dualism can take more or less extreme forms. An extreme form might have it that in some remote corner of the universe there are disembodied creatures with headaches, and that, next year, humans with firing c-fibres will no longer have headaches while erupting geysers will have headaches. Few scientifically minded people accept such an extreme form of dualism. According to a more moderate form of dualism, mental properties are tied to physical properties by laws of nature in a way that is structurally similar to, but modally weaker than, strong supervenience (see Chalmers 1996: 123–171). We can express this moderate form of dualism more precisely by introducing the notion of nomological supervenience:

Nomological supervenience: A set of properties A *nomologically supervenes* on a set of properties B if and only if it is nomologically necessary that if anything instantiates some property F in A at a given time, then there is a property G in B such that that thing instantiates G at that time, and it is nomologically necessary that everything that instantiates G at a given time also instantiates F at that time.

The definition of nomological supervenience is just like the definition of strong supervenience, except that the two occurrences of 'necessarily' (which, remember, we stipulated to mean metaphysical necessity) are

---

[10] The doctrine of non-reductive physicalism is often associated with the view that particular, token mental events are identical to particular physical events. We shall see in the following section, however, that not all accounts of token events allow this. For further discussion of the relation between non-reductive physicalism and token identity, see Schneider 2012.

replaced by 'it is nomologically necessary that'.[11] Nomological necessity is necessity in view of the laws of nature: something is nomologically necessary just in case it is strictly implied by the actual laws of nature. (Equivalently, something is nomologically necessary just in case it is true in all possible worlds in which all actual laws of nature hold.) We can use the notion of nomological supervenience to formulate the moderate form of dualism, which, following Chalmers (1996), I will call naturalistic dualism:

Naturalistic dualism: Each mental property is distinct from all physical properties. No subset of mental properties strongly supervenes on physical properties, but mental properties nomologically supervene on physical properties.

Naturalistic dualism is obviously a version of dualism as we have defined it. Both reductive physicalism and non-reductive physicalism are versions of physicalism about mental properties, but do not exhaust it. One could hold that some but not all mental properties are identical to physical properties, while the remaining mental properties strongly supervene on physical properties. Then one would neither be a reductive physicalist nor a non-reductive physicalist. The best way to describe such a view is to divide the subject-matter and say that its adherents are reductive physicalists about those mental properties that they take to be identical to physical properties, but non-reductive physicalists about those mental properties that they take to merely strongly supervene on physical properties. Similarly, dualism and physicalism do not exhaust logical space. One could hold that some subset of mental properties strongly supervenes on physical properties (perhaps even that the members of this subset are identical to physical properties), while some other subset of mental properties does not strongly supervene on physical properties. Then one would be neither a physicalist nor a dualist. This kind of view seems odder than the version of physicalism that is neither reductive nor non-reductive, but one could again say that its adherents are physicalists about the first subset of mental properties and dualists about the second.

---

[11] Indeed, if it weren't for the stipulation that 'necessarily' mean metaphysical necessity, nomological supervenience would be a kind of strong supervenience, for without the stipulation, strong supervenience could accommodate different kinds of necessity, including nomological necessity. If one preferred this more flexible notion of strong supervenience, one could define two species of this genus, say 'metaphysical strong supervenience' and 'nomological strong supervenience', which would correspond to our notions of strong supervenience and nomological supervenience, respectively. Our terminology has the advantage of brevity, however.

One could avoid the possibility of hybrid views by defining the positions differently. In particular, one could define non-reductive physicalism as the strong supervenience thesis conjoined with the claim that *some* mental properties are distinct from physical properties. Similarly, one could define dualism as the claim that *some* mental properties are distinct from physical properties conjoined with the claim that *some* subset of mental properties does not even strongly supervene on physical properties. The resulting positions would exhaust logical space, and they would be entailed by, but not entail, the corresponding positions according to the definitions I have given.[12] It seems to me that the stronger, albeit non-exhaustive, definitions capture the general usage better, but one could make a different terminological choice.

Setting aside the issue of whether or not the definitions should exhaust logical space, there is also some controversy about whether the labels 'reductive physicalism', 'non-reductive physicalism' and 'dualism' are apt for the positions to which I have attached them. Some would object to the definition of reductive physicalism because they think that reduction requires more than identity.[13] Some would object to the definition of non-reductive physicalism because they think that physicalism (non-reductive or otherwise) requires more than strong supervenience.[14] Some would object to the definition of naturalistic dualism because they think that nomological supervenience is sufficient for physicalism and hence for the falsity of dualism (see Kim 2005: 49). (Consequently, they would also object to the definition of dualism *simpliciter*, since, according to the definition, naturalistic dualism is a species of dualism.) I will not address these objections here. It suffices for our purposes that the positions that I have labelled 'reductive physicalism', 'non-reductive physicalism' and 'dualism' have been sufficiently prominent in the philosophy of mind. It does not matter for our purposes whether they really deserve these labels.

There are certain standard objections to each of the positions about the nature of mind. There is one class of objections that have nothing to do with mental causation. Non-reductive physicalists argue that reductive

---

[12] Strictly speaking, the entailments hold only on the assumption that there are mental properties, which I take for granted here.

[13] See van Riel 2013. Kim (2005: 34) defines non-reductive physicalism (*inter alia*) as the conjunction of the claim that mental properties are not reducible to physical properties and the claim that they are not identical to physical properties. He explicitly acknowledges that identity is necessary for reduction, however (2005: 34), and his arguments for reductive physicalism (2005: 32–69) suggest that he takes it to be sufficient for reduction too. For discussion of the notion of reduction in the context of emergentism, see Stephan 2002.

[14] See Wilson 2005; see also Jackson 1998: 22–23 and Melnyk 2003: 49–70.

physicalists cannot explain the multiple realizability of mental properties, such as the fact that headaches can be accompanied by c-fibre firings as well as x-fibre firings. Dualists argue that reductive physicalists and non-reductive physicalists cannot explain the possibility of zombies, that is, beings that are physically exactly like us but without any conscious thoughts. I am not going to discuss this class of objections. The comparative merits and difficulties of the different views about the nature of mind will occupy us only where mental causation is concerned.

1.3 The Relata of Causation

Statements of causation come in many stripes. We say that my throwing the stone caused the shattering of the bottle (more idiomatically: that it caused the bottle to shatter); that the reef caused the leakage; that smoking causes cancer. When we say that the throwing caused the shattering, we are talking about token events, that is, particular events (the throwing and the shattering). When we say that the reef caused the leakage, we are talking about a particular thing (the reef) and a particular event (the leakage). When we say that smoking causes cancer, we are talking about general phenomena (smoking, cancer); these might in turn be event types or properties. Perhaps these different statements of causation talk about different kinds of causation that are mutually irreducible; perhaps they do not.[15] In any event, the problems of mental causation are primarily problems about causation between particular events, so my focus will be on this. The interaction problem is about how, in principle, particular mental events such as my headache can cause particular physical events such as my hand's moving towards the aspirin. The exclusion problem is about how a particular physical event such as my hand's moving towards the aspirin can have both a particular mental event and a simultaneous particular physical event as its cause without being like a case of overdetermination.[16] This is not to say that properties play no role in these causal relations – indeed, we shall see that they play a crucial role – but the causal relata are best taken to be particular events. Henceforth, when talking about events without further qualification, I shall mean particular events.

---

[15] One promising approach analyses claims such as 'Smoking causes cancer' as generic statements about token events. See Carroll 1988, 1991 and Swanson 2012b for further discussion.

[16] Lowe (2000, 2008: 41–57) advocates a solution to the exclusion problem according to which mental events cause not physical *events* but *facts* about intra-physical causal relations. If this kind of solution could be made to work, it would still be only a second-best solution. It would be better to have a solution in terms of causation between events.

Theories of the Mind and Theories of Causation

What are events? In particular, when are we dealing with a single event and when with several events? W.V.O. Quine and others think that events are identical just in case they occur in the same spatiotemporal region.[17] This account individuates events in a rather coarse-grained way. I stroll leisurely. By virtue of strolling leisurely, I stroll. My strolling and my strolling leisurely take place in the same spatiotemporal region. Therefore, according to the Quinean account, my strolling and my strolling leisurely are one and the same event. Someone who is worried about multiplying events beyond necessity will welcome this result. But there are problems. Perhaps my strolling leisurely, but not my strolling *per se*, causes me to feel refreshed afterwards. How can my strolling leisurely cause something that my strolling does not cause, yet be the very same event as my strolling? By Leibniz's law, identical events must have the same effects (and the same causes). Other examples bring out this issue more sharply. A metal sphere rotates and heats up at the same time. (The heating is due to an external source.)[18] The sphere's rotating and the sphere's heating up take place in the same spatiotemporal region. Therefore, according to the Quinean account, the sphere's rotating and the sphere's heating up are one and the same event. This should sound strange even to those who are inclined towards ontological parsimony. And to say that the sphere's rotating and the sphere's heating up have all their causes and effects in common sounds even less plausible than the parallel claim in the case of my stroll. If I place a funny hat on the sphere, it will start rotating too, but the hat's rotation will be caused by the sphere's rotating, not by the sphere's heating up.

These problems force us, I think, to reject the Quinean account. This may seem unfortunate, for the account seems to offer an attractive solution to the problems of mental causation. Suppose that my headache takes place in the same spatiotemporal region as my c-fibre firing does. (The claim that headaches have spatial location is not completely uncontentious, but anyone who is a substance physicalist should find it acceptable.) Then, according to the Quinean account, my headache and my c-fibre firing are one and the same event.[19] Thus, my headache and my c-fibre firing have all their causes and effects in common. The interaction problem

---

[17] See Lemmon 1967, Smart 1972, Quine 1970: 31–32, Quine 1974: 5, 131–132, and Davidson 1985. Previously, Davidson (1969) had endorsed the individuation of events in terms of sameness of causes and effects, which critics had claimed to be covertly circular.

[18] The example is from Davidson 1969.

[19] This result is a token identity claim, albeit one that, if generalized, remains weaker than Davidson's (1970) famous Anomalous Monism, because it does not claim that the mental is anomalous.

disappears. No one denies that my c-fibre firing can cause my hand to move towards the aspirin; if it does, then *ipso facto* my headache causes my hand to move towards the aspirin. The exclusion problem disappears, too. Since my headache and my c-fibre firing are one and the same cause of my hand's moving towards the aspirin, my hand's moving is not caused twice over. Even non-reductive physicalists and dualists about mental properties could invoke this solution to problems of mental causation, for what matters is merely that particular mental and physical events are identical; the mental and physical properties that are involved can be distinct and need not even stand in a relation of strong supervenience.

Apart from requiring an implausible conception of events, however, this solution to the problems of mental causation loses its appeal on closer scrutiny. When we demand an explanation of how physical effects can have mental causes, we want to know how mental events can cause physical events by virtue of their mental properties. The explanation that has been suggested provides at most an account of how mental events cause physical events by virtue of their physical properties. According to the explanation, my headache causes my hand to move towards the aspirin because it is identical to my c-fibre firing. Presumably, how my c-fibre firing causes my hand to move is in turn explained by the physical properties involved in my c-fibre firing. So we are still lacking an explanation of how mental events can be causes *qua* mental. For all we know, the situation might be like the following: I put an apple on a scale. The apple weighs 100 grams and has a temperature of 20 degrees Celsius. Shortly after putting the apple on the scale, the display flashes '100'.[20] Quineans have to say that the apple's weighing 100 grams (at a certain time shortly before the flashing) is identical to the apple's having a temperature of 20 degrees (at that time), since these events take place in the same spatiotemporal region.[21] We may assume that the apple's weighing 100 grams caused the display to flash '100'. If the apple's weighing 100 grams is identical to the apple's having a temperature of 20 degrees, it follows that the apple's having a temperature of 20 degrees caused the display to flash '100'. This is an implausible result similar to the result that the sphere's heating up caused the hat to turn, but let us accept it for the sake of argument. The temperature causes the flashing, then, but we have not yet explained how it causes the flashing *qua* temperature.

---

[20] This example is a variation of an example from Honderich 1982.

[21] I am assuming here and throughout that events can be static, that is, that events need not involve change.

One might think that the foregoing considerations do not tell against a coarse-grained individuation of events like the Quinean account as such. Rather, one might think, they show that we should marry a coarse-grained individuation of events to a permissive notion of causation that allows the sphere's warming to cause the hat to rotate and the apple's having a temperature of 20 degrees to cause the display to flash '100'. One might concede that one needs another causal relation, causation-*qua*, that is less permissive and that does not merely relate events, but events together with certain of their aspects. Thus, while the apple's having a temperature of 20 degrees (which is identical to the apple's weighing 100 grams according to the Quinean account of events) does cause the display to flash '100' in the permissive sense, it does not cause the display to flash '100' *qua* temperature, but *qua* mass. Similarly, while the sphere's warming up (which is identical to the sphere's rotating according to the Quinean account of events) does cause the hat to rotate in the permissive sense, it does not cause the hat to rotate *qua* warming up, but *qua* rotating.[22]

Such a view is consistent, but not attractive. First, the problems of mental causation reappear at the level of causation-*qua*. Perhaps my head-ache causes my hand to move towards the aspirin in the permissive sense, but how can it cause my hand to move *qua* mental? And how can my headache cause my hand to move both *qua* mental and *qua* physical without there being overdetermination at the *qua*-level? Second, the onto-logical parsimony about events that the Quinean account of events had boasted is outweighed by a proliferation of causal relations. We have few events, but we need an extra kind of causal relation.[23] Proliferating kinds, however, seems worse than proliferating entities *simpliciter* (see Lewis 1973b: 87).

One might try to augment the claim that individual mental events are identical to individual physical events (owing to the Quinean identity condition or for other reasons) in order to save the causal relevance of mental events *qua* mental by adding another ontological layer. Specifically, one could introduce a layer of particularized properties and claim that mental events have physical effects because particularized mental proper-ties are identical to particularized physical properties.

---

[22] See Horgan 1989 for discussion.

[23] Perhaps one could eschew the permissive notion of causation and hold that causation-*qua* is the only causal relation. But then one would still incur a commitment to extra complexity owing to the higher adicity of causation-*qua*, which seems to outweigh, or at least neutralize, the simplicity of the Quinean account of events.

One way of elaborating this idea is due to David Robb.[24] The details of Robb's suggestion are as follows. Particular mental events are identical to particular physical events. My headache, for instance, is identical to my c-fibres' firing.[25] Whether mental properties are identical to physical properties, Robb holds, depends on what we mean by 'property'. He thinks that 'property' is ambiguous between something particular and something universal (Robb 1997: 186–187). In the particular sense, 'property' means what Robb calls an 'abstract particular' or a 'trope'. Properties in the sense of abstract particulars are supposed to be wholly present in the things that instantiate them, but nowhere else. In the universal sense, 'property' means a universal or a unifying entity; this is (roughly) the sense in which 'property' has been used in this book so far. Robb calls properties in the sense of universals 'types'. To illustrate the difference between types and tropes, consider a case of two wise women, Anna and Hannah.[26] Is Anna's wisdom identical to Hannah's wisdom? If we conceive of Anna's wisdom and Hannah's wisdom as a type, that is, as a property in the sense of a universal, the answer is 'Yes'. If we conceive of Anna's wisdom and of Hannah's wisdom as a trope, that is, as a property in the sense of an abstract particular, the answer is 'No'. Robb holds that mental types are distinct from physical types. In our terminology, Robb denies reductive physicalism. He does, however, hold that each mental trope is identical to a physical trope (1997: 187).

Identifying mental and physical tropes is supposed to ensure not only that mental events cause physical events, but that they do so *qua* mental. They do so, according to Robb, because it is the tropes, not the types, that are responsible for the causal relevance of properties (1997: 187). Thus, for example, the event that is my headache is characterized by a headache-trope, which is identical to a c-fibre-firing-trope. The event has a physical effect, namely my hand's reaching towards the aspirin. The earlier event causes this physical event *qua* mental because it is characterized by a mental trope (which, like all mental tropes, is also a physical trope). It is, as it were, the job of tropes to guarantee causal relevance and, Robb holds, it does not make sense to ask whether tropes in turn get their causal relevance from something else: 'Tropes are not causally relevant *qua* this or that, they are

---

[24] See Robb 1997. Similar views are defended in MacDonald and MacDonald 1986, Heil 1992: 135–139, Heil and Robb 2003, and Robb 2013. I focus on Robb's position here because it ties in best with the above discussion of event identity.

[25] Robb (1997: 187) endorses this identity claim, but does not derive it from the Quinean identity condition for events.

[26] The example is a variant of an example of Robb's (1997: 186).

Theories of the Mind and Theories of Causation   25

causally relevant (or not), period' (1997: 191). The overall picture that Robb advocates is that there are three kinds of entities that are in play in causal relations: events, tropes, and types. Mental events are identical to physical events, and mental tropes are identical to physical tropes, but mental types are distinct from physical types. Tropes are responsible for causal relevance. In particular, they are responsible for mental events being causes *qua* mental.

One might object to Robb's suggestion by saying that, like the earlier suggestion that there is a separate causal relation, causation-*qua*, it needlessly proliferates kinds of entities by postulating the existence of tropes. But this objection could be countered by offering independent arguments for the existence of tropes.[27] It could also be countered by claiming that types reduce to tropes because types are nothing but sets of tropes that resemble one another.[28] A more serious problem for Robb's suggestion is that it is doubtful that it has really solved the problem of how mental events can be efficacious *qua* mental. Any solution to this problem should appeal to something general: when we ask by virtue of what, or *qua* what, a certain event had a certain effect, we expect the answer to tell us something general about that event. Saying that the event caused the effect by virtue of belonging to a certain type would satisfy this expectation, but this answer is not available to Robb, because he holds that mental and physical types are distinct. Saying that the event caused the effect by virtue of being characterized by a certain trope does not satisfy the expectation, for tropes are by definition particular, not general. Locating the causal relevance of events at the level of tropes seems merely to define the *qua* problem away instead of solving it.[29]

Let us return to identity conditions for events. Let us also, from now on, read 'property' in the universal or type sense and not in the trope sense, unless specified otherwise.

Jaegwon Kim thinks that events are constituted by an object, a property that is instantiated by the object, and the time at which the object instantiates the property.[30] Kim endorses the following two conditions,

---

[27] See Campbell 1990, Heil 2003, and Ehring 2011.

[28] Robb endorses the identity of types with sets of tropes, but holds that his theory of mental causation does not depend on it (1997: 186–188).

[29] A similar worry is expressed in MacDonald and MacDonald 2006; see also Noordhof 1998 and Shoemaker 2001. For further discussion of Robb's view, see Robb 2001, Ehring 2003, Gibb 2004, and Robb 2013.

[30] See Kim 1976. Kim uses 'substance' instead of 'object', but it is clear from his examples that he is not using 'substance' in a metaphysically laden sense. Here and throughout, I will confine myself to monadic events, that is, events that involve a single object (as opposed to multiple objects) and

Mental Causation

where '$[x, P, t]$' stands for the event that is constituted by object x, property P, and time t:

Existence condition: Event $[x, P, t]$ exists [i.e., occurs] just in case object x has property P at time t.

Identity condition: $[x, P, t] = [y, Q, t']$ just in case $x = y$, $P = Q$, and $t = t'$. (1976: 160–161)

Kim's conditions individuate events more finely than the Quinean account does. The property of rotating is distinct from the property of warming up. Hence, by the identity condition, the sphere's rotating is distinct from the sphere's warming up. Similarly for the apple's weighing 100 grams and the apple's having a temperature of 20 degrees. (The case of my strolling vs my strolling leisurely will be discussed in a moment.) Similarly, too, for my headache and my c-fibre firing if one is a non-reductive physicalist or a dualist: proponents of these positions deem the properties of having a headache and of having firing c-fibres to be distinct; hence, they have to deny the identity of the corresponding events if they accept Kim's identity condition.

Kim's existence and identity conditions allow for a weak and a strong reading. According to the weak reading, the conditions apply only to actual events, objects, properties, and times. According to the strong reading, they apply to all possible events, objects, properties, and times.[31] Let us call the resulting conception of events the *weak Kimian account* and the *strong Kimian account*, respectively.

On the strong reading, Kim's existence condition says that, in any possible world, event $[x, P, t]$ occurs just in case x has P at t in this world. The identity condition says that event $[x, P, t]$ at a possible world w is identical to event $[y, Q, t']$ at a possible world v (which may or may not be identical to w) just in case x is identical to y, P is identical to Q, and t is identical to t'.[32] On the strong reading, each event has its object, property, and time essentially. That is, no event could have occurred while being constituted by a different object or a different property; nor could any event have occurred at a different time. To see this, take some event $[x, P, t]$ that actually occurs. Assume that object y has property Q at time t' at

---

a property (as opposed to a relation). I will allow the constitutive time to be an interval that is larger than a point.

[31] Presumably, properties exist at possible worlds at which they are not instantiated. If so, the two readings do not differ with respect to what properties they quantify over.

[32] If one prefers the counterpart relation over trans-world identity, one can substitute 'is a counterpart of' for 'is identical to'.

a different world. Then, by the existence condition, the event $[y, Q, t']$ occurs at that world. But, by the identity condition, $[y, Q, t']$ is identical to $[x, P, t]$ only if y is identical to x, Q is identical to P, and t' is identical to t. In other words, $[x, P, t]$ can occur at different possible worlds only if it involves the same object, property, and time there.

Making the object, property, and time essential to an event is problematic, albeit not equally problematic for all the constituents. Suppose that in fact I strolled leisurely between noon and half past noon yesterday. If the object is essential to an event, then my strolling leisurely could not have been someone else's strolling leisurely. This sounds plausible.[33] If the property is essential to an event, then my strolling leisurely could not have happened while I had a property incompatible with strolling leisurely, such as strolling non-leisurely. This may sound less plausible. But we can say that the expression 'my strolling leisurely at noon' can pick out either of two events, one of which involves the property of strolling leisurely and one of which involves the property of strolling *simpliciter*. The former event is essentially a leisurely strolling according to the strong Kimian account; the latter event is merely essentially a strolling and could have happened in a non-leisurely way (see Kim 1976: 163). If the time is essential to an event, then my strolling leisurely could not have occurred at a different time. If I had started to stroll leisurely a second after noon yesterday, I would have strolled a different stroll. This may sound implausible. At least sometimes, it seems, events can be postponed or antedated without being replaced by different events. While the result that events have their time of occurrence essentially is a shortcoming of the strong Kimian account of events, we shall see that this account is still attractive overall.

On the weak reading, Kim's existence condition says that, in the actual world, event $[x, P, t]$ occurs just in case object x has property P at time t in the actual world. The identity condition says that an actual event $[x, P, t]$ is identical to an actual event $[y, Q, t']$ just in case x is identical to y, P is identical to Q, and t is identical to t'. The weak reading remains silent on whether or not events have their object, property, or time essentially. If an event that differs in one of these constituents from some actual event occurs at a possible world, it may or may not be identical to the actual event. If the possible event is identical to the actual event despite differing

---

[33] Which is not to say that there are no objections. Kim (1976: 171) discusses the case in which the stroll is a ritual of a secret society that chooses by lottery the person who will stroll. In this case it might seem that, had someone else been chosen, she would have strolled the same stroll.

in some constituent, that constituent is not essential to the event. One can, of course, supplement the weak Kimian account with claims to the effect that certain constituents of events are essential to them.[34] Kim himself sympathizes with the idea that the object is essential to an event, but not the property or the time (1976: 172).

If one endorses the weak Kimian account of events, but, unlike Kim, thinks that properties are essential to events, one can even go further than claiming that it is the constituent property that is essential to an event. One can make the stronger claim that some more specific property is essential to the event. For instance, one could claim that it is not merely essential to the sphere's rotating that the sphere rotates, but that it is essential that the sphere rotates with a certain angular velocity, or with an angular velocity that lies within a certain range. (That range should of course contain the sphere's actual angular velocity.) I shall leave it open for now whether making more specific properties essential to events is a good idea, but at any rate the weak Kimian account of events allows a lot of flexibility with respect to the modal relation between an event and its constituents (and more specific variants of the constituents). Thus, the weak Kimian account of events can be tailored to one's views about the essential and modal properties of events.

David Lewis thinks that events necessarily occur in spatiotemporal regions (1986b). Indeed, he thinks that actual and possible events are identical just in case they occur in the same actual and possible spatiotemporal regions.[35] 'Regions', not 'region': one and the same event may well occur in different spatiotemporal regions in different worlds. According to Lewis, events may have essential features, but we cannot read off these features from the nominalization that we use to pick out events. We use 'my strolling leisurely between noon and half past noon yesterday' to pick out a certain event, but it does not follow that this event necessarily involves me or a leisurely stroll; nor does it follow that this event necessarily occurs between noon and half past noon yesterday.

The Lewisian account and the weak Kimian account are very similar. They are in conflict only if in the actual world (i) a putative event occurs in a spatiotemporal region without being constituted (*inter alia*) by an object and a property or (ii) a non-spatial object has a property at a time.

---

[34] Strictly speaking, one could endorse a *weak* Kimian account and yet hold that all three constituents are essential to an event. Then some events in different worlds that have all three constituents in common could nonetheless be distinct. It is hard to see the motivation for such a view, however.

[35] In Lewis's own terminology, events correspond to properties, that is (according to Lewis), sets of spatiotemporal regions – those spatiotemporal regions in which the events occur (1986b: 244).

Theories of the Mind and Theories of Causation 29

According to the Lewisian account, a genuine event occurs in case (i), but not in case (ii). According to the weak Kimian account (or the strong Kimian account, for that matter), a genuine event occurs in case (ii), but not in case (i). Case (i) is impossible if we can find a suitable property to ascribe to the spatiotemporal region itself.[36] The best candidates for case (ii) seem to be Cartesian souls that exist in time but not in space. Few contemporary philosophers, including contemporary dualists, endorse their existence, however, and it is not even clear that the advocates of Cartesian souls can uphold that they are not spatial (see Lycan 2009, Bailey *et al.* 2011).

Given their similarity, it does not come as a surprise that the weak Kimian account and the Lewisian account of events share strengths and weaknesses. Like the weak Kimian account (and the strong Kimian account), the Lewisian account has the advantage of ruling the sphere's rotating and the sphere's warming up to be distinct events. While they occur in the same spatiotemporal region in the actual world, presumably there are possible regions where either event occurs without the other. Hence, by Lewis's identity condition, they are distinct. Like the weak Kimian account of events, the Lewisian account allows events to have essential features. Like the weak Kimian account, but unlike the strong Kimian account, the Lewisian account does not entail that events have certain specific essential features.

All this seems to tell in favour of the weak Kimian account and the Lewisian account vis-à-vis the strong Kimian account. The strong Kimian account has an advantage over these two views, however: it states necessary and sufficient conditions for the occurrence of a given event that hold in all possible worlds, not merely in the actual world. Moreover, it states these conditions in terms of objects, properties, and times. These two features of the strong Kimian account greatly facilitate the squaring of claims about the occurrence or non-occurrence of events in possible situations with claims about supervenience, which are also formulated in terms of objects, properties, and times. Many of the arguments in the following chapters will derive claims about the occurrence or non-occurrence of events in certain possible situations, and subsequently claims about causation, from claims about supervenience. It will therefore be convenient to assume a strong Kimian account of events. I will not overindulge in convenience, however. Sometimes the weak Kimian account and the Lewisian account will yield different results than the strong Kimian account. In these cases,

---

[36] For a similar suggestion, see Brand 1977: 335.

30 Mental Causation

I will consider the ramifications that ensue if one of these accounts of events is accepted instead.

1.4 Causation and the Logic of Counterfactuals

What makes a difference is a cause. This is the central principle about causation that I shall use in this book. An event occurs, followed by another event. If the earlier event had not occurred, the later event would not have occurred. Therefore, by the principle, the earlier event caused the later event. For example, I throw a dart at a balloon; an instant later the balloon bursts. If I had not thrown the dart, the balloon would not have burst. Therefore, by the principle, my throw causes the balloon to burst. We can formulate the principle more concisely by using the notion of counterfactual dependence. Say that event e *counterfactually depends* on event c just in case e would not have occurred if c had not occurred.[37] Then the principle says that for any two events c and e that actually occur, if e occurs later than c, and e counterfactually depends on c, then c causes e.[38]

The principle states a sufficient condition for causation in terms of counterfactual dependence. If there are any plausible claims about causation, the principle is one of them.[39] Its plausibility might, however, be obscured by problems that beset the more ambitious project of giving not merely sufficient conditions for causation in terms of counterfactuals, but necessary conditions as well. There are two kinds of cases that are particularly troublesome for the more ambitious project. First, there are cases of so-called late pre-emption. Billy and Suzy each throw a rock at a bottle at the same time. Billy's rock arrives there first and shatters the bottle. But if Billy had not thrown, Suzy's rock would have shattered the bottle anyway.[40] Second, there are cases of overdetermination. Both members of a firing squad of two simultaneously fire at the victim. The victim dies. Each firing killed the victim, it seems, but if either member had not shot, the victim would still

[37] I follow the common practice of taking counterfactual dependence to capture our informal notion of difference-making. Sartorio (2005, 2016: 94) has a different notion of difference-making that can apply in the absence of counterfactual dependence.

[38] Sometimes the counterfactual dependence of e on c is taken to require not just that e would not have occurred if c had not occurred, but also that e would have occurred if c had occurred. Given Lewis's truth-conditions for counterfactual conditionals, which will be presented shortly, the second counterfactual conditional is redundant given that (i) c and e actually occur and that (ii) any world (including the actual world) is closer to itself than any other worlds are. The assumption that any world is closer to itself than any other world is known as Strong Centring (see Lewis 1973b: 120). The account of mental causation developed in List and Menzies 2009 rejects Strong Centring.

[39] See Lewis 2004: 78, Schaffer 2004b: 240.

[40] So-called cases of trumping pre-emption give rise to similar problems; see Schaffer 2000b.

Theories of the Mind and Theories of Causation 31

have died.[41] These cases show that counterfactual dependence is not necessary for causation. Billy's throw causes the bottle to shatter, but the bottle would have shattered even if Billy had not thrown. The firing of each squad member causes the victim to die, but if either squad member had not fired, the victim would have died anyway from the other member's shot.[42] The cases are not counterexamples to the sufficiency of counterfactual dependence for causation, however, which is all that our principle claims.

In order to apply the principle, we need to know more about how counterfactual conditionals ('counterfactuals' for short), the claims that express counterfactual dependence, work. The counterfactuals we have considered so far have had the specific form 'If this event had not occurred, then that event would not have occurred', but it will be useful to have a general account that can handle any claims of the form 'If ϕ were the case, then ψ would be the case' (in symbols, $\phi \mathbin{\Box\!\!\rightarrow} \psi$), irrespective of what the antecedent ϕ and the consequent ψ look like. I shall assume Lewis's (1973b) truth-conditions for counterfactual conditionals. Assume that we can order all possible worlds according to how similar they are, overall, to the actual world. Let us think of the less similar worlds as more distant from the actual world. Lewis's idea is that a counterfactual is true just in case we have to depart further from the actual world to find a world where the antecedent of the conditional is true while its consequent is false than we have to in order to find a world where both the antecedent and the consequent are true. For example, the counterfactual 'If there had been no water on Earth, then no life would have developed there' is true just in case we have to depart further from actuality in order to find a world with a dry Earth where life still developed than we have to in order to find a world with a dry Earth where no life developed.[43] Lewis's idea can be applied only if the antecedent is metaphysically possible; otherwise, Lewis stipulates, the conditional is always vacuously true. More technically, Lewis's truth-conditions are as follows: a counterfactual 'If ϕ were the case, then ψ would be the case' ($\phi \mathbin{\Box\!\!\rightarrow} \psi$) is true if and only if either

(i) there is no possible world where ϕ is true; or
(ii) there is a possible world where ϕ and ψ are true that is closer

[41] For an argument for the claim that the individual overdetermining events cause the overdetermined event, see Schaffer 2003. Lewis remains neutral on this claim (1973a: 567 n. 12).

[42] In order to deal with certain other cases of pre-emption, Lewis suggests that not counterfactual dependence by itself, but the existence of a chain of events that are related by stepwise counterfactual dependence, is necessary and sufficient for causation (1973a: 567). This condition is violated in cases of late pre-emption and overdetermination, however. See Lewis 1986d for further discussion.

[43] The imagined journey takes place in the modal universe of possible worlds (sometimes called a pluriverse) and not in the actual universe, so the features of nearby earthlike planets in our actual galaxy have at best an indirect bearing on the truth of the present counterfactual.

(that is, more similar overall) to the actual world than any worlds where ϕ is true while ψ is false.

The truth-conditions also allow us to formulate truth-conditions for another kind of counterfactual conditional, namely conditionals of the form 'If ϕ were the case, then ψ might be the case.' Such 'might' conditionals are not directly relevant to the counterfactual dependence between events, but they will play a role in later arguments. I will follow Lewis in taking 'If ϕ were the case, then ψ might be the case' ($\phi \diamondsuit\!\!\rightarrow \psi$) to be equivalent to the negation of 'If ϕ were the case, then ψ would *not* be the case.' Thus 'If ϕ were the case, then ψ might be the case' is true just in case there is a world where both ϕ and ψ are true which is at least as close to the actual world as any worlds where ϕ is true while ψ is false. For example, the 'might' conditional 'If the coin had been tossed, it might have fallen heads' is true just in case there is a world where the coin is tossed and it falls heads that is at least as close as any worlds where the coin is tossed but it does not fall heads. Most of the counterfactual conditionals we shall be concerned with are 'would' conditionals rather than 'might' conditionals; I will therefore use 'counterfactual' without qualification to refer to the former kind of conditional.

It is tempting to paraphrase Lewis's truth-conditions for counterfactuals and 'might' conditionals by speaking about the closest worlds where their antecedents are true. According to this paraphrase, a counterfactual is non-vacuously true just in case its consequent is true at the closest worlds where its antecedent is true (for short: at the closest antecedent-worlds). For example, 'If there had been no water on Earth, then no life would have developed there' is non-vacuously true just in case no life developed at the closest worlds where there is no water on Earth. Similarly, a 'might' conditional is true according to the paraphrase just in case its consequent is true in some of the closest antecedent-worlds. 'If the coin had been tossed, it might have fallen heads', for example, is true just in case the coin falls heads in some of the closest worlds at which it is tossed.

The 'closest worlds' paraphrases presuppose that there is a set of closest antecedent-worlds for any 'would' or 'might' conditional. It presupposes, that is, that for any such conditional there is a set of antecedent-worlds such that no worlds are closer to the actual world than the members of this set.[44] It is doubtful whether we can always find such a set, however. Consider the following example. The counterfactual 'If I were nearer to Hammerfest

---

[44] The claim that there is such a set for each 'would' and 'might' conditional is the so-called Limit Assumption. See Lewis 1973b: 19–21 and Swanson 2012a for further discussion.

Theories of the Mind and Theories of Causation 33

now, I would still be alive' is true (I hope). Thus, according to the truth-conditions, there is a world – that is, there is at least one world – in which I am nearer to Hammerfest now and I am alive that is closer to the actual world than any worlds in which I am nearer to Hammerfest now without being alive. According to the 'closest worlds' paraphrase, there is also a set of worlds in which I am nearer to Hammerfest now (and in which I am alive) that are closer to the actual world than any other worlds in which I am nearer to Hammerfest now. There need not be any such set of worlds, however (let alone a unique such world). Presumably, there is a world where I am one metre nearer to Hammerfest now and still alive that is closer to the actual world than any worlds where I am nearer to Hammerfest now without being alive. The existence of such a world suffices to satisfy the truth-conditions for counterfactuals, but it does not suffice for the existence of a set of closest antecedent-worlds for our conditional. For it might well be the case that how close worlds in which I am nearer to Hammerfest now are to the actual world varies with how near I am to my actual position in those worlds. It might well be, that is, that worlds where I am one centimetre nearer to Hammerfest now are closer to the actual world than worlds where I am one metre nearer to Hammerfest now; that worlds where I am one millimetre nearer to Hammerfest now are closer to the actual world than worlds where I am one centimetre nearer to Hammerfest now; etc. Thus, it might well be that for all worlds where I am nearer to Hammerfest now, there are other worlds where I am nearer to Hammerfest now that are closer still to the actual world because in these other worlds I am nearer to where I actually am. If so, there is no set of closest antecedent-worlds, as the 'closest worlds' paraphrase has it. Despite this complication, I will use the paraphrase for convenience in cases where the presupposition is harmless.

From Lewis's truth-conditions for counterfactuals and 'might' conditionals we can assess various inferences that involve counterfactuals as valid or invalid. Having a repertoire of valid inferences that involve counterfactuals to hand will allow us to formulate arguments for claims about counterfactual dependence between mental and physical events and related claims in later chapters.

One inference that we will use repeatedly is the implication of a counterfactual by the corresponding strict conditional (where a strict conditional is a material conditional that is prefixed by 'Necessarily'):

(1)   Necessarily, if ϕ is the case, then ψ is the case. ($\Box[\phi \supset \psi]$)

---

(2)   If ϕ were the case, then ψ would be the case. ($\phi \, \Box\!\!\rightarrow \psi$)

Mental Causation

(In the notation, $\supset$ is the material conditional and $\square$ the metaphysical necessity operator.) The inference from (1) to (2) is valid because if ψ is true in all ϕ-worlds, as (1) says, then *a fortiori* ψ is true in all closest ϕ-worlds, as (2) says.[45]

Certain inferences that are valid for material conditionals and strict conditionals are invalid for counterfactuals. For our purposes, issues of transitivity will be particularly relevant. Material conditionals and strict conditionals are transitive; that is, the following inferences are valid:

(3) If ϕ is the case, then χ is the case. $(\phi \supset \chi)$[46]
(4) If χ is the case, then ψ is the case. $(\chi \supset \psi)$

----

(5) If ϕ is the case, then ψ is the case. $(\phi \supset \psi)$

(6) Necessarily, if ϕ is the case, then χ is the case. $(\square[\phi \supset \chi])$
(7) Necessarily, if χ is the case, then ψ is the case. $(\square[\chi \supset \psi])$

----

(8) Necessarily, if ϕ is the case, then ψ is the case. $(\square[\phi \supset \psi])$

Counterfactuals, by contrast, are not transitive; that is, the following inference is invalid (see Lewis 1973b: 32):

(9) If ϕ were the case, then χ would be the case. $(\phi \;\square\!\!\rightarrow\; \chi)$
(10) If χ were the case, then ψ would be the case. $(\chi \;\square\!\!\rightarrow\; \psi)$

----

(11) If ϕ were the case, then ψ would be the case. $(\phi \;\square\!\!\rightarrow\; \psi)$

That counterfactuals fail to be transitive can be shown abstractly from their truth-conditions, but can also readily be seen from concrete examples, such as the following:

(12) If I were king, I would wear a crown.
(13) If I wore a crown, people would find me ridiculous.

----

(14) If I were king, people would find me ridiculous.

----

[45] Friends of false counterpossibles, that is, false counterfactuals with impossible antecedents, will disagree. For a given (allegedly) false counterpossible, they cannot accept that it is logically implied by the corresponding strict conditional, which is trivially true owing to the impossible antecedent. Friends of false counterpossibles can still accept the weaker claim that strict conditionals with possible antecedents logically imply the corresponding counterfactuals. But in any event the existence of false counterpossibles is incompatible with Lewis's truth-conditions, which are assumed here. For further discussion, see Williamson (forthcoming).

[46] For simplicity, I am expressing material conditionals by indicative conditionals in natural language here, but the relation between these two kinds of conditional is notoriously difficult; see Jonathan Bennett 2003 for discussion.

Theories of the Mind and Theories of Causation   35

The closest possible worlds where I am king are rather remote from the actual world. In these closest worlds I use the usual insignia of the monarchy, including a crown. Thus, (12) is true. The closest worlds where I wear a crown are not quite so remote. Presumably, the closest worlds where I wear a crown are worlds where I buy one from a fancy dress shop and wear it on my way back home. In those worlds, people find me ridiculous, so (13) is true. But in the more distant worlds where I am king, people do not find me ridiculous, so (14) is false. More generally, counterfactuals can fail to be transitive when the antecedent of the first premise takes us to more distant worlds than the antecedent of the second premise does. In such a case the shared consequent of the second premise and the conclusion can be true in the less distant worlds but false in the more distant worlds.

The failure of transitivity persists even if we strengthen the first premise of the inference by replacing the counterfactual by a strict conditional. This strengthening yields the following inference:

(15) Necessarily, if ϕ is the case, then χ is the case. ($\Box[\phi \supset \chi]$)
(16) If χ were the case, then ψ would be the case. ($\chi \,\Box\!\!\rightarrow \psi$)

(17) If ϕ were the case, then ψ would be the case. ($\phi \,\Box\!\!\rightarrow \psi$)

This inference is invalid, too. Again, this can be shown abstractly or illustrated by a counterexample such as the following:[47]

(18) Necessarily, if I got up at 3 a.m., I got up before 9 a.m.
(19) If I had got up before 9 a.m., I would still have been rested.

(20) If I had got up at 3 a.m., I would still have been rested.

Suppose that, actually, I get up at 9 a.m. after a long night's sleep, perfectly rested. Assuming that, if I had got up earlier, I would not have gone to bed earlier (more on this kind of assumption below), (20) is false, because, given this assumption, I am sleep-deprived in the closest worlds at which I get up at 3 a.m. By contrast, (19) is true. For we may assume that, first, the closer in time my getting up is to my actual getting up, the closer the corresponding world is to the actual world and that, second, in such a world I am still rested if I do not get up much earlier than 9 a.m.[48] The strict conditional (18) is obviously true. In sum, the premises of the inference are true, but the conclusion is false, so the inference is invalid.

---

[47] Lewis (1973b: 32) gives a similar counterexample.
[48] The first assumption makes (19) a temporal analogue of the Hammerfest example discussed above.

Mental Causation

That the above inferences involving counterfactuals are invalid should not mislead one into thinking that no interesting transitivity-like reasoning with counterfactuals is possible. For we can find substitutes for those inferences that are valid (see Lewis 1973b: 31–36, 1973c). The idea behind the substitute inferences is to patch up the premises so that the closest antecedent-worlds of the premises no longer come apart in a way that threatens the truth of the conclusion.

This can be done in several ways. The first inference, that from (9) and (10) to (11), can be repaired by adding another premise to the effect that the antecedent of the first premise not only counterfactually implies the antecedent of the old second premise, but that the converse is also true:

(9)   If ϕ were the case, then χ would be the case. ($\phi \mathbin{\Box\!\!\rightarrow} \chi$)
(21) If χ were the case, then ϕ would be the case. ($\chi \mathbin{\Box\!\!\rightarrow} \phi$)
(10) If χ were the case, then ψ would be the case. ($\chi \mathbin{\Box\!\!\rightarrow} \psi$)

---

(11) If ϕ were the case, then ψ would be the case. ($\phi \mathbin{\Box\!\!\rightarrow} \psi$)

Together, premises (9) and (21) guarantee that the closest ϕ-worlds coincide with the closest χ-worlds, for (9) says that the closest ϕ-worlds are χ-worlds, and (21) says that the closest χ-worlds are ϕ-worlds. By (10), the closest χ-worlds are ψ-worlds, so together with the coincidence claim it follows that the closest ϕ-worlds are ψ-worlds, as conclusion (11) says.[49]

Another way of repairing the inference from (9) and (10) to (11) is to replace (10) with a premise with a stronger antecedent, viz. claim (22) below; the resulting inference is sometimes called *restricted transitivity*:

(9)   If ϕ were the case, then χ would be the case. ($\phi \mathbin{\Box\!\!\rightarrow} \chi$)
(22) If ϕ and χ were the case, then ψ would be the case. ($\phi \mathbin{\&} \chi \mathbin{\Box\!\!\rightarrow} \psi$)

---

(11) If ϕ were the case, then ψ would be the case. ($\phi \mathbin{\Box\!\!\rightarrow} \psi$)

Again, this manoeuvre guarantees that the closest antecedent-worlds of the premises coincide. For if (9) is true, the closest ϕ-worlds are χ-worlds and thus are also the closest ϕ-and-χ-worlds, and the closest antecedent-worlds of (22) are trivially the closest ϕ-and-χ-worlds. The inference is valid because by (22) the closest ϕ-and-χ-worlds are ψ-worlds and by (9) the closest ϕ-worlds are also the closest ϕ-and-χ-worlds and so are ψ-worlds.

---

[49] For further discussion of the inference from (9), (21) and (10) to (11), see Stalnaker 1968, Lewis 1973b: 33, Tooley 2002 and Cross 2006.

Theories of the Mind and Theories of Causation

The inference that involved strict as well as counterfactual conditionals, that from (15) and (16) to (17), can be repaired by turning the strict conditional (15) into a strict biconditional, claim (23):

(23) Necessarily, ϕ is the case if and only if χ is the case. ($\Box[\phi \equiv \chi]$)
(16) If χ were the case, then ψ would be the case. ($\chi \,\Box\!\!\rightarrow \psi$)

---

(17) If ϕ were the case, then ψ would be the case. ($\phi \,\Box\!\!\rightarrow \psi$)

(In the additional symbolism, $\equiv$ is the material biconditional.) The manoeuvre of replacing (15) with (23) makes sure that the closest ϕ-worlds and the closest χ-worlds coincide. Indeed, by (23), *all* ϕ-worlds and χ-worlds coincide.[50] By (16), the closest χ-worlds are ψ-worlds, so with the coincidence result we get that the closest ϕ-worlds are ψ-worlds.

Another way of repairing the inference that involved both counterfactuals and strict conditionals is to switch the role of the counterfactual premise and the strict conditional premise. Thus, we get the following inference:

(24) If ϕ were the case, then χ would be the case. ($\phi \,\Box\!\!\rightarrow \chi$)
(25) Necessarily, if χ is the case, then ψ is the case. ($\Box[\chi \supset \psi]$)

---

(17) If ϕ were the case, then ψ would be the case. ($\phi \,\Box\!\!\rightarrow \psi$)

While (24) and (25) allow the closest ϕ-worlds to be more distant than the closest χ-worlds, they do not allow ψ to be true only in the relatively close χ-worlds. For by (25) ψ is true in all χ-worlds; *a fortiori* ψ is true in the closest ϕ-worlds, because those, by (24), are also χ-worlds. Thus, (17) follows from (24) and (25).

Besides transitivity, further inferences that are valid for material conditionals and strict conditionals are invalid for counterfactuals. For instance, unlike material conditionals and strict conditionals, counterfactuals do not allow strengthening of the antecedent. That is, the following inference is invalid:

(26) If ϕ were the case, then ψ would be the case. ($\phi \,\Box\!\!\rightarrow \psi$)

---

(27) If ϕ and χ were the case, then ψ would be the case. ($\phi \,\&\, \chi \,\Box\!\!\rightarrow \psi$)

The inference is invalid for reasons similar to the reasons why counterfactuals fail to be transitive: the closest worlds where both ϕ and χ are true may be more

---

[50] The inference from (23) and (16) to (17) is valid not only given Lewis's truth-conditions for counterfactuals, but in any logic for counterfactuals that creates non-hyperintensional contexts in Williamson's (2006: 312) sense. That is, the inference is valid in any logic for counterfactuals that allows the substitution of strictly equivalent propositions *salva veritate*.

remote and different in character from the closest worlds where merely φ is true.[51] For instance, at the closest worlds where I strike the match, the match is dry and it lights. But at the closest worlds where I strike the match and it is wet, it does not light. Thus, the premise of the following argument is true but its conclusion false:

> (28)   If I had struck the match, then it would have lit.

> (29)   If I had struck the match and the match had been wet, then it would have lit.

Like the transitivity-inferences, the inference from (26) to (27) can be repaired to restore validity. We can, for example, add the further premise that if φ were the case, χ might be the case, which yields the following argument (see Lewis 1973c):

> (26)   If φ were the case, then ψ would be the case. ($\phi \;\Box\!\!\!\rightarrow\; \psi$)
> (30)   If φ were the case, then χ might be that case. ($\phi \;\Diamond\!\!\!\rightarrow\; \chi$)

> (27)   If φ and χ were the case, then ψ would be the case. ($\phi \;\&\; \chi \;\Box\!\!\!\rightarrow\; \psi$)

Adding premise (30) makes sure that some of the closest φ-worlds, which, by (26), are all ψ-worlds, are χ-worlds. Thus, the closest φ-and-χ-worlds as well as the closest φ-worlds are ψ-worlds, and (27) is true.

The lesson to be learned from the logical peculiarities of counterfactuals is twofold. First, we may not simply use familiar inferences that are valid for other kinds of conditional, for these inferences may fail for counterfactuals. Second, we can find similar inferences that are valid for counterfactuals and that we can substitute for the invalid ones. In philosophical debates the first point has received more attention than the second. But this should not make us pessimistic about reasoning with counterfactuals, because the second point shows that, if we are sufficiently careful, we can still build powerful arguments with counterfactuals.

The following chapters capitalize on the logic of counterfactuals in order to solve the problems of mental causation. In particular, they derive claims about counterfactual dependence, and thence claims about causation, between mental and physical events from other counterfactuals or from other counterfactuals together with claims about necessity. For this strategy, the substitute inferences for transitivity will be especially relevant, but other inferences will also play a role. New inferences will be explained

---

[51] Lewis (1973b: 31–36) holds that the transitivity failures of counterfactuals can be regarded as generalizations from the failure of the present inference.

Theories of the Mind and Theories of Causation

when they first appear in the text. Appendix 2 contains a list of valid and invalid inferences involving counterfactuals for easy reference.

1.5 Counterfactual Dependence and Similarity between Worlds

The central ingredient in the truth-conditions for counterfactuals is the relation of comparative overall similarity or closeness between worlds, that is, the relation expressed by 'world w is more similar overall to the actual world than world v is' and (equivalently) by 'world w is closer to the actual world than world v is'. The truth-conditions enable us to classify inferences involving counterfactuals as valid or invalid even if we do not know anything about the relation of comparative overall similarity or closeness apart from its structural features. In order to evaluate individual counterfactuals as true or false, however, we need to specify the details of the relation. This section discusses how we should spell out these details. The results will be important for the arguments in later chapters. In particular, the results will enable us to evaluate counterfactuals about the synchronic relation between the mental and the physical as well as claims about the counterfactual dependence of later physical events on earlier events.

The relation of comparative overall similarity or closeness should not have the result that the past counterfactually depends on the present or on the future. The air pressure drops. A little later, the barometer reading falls. Suppose that our similarity relation had the result that if the barometer reading had not fallen, then the air pressure would not have dropped. We would not like to say that the falling of the barometer reading causes the earlier drop in air pressure, and we do not have to say this, for our principle about causation is restricted to putative effects that occur after their putative causes. So far, so good. But suppose further that after the barometer reading falls, there is a storm. If it is true that the air pressure would not have dropped had the barometer reading not fallen, presumably it is also true that the storm would not have occurred had the barometer reading not fallen. Unlike the drop in air pressure, the storm occurs after the barometer reading falls, so it would follow from our principle that the falling of the barometer reading causes the storm. That claim, however, is almost as implausible as the claim that the falling of the barometer reading causes the earlier drop in air pressure.

Let us define a *backtracking* evaluation of a counterfactual as an evaluation that has the result that the past of the time that the antecedent talks about counterfactually depends on what is going on at that time. We just saw that backtracking can have the result that the future depends on the present or past in the wrong way. This, in turn, would make trouble for our principle about causation. We should therefore rule out backtracking evaluations at least in contexts where we are interested in causation.

Backtracking is well defined only for counterfactuals whose antecedents talk about a specific time, so let us confine our attention to such counterfactuals for now. Here is a simple suggestion that rules out backtracking. For a given counterfactual, let us stipulate that there is a set of antecedent-worlds that are closer to the actual world than any other antecedent-worlds and that have the following feature: the past of the worlds in the set exactly matches the past of the actual world until just before the time specified in the antecedent; then the antecedent is made true with minimal difference to the actual world, which might involve violations of the actual laws of nature; from the antecedent-time onwards, there are no more violations of the actual laws of nature. Let us call this approach to the similarity relation the *asymmetry-by-fiat approach*.[52]

The asymmetry-by-fiat approach avoids backtracking, because the closest antecedent-worlds match the actual world until just before the antecedent-time. Here is how the approach accounts for ordinary cases of counterfactual dependence, such as the dependence of the balloon's bursting on my throwing the dart: The closest antecedent-worlds for the counterfactual 'If I had not thrown the dart, then the balloon would not have burst' are like the actual world until just before the time at which I throw the dart in the actual world. Then my throwing is prevented in a way that minimized the difference to the actual world. Perhaps I have a change of heart, or perhaps a sudden cramp in my arm. Afterwards, the closest antecedent-worlds evolve in accordance with the actual laws of nature. Thus, the balloon remains intact. (Perhaps the balloon eventually bursts at a much later time, but this would be different bursting.)

The asymmetry-by-fiat approach has two disadvantages. First, it entails, at least for the kind of counterfactuals under consideration, that there is a set of closest antecedent-worlds in the sense that the worlds in that set are closer to the actual world than any other antecedent-worlds. We saw in the previous section that counterfactuals like 'If I were nearer to Hammerfest now, I would still be alive' show that there need not always be such a set and that instead there might be a series of antecedent-worlds that are ever closer

---

[52] I borrow the term from Lewis (1979), who uses it to refer to a slightly different account of counterfactuals that does not assume the truth-conditions in terms of the similarity of possible worlds. Similar approaches can be found in Maudlin 2007 and Paul and Hall 2013: 47–48.

Theories of the Mind and Theories of Causation 41

to the actual world.[53] A second disadvantage of the asymmetry-by-fiat approach is that it can be applied only to counterfactuals whose antecedents talk about what is (or is not) going on at specific times.

Neither disadvantage should worry us too much. The closest-worlds issue can be circumvented. Instead of stipulating that there is a set of such-and-such closest antecedent-worlds, we can rule out backtracking by fiat by formulating similarity criteria in the style of the miracles approach that will be discussed shortly.[54] But presumably the closest-world issue is not much of a problem to start with. In any event, for convenience I shall continue sometimes to talk about 'the closest antecedent-worlds' of a given counterfactual. The restriction to antecedents that talk about specific times is not a problem for us either, because the counterfactuals that we shall be concerned with, namely counterfactuals that express counterfactual dependence, have antecedents that talk about specific times in any case. (Likewise for the counterfactuals with more complex antecedents that will play a role in Chapter 3.)

The asymmetry-by-fiat approach gives a simple and convenient way to evaluate the counterfactuals that are relevant to causation. Sometimes, however, it will prove useful to have a more elaborate account of the similarity relation. Lewis suggests the following criteria for the comparative overall similarity between worlds:

(1) It is of the first importance to avoid big, widespread, diverse violations of law.

(2) It is of the second importance to maximize the spatiotemporal region throughout which perfect match of particular fact prevails.

(3) It is of the third importance to avoid even small, localized, simple violations of law.

(4) It is of little or no importance to secure approximate similarity of particular fact, even in matters that concern us greatly. (Lewis 1979: 472)

Following Lewis (1979, 471), let us call a big, widespread violation of law a *big miracle* and a small, localized, simple violation of law a *small miracle*. Let us call the way of spelling out comparative overall similarity between worlds by criteria like (1)–(4) the *miracles approach*. It is worth pointing out that the miracles that feature in this approach are not themselves very

---

[53] The asymmetry-by-fiat approach does not entail the Limit Assumption (see footnote 44), however, since the latter is more general: the Limit Assumption applies to counterfactuals irrespective of whether their antecedents are about specific times.

[54] These criteria would read: it is of the first importance to match the actual world perfectly in particular fact until just before the antecedent-time and not to involve miracles after antecedent-time; it is of the second importance to minimize the violations of law just before the antecedent-time.

miraculous. Nothing like witchcraft is required. If a miracle (big or small) occurs in a given world, *our* laws of nature are violated at that world, not the laws of nature of that very world. (Given that laws at least entail regularities without exceptions, it is impossible for the laws of nature of a given world to be violated in that very world; see Lewis 1979: 468–469.) Lewis's criteria (1)–(4) are most naturally read as exceptionless priorities, such that the criteria higher up on the list always trump the criteria further down.[55] Thus, a world where a big miracle occurs is always less similar overall to our world than a world without big miracles. Among worlds that are on a par with respect to big miracles, a world that matches the actual world perfectly in particular fact throughout a larger region of space–time than another one is always more similar overall to the actual world than the latter. Among worlds that are on a par with respect to all of the above, a world where a small miracle occurs is always less similar overall to our world than a world without a small miracle. Among worlds that are on a par with respect to all of the above, a world that matches the actual world approximately in particular fact throughout a larger region of space–time than another one is always more similar overall to the actual world than the latter (if we opt for the 'little importance' rather than the 'no importance' reading of criterion (4)).

To see how the miracles approach rules out backtracking, let us first assume that our laws of nature are deterministic. Let us assume, that is, that any worlds where our laws of nature hold are either always alike or never alike. (I will say more below about why I make this assumption.) It seems that we never need more than a small miracle to prevent the occurrence of a given event, even if we hold history fixed until just before the time at which the event actually occurred. Take the falling of the barometer reading. We can find a world where a small miracle prevents the falling of the barometer reading, owing to a tiny malfunctioning of the barometer just before its reading actually fell, say. We can also find a world where a small miracle prevents the earlier drop in air pressure. At that world, too, the barometer reading does not fall. The two worlds are on a par with respect to criterion (1), since neither involves a big miracle. The world

---

[55] We can think of aggregating aspects of similarity to overall similarity as an interpretation of social choice theory: the aspects of similarity play the role of the individual preferences, and overall similarity plays the role of the collective preference. In social choice terms, the similarity aspect of whether or not there is a big miracle is *dictatorial*, because it overrides any other aspects of similarity. While it seems implausible that there are always dictatorial aspects of similarity, such aspects may be tolerated in the special case of causal contexts; see Morreau 2010 and Kroedel and Huber 2013 for further discussion.

where the barometer malfunctions just before the time at which its reading actually fell has more perfect match of particular fact with the actual world than the world where there is no earlier drop in air pressure. By criterion (2), the world with the malfunctioning barometer wins the contest for similarity with the actual world. Since the world with the malfunctioning barometer matches the actual world perfectly in particular fact until just before the time at which the reading actually fell, no backtracking ensues (except perhaps into the very near past).

How does the miracles approach yield the truth of counterfactuals about ordinary cases of counterfactual dependence, such as 'If I had not thrown the dart, then the balloon would not have burst'? Like in the barometer case, we can find worlds whose history is exactly like the actual history until just before the time at which I actually threw and where a small miracle prevents my throw. By criterion (2), these worlds would be even closer to the actual world if they also matched the actual world perfectly after the antecedent-time. According to Lewis, such 'reconvergence' requires a big miracle, however.[56] All the traces of my failure to throw – my memories of not throwing, light rays reflected from my stationary arm, etc. – need to be erased. This requires a multitude of small miracles, which add up to a big miracle. By criterion (1), the worlds with perfect reconvergence that is due to a big miracle are less similar to the actual world than worlds that diverge from the actual world after the original small miracle. One could achieve less than perfect convergence at the cost of a few additional small miracles. In particular, a world could hold fixed the balloon's bursting at the cost of one extra small miracle. By criteria (3) and (4), however, avoiding small miracles is more important than increasing approximate match of particular fact.[57] Thus, there are antecedent-worlds where a single small miracle prevents my throw and where, consequently, the balloon does not burst. By Lewis's criteria, these worlds are closer to the actual world than any

---

[56] See Lewis 1979. Elga (2001) and Wasserman (2006) argue that sometimes a small miracle suffices to bring about perfect reconvergence.

[57] At least this is the canonical story. It raises some tricky issues, however. First, we cannot read criterion (3) as being an all-or-nothing matter about the occurrence of *some* small miracle, since the number of small miracles matters. This in turn raises questions about how to count small miracles, which is complicated by the fact that, according to Lewis, miracles have a mereological structure similar to that of events. Second, it might seem that a world where the bottle's shattering is brought back by a small miracle has extra *perfect* match of particular fact with the actual world, namely extra perfect match in the spatiotemporal region occupied by the shattering. By criterion (2), this result would jeopardize the desired truth of our counterfactual. We can avoid the result by reading 'spatiotemporal region' in (2) as 'spatiotemporal region that is not scattered along the spatial dimension', but stipulating such a reading raises complications of its own. See Kroedel 2018 for further discussion.

worlds with perfect or imperfect reconvergence where I do not throw and the bottle still shatters. The shattering counterfactually depends on the throw, as desired.

There is some controversy about whether the miracles approach always avoids backtracking. Consider the following case. A nuclear bomb explodes in the centre of our town. The blast first destroys my house; a fraction of a second later, it destroys your house, which is further away from the centre. It might seem that it takes a big miracle to prevent the destruction of my house given that the bomb explodes, but only a small miracle (a tiny malfunction in the fuse, say) to prevent the explosion. Hence, in the closest worlds where my house is not destroyed, the nuclear bomb does not explode and your house is not destroyed either. Consequently, the counterfactuals 'If my house had not been destroyed, then the bomb would not have exploded' and 'If my house had not been destroyed, then your house would not have been destroyed' both come out true.[58] But they should not come out true, of course, if we want to avoid the result that the destruction of my house causes the destruction of your house, which would follow by our principle about causation.

There is a bold and a modest response. The bold response denies that the counterfactuals are true and claims that it merely takes a small miracle to prevent the destruction of my house. Thus, the closest worlds where my house is not destroyed match the actual world until just before the time at which my house is destroyed in the actual world. In particular, in these worlds the nuclear bomb still explodes and, later, your house is still destroyed. Why should we say that the miracle that prevents the destruction of my house (given that the nuclear explosion occurs) is a small one? According to Lewis (1986e: 55–56), what distinguishes big miracles from small ones is that big miracles are spread out more broadly and have parts (themselves small miracles) that are varied.[59] Given that the nuclear explosion occurs, certain laws need to be broken throughout a spatial volume around my house for a short while in order to shield my house from the blast. While admittedly this volume has a substantial size, it is not spread

---

[58] Kment (2010: 84, 107 n. 10) credits this example to Peter Lipton. Woodward (2003: 133–145) raises a similar issue. See also Jonathan Bennett 2003: 204–211. (All future references of the form 'Bennett 2003' are to Karen Bennett's 2003.)

[59] Lewis writes that '[a] big miracle consists of many little miracles together, *preferably* not all alike' (1986e: 56, my emphasis). The context of his discussion strongly suggests that the 'preferably' qualification can be dropped, however, for the following sentence states that '[w]hat makes the big miracle more of a miracle is . . . that it is divisible into many *and varied* parts, any one of which is on a par with the little miracle' (1986e: 56, my emphasis; see also Lewis 1979: 471).

Theories of the Mind and Theories of Causation 45

out in the sense of being scattered.[60] Further, the parts of this miracle are all alike, because they all involve violations of the same laws (namely whichever laws need to be broken in order to prevent the radiation, heat, and impact of the explosion from reaching my house).

The modest response is to tolerate cases of backtracking that allegedly result from the miracles approach and to weaken our principle about causation accordingly. Instead of claiming that counterfactual dependence as assessed according to the miracles approach is sufficient for (forward-in-time) causation, we can claim that counterfactual dependence as assessed according to the miracles approach is sufficient for causation *if* the relevant counterfactual is not evaluated in a backtracking way. Perhaps in the case of the nuclear explosion the truth of 'If my house had not been destroyed, then your house would not have been destroyed' is due to backtracking according to the miracles approach. If so, no causal consequences follow. By contrast, the truth of 'If I had not thrown the dart, then the balloon would not have burst' is not due to backtracking according to the miracles approach. Hence we may infer that my throw causes the balloon to burst. We shall see that in cases of mental causation the miracles approach will not yield backtracking either, so the modest response will be available in those cases too.

As it stands, the miracles approach requires determinism to yield the right verdicts about counterfactual dependence. (By determinism, I mean the claim that the laws of a given world are deterministic in the sense defined earlier in this section.) Without determinism, perfect reconvergence would not require another miracle (big or small), because it could occur by mere chance (see Lewis 1986e: 60). Similarly, imperfect reconvergence that merely guarantees the falsity of the consequent at the world in question could come about by chance. Thus, most counterfactuals about ordinary cases of counterfactual dependence would come out false (see Hawthorne 2005, Hájek ms.). The same holds for the asymmetry-by-fiat approach.[61] If we let an antecedent-world evolve lawfully and the laws are indeterministic, the consequent of the counterfactual may come out false by chance.

I will set aside the question of whether the falsity of ordinary counterfactuals under indeterminism would be a serious problem *per se*. We would not get counterexamples to our principle about causation, because the principle says that counterfactual dependence is sufficient for causation, not that it is necessary. While the principle would lose much of its utility if

---

[60] By contrast, Lewis's paradigmatic big miracles, the reconvergence miracles, are spread out in the sense of being scattered (1979: 471).
[61] *Pace* Lewis, who holds that the approach 'has no need of determinism' (1986e: 62).

there were few cases of counterfactual dependence under indeterminism, there is a similar principle that we could use as a substitute. The similar principle says that what we may call *probabilistic dependence* is sufficient for causation: event *c* causes a later event *e* just in case *e* would have had a much lower chance of occurring had *c* not occurred.[62] It seems that both the asymmetry-by-fiat approach and the miracles approach would evaluate enough counterfactuals that express probabilistic dependence as true to justify using a sufficient condition for causation in terms of counterfactuals.[63] Thus, in the end not much hinges on whether or not our laws of nature are deterministic. It is mainly for simplicity that, for the remainder of this book, I shall assume that they are.

The upshot so far is that the asymmetry-by-fiat approach is simple and straightforwardly rules out backtracking. The miracles approach is less simple (albeit more generally applicable), and it is less clear that it rules out backtracking. Owing to these advantages of the asymmetry-by-fiat approach over the miracles approach, I shall – at least *ceteris paribus* – prefer the asymmetry-by-fiat approach in later arguments. When we consider mental causation under dualism, however, the miracles approach will turn out to be superior, because it lends itself to making a modal distinction between different kinds of laws (in particular, between physical laws and psychophysical laws).

Backtracking is not the only threat to the sufficiency of counterfactual dependence for causation. Another one comes from strange causal relata. Here is an example. At midnight, a bottle shatters owing to sudden external forces. At 11:59 p.m., the bottle had the property of shattering-in-one-minute (call this property $S+$). If the bottle had not had $S+$ at 11:59 p.m., it would not have shattered at midnight. But it does not seem that the bottle's having $S+$ at 11:59 p.m. causes the bottle's shattering at midnight.

The appropriate response is to rule out events that involve certain kinds of properties. We should allow only properties that are sufficiently intrinsic and temporally intrinsic, that is, roughly, properties that are about how things are with the object in question itself and about how things are with that object at the time of instantiation.[64] Property $S+$ is not about how things are with the object at the time of instantiation, but rather about how things will be with the object a minute after the time of instantiation. We can spell out the envisaged response in two ways. We can say that only

---

[62] See Lewis 1986d. For further discussion, see Hitchcock 2004a.
[63] The miracles approach requires some modifications for the indeterministic case; see Lewis 1986e.
[64] See Lewis 2004: 78. Cases where merely the requirement of intrinsicness is violated, not the requirement of temporal intrinsicness, are discussed in Lewis 1986b: 262–266 and 1986d: 189–193.

Theories of the Mind and Theories of Causation 47

instantiations of properties that are sufficiently (temporally) intrinsic are genuine events. Or we can say that only counterfactual dependence between events that involve properties that are sufficiently (temporally) intrinsic suffices for causation. I have no firm opinion about how (temporally) intrinsic the properties in genuine events have to be and will therefore embrace the second option.[65]

It might seem that instances of properties that are highly temporally extrinsic still sometimes qualify as causes. Suppose that, at noon, a celebrity has the property of dying at midnight from a prolonged illness. Call the property of dying-at-midnight $D+$. Property $D+$ is highly temporally extrinsic (at least when instantiated at a time other than midnight). Having learned about the impending death, a journalist writes an obituary in the afternoon. Does the celebrity's having $D+$ cause the journalist's writing? It might seem so at first sight, but a better diagnosis of the case is that the journalist's writing and the celebrity's death have a common cause, namely the celebrity's medical condition before noon. This is consistent with citing the fact that the celebrity has $D+$ – more idiomatically, the fact the celebrity is going to die – as a reason for the journalist's writing the obituary.[66] For the fact can be a reason for the journalist to write by virtue of being the content of a belief of the journalist, which in turn is a cause of the writing; the fact need not itself be such a cause.

Lastly, alleged causes that seem far-fetched pose a threat to the sufficiency of counterfactual dependence for causation. On the street I bump into a stranger, Albert, who subsequently misses his bus. On the next bus, Albert meets his future wife. They have a child, Berta, who dies 90 years later. If I had not bumped into Albert, then Berta

---

[65] A related worry is about omissions. Lots of events counterfactually depend on omissions, but one might not want to accept that they are caused by those omissions. That omissions cannot be causes is more controversial than that properties like $S+$ cannot be causes. If one wants to rule out omissions as causes, one could pursue a similar strategy: restrict our sufficient condition for causation to instances of 'positive' properties and disallow instances of 'negative' properties. I will remain neutral on questions about omissions as causes, but in Section 3.4 I will discuss ways of dealing with omission in the causal modelling framework. For further discussion, see Lewis 1986d: 189–193 and McGrath 2005. Should we also demand that only instances of *natural* properties in Lewis's (1983) sense can be causes and effects? We had better not without good reason. Arbitrary disjunctions of intrinsic properties are still intrinsic (see Weatherson 2001) – not so for natural properties. Given non-reductive physicalism, mental properties turn out to be – or at least to be strictly equivalent to – long disjunctions of physical properties (see Section 2.2). Perhaps this makes mental properties somewhat unnatural, but we would still like to maintain that their instances can be causes and effects. For further discussion of disjunctive causes, see Sartorio 2006 and Beebee 2017.

[66] On the related issue of corresponding 'because'-sentences, see Jenkins and Nolan 2008 and Schnieder 2015.

would not have died.[67] But it might seem that my bumping into Albert does not cause Berta's death.

The appropriate response is to accept that my bumping into Albert does cause Berta's death and to explain away appearances to the contrary as a pragmatic phenomenon. Counterfactual dependence is sufficient for a kind of causation that is 'broad and non-discriminatory' (Lewis 1973a: 559). If event e counterfactually depends on an earlier event c, it follows that c is a cause of e. It does not follow that c is among those causes of e that are explanatorily relevant, and hence worth mentioning, in any given context. (*A fortiori*, it does not follow that c is *the* cause of e, if the definite article is supposed to single out the most explanatorily relevant one among e's causes.) In most contexts, my bumping into Albert counts as irrelevant for a causal explanation of Berta's death. In those contexts, it would sound strange to say that my bumping into Albert causes Berta's death, but it remains true that it is among the causes of Berta's death.[68]

For completeness I should mention another type of case that is often cited in objections to Lewis's theory of causation. I write 'Larry'. By writing 'Larry', I *ipso facto* write 'rr'. Thus, if I had not written 'rr' I would not – indeed, could not – have written 'Larry'. But it sounds strange to say that my writing 'rr' causes me to write 'Larry' (see Kim 1973). This result does not follow from our principle about causation, however. The principle is restricted to cases where the putative cause occurs before the putative effect.[69] My writing 'rr' does not, however, occur before my writing 'Larry' (although it ends earlier). More generally, if two events occur at times that do not overlap and they involve only properties that are temporally intrinsic, we never get the kind of necessary connection between those events that give rise to 'Larry'-style counterexamples.[70]

---

[67] That is, the event of Berta's death would not have occurred, because Berta would not have existed in the first place. The example is a variation of an example from Lewis 1986d: 184. Thomson (2003) takes cases of this kind to refute the sufficiency of counterfactual dependence for causation.

[68] See Lewis 2004: 101. For a recent elaboration of this approach, see Swanson 2010. According to Sartorio 2010, there are further cases, which indirectly involve omissions, that are counterexamples to the sufficiency of counterfactual dependence for causation. Weslake 2013 argues that they can be defused by a strategy that is similar to the one used here.

[69] Thus, the principle remains neutral on whether there can be simultaneous causation. See Section 3.6 for further discussion.

[70] Lewis's own response is to restrict causal claims to cases where cause and effect are wholly distinct events, that is, events that occur in non-overlapping spatiotemporal regions (see Lewis 1986b: 259 for discussion). It is not entirely clear that cause and effect can never overlap. Perhaps the First World War caused a famine that started before the war ended. For our purposes we need not settle this issue, however.

1.6   Transference Views, Double Prevention, and Powers

A rival view of causation requires that a certain physical quantity be transferred from cause to effect. This view can be spelled out in different ways. One might remain neutral on what physical quantity is transferred (see Aronson 1971) or allow only quantities that obey a physical conservation law (see Dowe 2000, Salmon 1994), especially energy (see Fair 1979). In typical cases of causation, such a transfer indeed takes place. A thrown rock transfers energy to a bottle, thereby shattering it. A moving billiard ball transfers momentum to another ball, thereby making it roll into the pocket. A lightning strike transfers energy to a house, thereby igniting it. Transfer accounts also give the right verdicts (or at least no wrong verdicts) about cases that full-blown accounts of causation in terms of counterfactuals have found hard to cope with, namely cases of late pre-emption and overdetermination. Only Billy's throw, which actually hits the bottle, transfers energy to it; Suzy's throw, which actually arrives at the bottle's place only after it is destroyed by Billy's throw, does not. And all bullets from the firing squad transfer energy to the victim.

The cases we have just considered make it *prima facie* plausible that transfer of a physical quantity is necessary for causation. The converse claim, that transfer of a physical quantity is sufficient for causation, does not seem plausible. Let us modify the example of the rock that shatters the bottle a bit. Suppose that the rock is first heated over a fire and then thrown at the bottle, which shatters. The fire transfers a physical quantity (namely heat) to the bottle via the rock, but does not seem to qualify as a cause of the shattering in any interesting sense.[71] Since friends of explaining causation in terms of transfer are well advised not to endorse the claim that transfer of a physical quantity is sufficient for causation, by 'transference views' I shall merely mean views according to which the transfer of a physical quantity is necessary for causation.

There is a family of cases that make trouble for transference views of causation. A pillar is propped up on a rack. I kick the rack aside, and the pillar falls down.[72] A catch holds a stretched spring in position. I release the catch, and the spring accelerates (see Aronson 1971: 425). There are many more cases of this kind (see Schaffer 2000a, 2004a). They all have the following structure: something happens that would have been prevented by something else, which is itself prevented. (Such cases have become

---

[71]   For a similar example, see Hitchcock 1995: 316. One can easily find examples of this kind where the transferred physical quantity that is seemingly irrelevant is a *conserved* quantity, such as charge.

[72]   See Paul and Hall 2013: 191 for a similar example.

known as cases of *double prevention*.) By kicking the rack aside, I prevent it from preventing the pillar from falling. By releasing the catch, I prevent it from preventing the spring from accelerating.

On the face of it, my kicking the rack aside causes the pillar to fall down, and my releasing the catch causes the spring to accelerate. Our counterfactual principle about causation says so too. If I had not kicked the rack aside, the pillar would not have fallen down. If I had not released the catch, the spring would not have accelerated. By our principle, the kicking causes the falling, and the releasing causes the accelerating. (The condition that the putative effect occurs after the putative cause is satisfied here too. For simplicity, I suppress reference to the events' time order here and in what follows.) This is bad news for transference views of causation. For in cases of double prevention like the ones we have considered, no transfer takes place between what seems to be the cause and what seems to be the effect. In kicking away the rack, I do not transfer anything to the pillar. In releasing the catch, I do not transfer anything to the spring.[73] (Of course, energy was transferred on the pillar when it was propped up, and energy was transferred to the spring when it was stretched, but this is not the issue here.) Thus, our counterfactual principle about causation and transference views are in conflict, and it seems that, at least with respect to the double-prevention cases we have considered so far, the counterfactual principle has the upper hand.

We can use so-called neuron diagrams to illustrate the structure of double-prevention cases.[74] The conventions for these diagrams are as follows. Circles represent neurons; specifically, shaded circles represent neurons that fire, and non-shaded circles represent neurons that do not fire. Arrows represent excitatory connections, lines with dots inhibitory connections. A neuron that has incoming connections fires just in case it is excited by other neurons and it is not inhibited by any other neuron.[75] In the case depicted in Figure 1.1, the relation of the firing of neuron c to the firing of neuron e is that of double prevention. The firing of c prevents the firing of d, which, had it not been prevented, would have prevented the firing of e. Figure 1.2 shows what would have happened if c had not fired. In this case, e would not have fired either, because it would have been

---

[73] Perhaps in some possible realizations of these cases, I also cause the pillar to fall to the side by transferring momentum to it or cause the spring to heat up by transferring body heat from my hand to it via the catch. We can, however, easily imagine realizations that are sufficiently idealized so that no such transfers take place.

[74] See Schaffer 2000a, 2004a, and Paul and Hall 2013: 175. My neuron diagrams differ slightly in structure from those of Schaffer and Paul and Hall, but in inessential ways.

[75] For a critical discussion of the use of neuron diagrams in the philosophy of causation, see Hitchcock 2007b.

Theories of the Mind and Theories of Causation 51

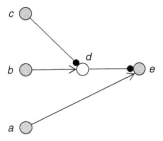

Figure 1.1. A neuron case of double prevention

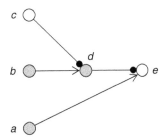

Figure 1.2. If c had not fired ...

prevented by the firing of *d*. On the face of it, the firing of *c* causes the firing of *e*. Again, our counterfactual principle agrees, because the firing of *e* counterfactually depends on the firing of *c*. But again, there is no transference from the firing of *c* to the firing of *e* (if we assume that no relevant quantity passes through a neuron that does not fire), so we seem to have another counterexample to the transference view.

We can use neuron diagrams to illustrate not just causal relations between the firings of (idealized) neurons, but also causal relations between ordinary events. Thus, we can map the other cases of double prevention onto the neuron structure depicted in Figures 1.1 and 1.2. Figure 1.3 shows a neuron representation of the pillar example.[76] What used to represent the firing of neuron *c* now represents my kicking the rack aside, and what used to represent the firing of neuron *e* now represents the falling down of the pillar. The firing of neuron *b* is now the event of the rack's being in place at a time before my kicking, while the firing of neuron *d* is now the event of the rack's being in place at a time just after my kicking. What used to be the

---

[76] For similar representations, see Schaffer 2000a and 2004a.

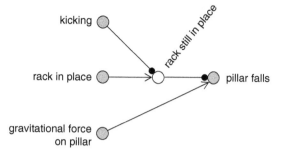

Figure 1.3. A real-life case of double prevention

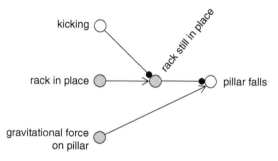

Figure 1.4. If I had not kicked away the rack ...

firing of neuron a is now a (non-double-preventive) cause of the pillar's falling down, such as the presence of a gravitational force that acts on the pillar. Figure 1.4 shows what would have happened if I had not kicked away the rack. In this case, the rack would have remained in place, which would have prevented the pillar from accelerating and thus from falling down.

Our double-prevention cases involve omissions as intermediaries. My kicking is followed by the absence of the rack underneath the pillar, which is followed by the falling of the pillar. My releasing of the catch is followed by its absence from its original position, which is followed by the acceleration of the spring. The firing of neuron c is followed by the non-firing of neuron d. One might be sceptical about whether omissions can be causes or effects. But this scepticism does not make the counterexamples to transference views go away, for the counterexamples are cases where one genuine event (my kicking the rack aside / my releasing the catch) causes another genuine event (the falling of the pillar / the acceleration of the spring) (see Paul and Hall 2013: 190).

Theories of the Mind and Theories of Causation 53

Admittedly, conflict between our counterfactual principle about causation and transference views also arises in cases of double prevention where it is more controversial how to resolve it. I shoot down an interceptor that would otherwise have shot down a bomber. The bomber destroys the target. As in the rack and spring cases, I prevent something from happening (namely the shooting down of the bomber) which in turn would have prevented something else from happening (the destruction of the target). Unlike in the other double-prevention cases, however, the different events in the story are not even continuous in space–time. Perhaps the bomber crew knew nothing about the threat to their mission, because I shot down the interceptor hundreds of miles from the bomber's course (see Hall 2004b). Our counterfactual principle says that my shooting down the interceptor causes the destruction of the target, because the target would not have been destroyed if I had not shot down the interceptor. Transference views say that my shooting down the interceptor does not cause the destruction of the target, because I do not transfer anything to it. It might seem more plausible to side with the transference views here because there is no spatiotemporal continuity between my actions and the destruction of the target.[77]

It is one peculiar feature of double-prevention cases that they allow for spatiotemporal discontinuity. Another peculiar feature is that, if they involve causation between the double preventer (that is, the event that prevents the prevention, such as my kicking away the rack) and the event whose prevention is prevented (such as the pillar's falling down), they also show that causation is not a matter of the intrinsic connection between events. The idea that causation is an intrinsic matter can be spelled out as follows. Take a case where, in the actual world, event c causes event e. Take all the events that, in the actual world, cause e and that occur from a certain time before c onwards. (These events of course include c.) Embed these events in an arbitrary nomologically possible situation. According to the intrinsicness idea, in the new situation c still causes e (see Paul and Hall 2013: 196–197). We can easily construct a counterexample to the intrinsicness thesis on the basis of our original neuron example if we assume, at least for the sake of the argument, that the firing of neuron c causes the firing of neuron e. In the example, the firing of neuron b does not seem to be among the causes of the firing of e. Thus, if the intrinsicness thesis holds,

---

[77] Hall's own diagnosis is that we should distinguish two concepts of causation and that counterfactual dependence is sufficient for only one of them, which applies in cases of double prevention (2004b). Won (2014: 215) holds that in double-prevention cases the event that prevents the preventer is not a cause at all.

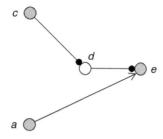

Figure 1.5. An intrinsic duplicate of the neuron case

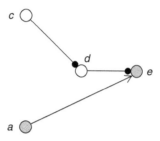

Figure 1.6. The intrinsic duplicate if *c* had not fired

duplicating our neuron structure while omitting neuron *b* should leave all the causal relations intact. Figure 1.5 shows this new structure.

Contrary to what the intrinsicness thesis predicts, in the new structure the firing of *c* does not cause the firing of *e* (Paul and Hall 2013: 196–197). This seems clear without assuming any particular theory of causation. In particular, friends of the counterfactual approach will reach this verdict. The firing of *e* no longer counterfactually depends on the firing of *c*. (Figure 1.6 shows the case where *c* does not fire.) This lack of counterfactual dependence does not by itself entail that there is no causation, because counterfactual dependence was never assumed to be necessary for causation. But, unlike in cases of pre-emption and overdetermination, where we also have causation without counterfactual dependence, it is unclear how the firing of *c* should otherwise cause the firing of *e* in the new situation where neuron *b* is absent.

We have assumed that, in the original neuron example, the firing of *c* causes the firing of *e*. In the intrinsic duplicate of the example shown in Figure 1.5, the firing of *c* does not cause the firing of *e*. Thus, if double prevention involves causation between the double preventer and the event whose prevention is prevented, then causation cannot always be a matter of the intrinsic connection between cause and effect. More specifically, if double prevention involves causation between the two events in question that is due to counterfactual dependence, then causation that is due to counterfactual dependence cannot always be a matter of the intrinsic connection between cause and effect.

The upshot so far is this. According to our counterfactual principle about causation, cases of double prevention are cases of causation. According to transference views, they are not. On the face of it, certain cases of double prevention, such as the pillar, spring, and neuron examples, seem to be cases of causation. For other cases, such as the bomber example, it is less plausible that they are cases of causation, because there is no spatiotemporal continuity between the events in question.[78] If one thinks that causation is an intrinsic matter, one also has reason to deny that cases of double prevention are cases of causation.

What should we make of this situation? I think we can still make a very strong case for the claim that double preventers are causes, which is *ipso facto* a very strong case against transference views of causation.

First, the worries about discontinuity and failures of intrinsicness can be explained away or at least attenuated. On reflection, it does not seem so implausible that my shooting down the interceptor causes the destruction of the target. Recall that we are reading 'causes' in the sense of being *a* cause of the effect, not in the sense of being a cause that has a particular explanatory relevance for the effect or that even is *the* cause of the effect. If we had to list the causes of the target's destruction in the order of their explanatory relevance, the bombing of the target would come first. But it does not follow that my shooting down of the interceptor is not to be found on the list at all. Perhaps I get a medal for my role in the successful destruction of the target, or perhaps I get blamed for it. How could this be justified if my action is not a cause of the target's destruction? According to a standard assumption, causation is necessary (though not sufficient) for moral responsibility, so I could rightly be praised or blamed for my role in the destruction only if my action caused it.[79] That there is no spatiotemporal continuity between cause and effect in our example may be unusual, but it is hard to see why it should make causation impossible.[80] The result that causation is not a matter of the intrinsic connection between cause and

---

[78] Examples like the bomber case can be multiplied. See, for instance, Lewis 2004: 83–84.

[79] On the standard assumption, see Sartorio 2007. Schaffer (2000a) also uses considerations of moral responsibility in support of the claim that double prevention involves causation.

[80] Arguably, cases of 'action at a distance' also arise in cases of quantum entanglement; see Fenton-Glynn and Kroedel 2015 for discussion.

effect does not have to be regarded as especially problematic, either. Few people, I take it, have a strong intuition that intrinsicness is a non-negotiable feature of causation, especially a strong intuition that is not parasitic on prior beliefs in transference views about causation.[81]

Second, as Schaffer points out, cases of double prevention display various features that are typically associated with causation (without having to be present in all cases of causation). For instance, knowing that the double preventer occurs licenses the prediction that the event that would have been prevented if the double preventer had not occurred will occur too, and bringing about the occurrence of the double preventer is an effective strategy for bringing about the event that would have been prevented.[82] Knowing that someone kicked away the rack, say, licenses the prediction that the pillar is going to fall, and kicking away the rack is an effective strategy for making the pillar fall.

Third, there are cases that seem to be among the most paradigmatic cases of causation and yet involve double prevention. The actions of modern firearms work much like our example of the spring (except that in firearms the spring starts out compressed rather than stretched out) (see Schaffer 2000a). In a cocked gun, the sear holds back the coiled spring. When the trigger is pulled, the sear is removed. No longer held back by the sear, the spring uncoils and causes the hammer to hit the cartridge, which causes the propellant to explode, which in turn causes the acceleration of the bullet. The pulling of the trigger is related to the acceleration of the bullet by double prevention. The pulling of the trigger prevents the sear's holding back of the spring, which, if it had not been prevented, would have prevented the spring from uncoiling and thus would have prevented the bullet from accelerating. If someone kills someone else by pulling the trigger of a gun, the relation between the pulling of the trigger and the death of the victim seems as causal as it ever gets. Our counterfactual principle agrees, because the victim would not have died if the trigger had not been pulled (assuming that there are no further redundant causes). Transference views disagree, because the pulling of the trigger does not transfer anything to the victim owing to the double-prevention structure of the case.

In sum, it seems much more plausible that some double-prevention cases are cases of causation than that some double-prevention cases are not cases of

---

[81] Lewis finds it intuitive that causation is a matter of an intrinsic relation between cause and effect, but adds that intuitions about what is intrinsic should be mistrusted (1986d: 205). For further discussion, see Schaffer 2000a, Hall 2004a, Hawthorne 2004, Lewis 2004, and Weatherson 2007.

[82] See Schaffer 2000a: 285. Lombrozo (2010) and Woodward (2012, 2014) discuss a feature that is present in some, but not all, cases of double prevention, viz. the feature they dub 'stability'.

Theories of the Mind and Theories of Causation 57

causation. If we treat double-prevention cases uniformly, we should therefore accept that all of them are cases of causation. Unlike our counterfactual principle about causation, transference views reach the opposite verdict. We should therefore reject transference views of causation.

The argument from double prevention also applies to certain powers theories of causation. Explaining causation in terms of powers or dispositions has become increasingly popular. One of the most detailed and influential powers theories of causation is due to Stephen Mumford and Rani Lill Anjum (2011).[83] According to their theory, there is causation when powers exercise themselves (2011: 6). More specifically, they hold that causation is the passing around of powers. For example, when the heat of a fire causes my body to warm up, it passes the power of warming things up to by body (see Mumford and Anjum 2009: 283). It does not always have to be the same power that is passed on, however. When a fragile glass is dropped and breaks, the pieces of glass have powers they did not have before, such as the power to cut (see Mumford and Anjum 2009: 284; 2011: 6–7).

According to Mumford and Anjum's powers theory, double prevention is not causation:

> Double prevention concerns the non-exercise of powers: twice over. A power is prevented from exercising when another also fails to exercise. We have, therefore, two failures of causation. Just as two wrongs do not make a right, two failures of causation do not make a cause. (Mumford and Anjum 2009: 287)

Applied to one of our examples, we can presumably locate the two failures of causation that Mumford and Anjum diagnose as follows: in the neuron example, the power of neuron b to simulate neuron d is prevented from exercising by the firing of neuron c, and neuron d fails to exercise its power to inhibit neuron e.

Why is there no exercise of powers in cases of double prevention? Why not say that, in the neuron example, it is still the case that neuron c exercises a causal power vis-à-vis neuron e, even though neuron b fails to exercise its power to stimulate neuron d, and d fails to exercise its power to inhibit neuron e? The deeper reason, according to Mumford and Anjum, for why c fails to exercise a causal power vis-à-vis e is that no power is passed from c to e. We can think of this passing as a kind of transference. Indeed, Mumford and Anjum hold that their theory is a transference theory, where

---

[83] Earlier powers theories are presented in Harré and Madden 1975, Bhaskar 1975, Cartwright 1989, Ellis 2001, Heil 2003, Molnar 2003, and Martin 2008.

what is transferred is powers and not necessarily conserved quantities (2011: 102). No transfer of causal powers takes place between a double preventer and the event whose prevention is prevented. For instance, no causal power is transferred from the firing of neuron c to the firing of neuron e. So, by Mumford and Anjum's theory, the firing of c does not cause the firing of e. Likewise for other cases of double prevention.[84]

Let us call theories of causation according to which causation requires transfer of causal powers *powers transference views*.[85] For the reasons just given, powers transference theories, just like transference views that talk about physical quantities, are committed to the claim that double prevention is not causation. Mumford and Anjum think it is a welcome result that their theory denies that double-prevention cases are cases of causation. They focus on cases like the bomber example where this denial is *prima facie* plausible. But, if we take all the considerations into account, the result is just as bad as it is for transference views in general. In particular, denying that there is causation in the bomber example comes at the cost of denying that one can cause people to die by pulling the trigger of a gun. This is too high a price to pay.[86]

In this section we have investigated transference and powers transference views of causation and discussed how they fare vis-à-vis cases of double prevention. We have seen that, all things considered, a strong case can be made for the claim that cases of double prevention are cases of causation. Transference and powers transference views of causation cannot accommodate this claim; our counterfactual principle can. This strongly speaks against transference and powers transference views, while speaking in favour of the counterfactual principle.

Proponents of transference or powers transference views might not be convinced by the argument from double prevention. Indeed, it would be surprising if they were, for philosophical debate tends to end in deadlock

---

[84] Mumford and Anjum do not quite make the point about the relation between the passing of powers on the one hand and double prevention on the other in these general terms, but they come close to it when they discuss double-prevention cases that involve spatiotemporal discontinuity. In this context, they write that '[c]ause and effect are to be understood as power and manifestation where one merges into another in a continuous process' (Mumford and Anjum 2009: 287).

[85] For continuity with the definition of transference views, I define powers transference views such that they merely claim that transfer of power is necessary for causation. Thus, Mumford and Anjum's view that causation *is* the transfer of powers is stronger than a mere powers transference view as defined here.

[86] Hüttemann (2013) defends a version of the powers theory of causation according to which double preventers *are* causes and thinks – rightly, by our lights – that this is a virtue of his theory. Vetter (2015) develops a theory of powers ('potentialities' in her terminology) that she claims is able to support both a Mumford-and-Anjum-style and a Hüttemann-style powers theory of causation (98–100).

rather than conversion.[87] They can, however, still read the remainder of this book as showing how far one can get in solving the problems of mental causation if one adopts our counterfactual principle about causation rather than a transference or powers transference view and as laying out the challenge for the competitor views. As we shall see, the troubles for transference and powers transference views are far from over. Difficulties, including difficulties from double prevention, will reappear in the context of mental causation.

1.7 Conclusion

This chapter has introduced different theories about the nature of mind, in particular reductive physicalism, non-reductive physicalism, and dualism, including naturalistic dualism. It has argued that, in the context of mental causation, causal relata are best conceived of as particular events. It has also argued that, in that context, the best account of particular events is the strong Kimian account, according to which events are constituted by triples of an object, a property, and a time, and according to which events have their identity (including their trans-world identity) determined by the object, the property, and the time. The chapter has introduced the truth-conditions for counterfactual conditionals and some of the logical peculiarities of these conditionals. It has defended a principle that states a sufficient condition for causation in terms of counterfactual dependence: an event causes a later event if the second event would not have occurred had the first event not occurred. In order for this principle to defy some *prima facie* problems, certain assumptions need to be made about how the relevant counterfactuals are evaluated. In particular, backtracking readings of those counterfactuals must be ruled out. This can be done either by following the asymmetry-by-fiat approach or by following the miracles approach. The principle also needs to be restricted to instances of properties that are sufficiently intrinsic and temporally intrinsic. In a different application of the notion of intrinsicness, cases of double prevention showed causation by counterfactual dependence not to be a matter of an intrinsic connection between cause and effect. These cases also showed the principle about causation in terms of counterfactual dependence to be in conflict with transference views and powers transference views of causation: according to the principle, cases of double prevention are cases of causation; according to transference and powers transference views, they are not. A strong case can be made for resolving the conflict in favour of the principle in terms of counterfactuals.

---

[87] At least that is what Lewis thought: see Lewis 2000: 102.

CHAPTER 2

Mental Causation by Counterfactual Dependence

2.1 Introduction

Mental events cause physical events because they make a difference to whether or not these physical events occur. This is the idea that is elaborated in this chapter. We saw in the previous chapter that an event causes a later event if it makes a difference to the occurrence of that event. The main task of this chapter is to show that mental events do in fact make a difference to physical events (technically speaking, to show that physical events counterfactually depend on mental events). If non-reductive physicalism is true, showing this is straightforward. If dualism is true, it is less straightforward but still manageable. Dualists will have to assume not just a naturalistic version of their view, but also a special status of the laws that connect mental and physical properties. The strategy of the argument for the counterfactual dependence of physical events on mental events is similar in the non-reductive physicalist case and the dualist case. In both cases, the argument proceeds as follows: the instantiation of a mental property is equivalent, in a sense to be spelled out in more detail, to the instantiation of some physical realizer or base of that mental property. Whether or not a realizer or base is instantiated makes a difference to whether or not future physical events occur. It follows that the instantiation of the mental property makes a difference to whether or not those physical events occur.

Section 2.2 presents the argument for the non-reductive physicalist case. We shall see that the argument generalizes to virtually all properties that supervene on physical properties: virtually all of these properties can also be shown to make a difference to the physical future and hence to have physical effects. For some supervenient properties this result is an interesting corollary. For others it looks more problematic. Section 2.3 discusses one of the more problematic cases and suggests several responses. A recent

60

Mental Causation by Counterfactual Dependence 61

argument by Lei Zhong (2011, 2012) also attempts to show that supervenient mental property-instances have physical effects by drawing on certain counterfactuals. Section 2.4 argues that the argument presented here is superior to Zhong's in several respects. The dualist case is discussed in Section 2.5, which argues that dualists can show the efficacy of the mental and thus solve the interaction problem if they adopt what I shall call super-nomological dualism, that is, a version of dualism that assigns a special modal status to the psychophysical laws. Section 2.6 discusses an objection according to which the account of mental causation presented here falls short of explaining genuine agency.

2.2 Non-Reductive Physicalism

If non-reductive physicalism is true, then many physical events counterfactually depend on mental events and, therefore, are caused by these mental events. This section presents a simple argument for that conclusion. Some authors have invoked counterfactuals in order to show that non-reductive physicalism allows the mind to have physical effects,[1] but in general they have not attempted to show why the relevant counterfactuals are true (see Kim 1998: 71). The argument presented here gives a rigorous derivation of those counterfactuals.

The argument employs some of the assumptions that were defended in the previous chapter. It uses the strong Kimian account of events, according to which events are constituted by an object, a property, and a time and according to which actual and possible events are identical just in case they are constituted by the same object, property, and time. (For simplicity I will sometimes suppress reference to the object and the time in question and simply refer to events by talking about the instance of the property.) The argument uses Lewis's truth-conditions for counterfactuals and the logic that results from them. Recall that, according to the truth-conditions, a counterfactual is non-vacuously true just in case there is a world where both the antecedent and the consequent are true that is closer (that is, more similar overall) to the actual world than any worlds where the antecedent is true while the consequent is false; if there is no world where the antecedent is true, the counterfactual is vacuously true. As an account of the relation of overall similarity, the simple asymmetry-by-fiat approach will suffice. According to this approach, the closest antecedent-worlds of a given

---

[1] For instance, Baker (1993), Lepore and Loewer (1987), Keil (2001), Loewer (2007), and List and Menzies (2009).

62 Mental Causation

counterfactual whose antecedent is actually false are exactly like the actual world until just before the time that the antecedent talks about; then the truth of the antecedent is brought about with minimal difference to the actual world; then things evolve lawfully again. (The asymmetry-by-fiat approach will suffice at least while we are dealing with non-reductive physicalism. For the dualist case that will be discussed in Section 2.5, the more elaborate miracles approach will prove more useful.) The argument uses our principle about causation according to which an event c causes a later event e if e counterfactually depends on c, that is, if e would not have occurred had c not occurred.

The argument draws on a consequence of the definition of strong supervenience, namely that the instantiation of a supervening property is strictly equivalent to the instantiation of some or other subvening property. Recall the definition from Section 1.2: a set of properties **A** *strongly supervenes* on a set of properties **B** if and only if, necessarily, if anything instantiates some property F in **A** at a given time, then there is a property G in **B** such that that thing instantiates G at that time, and, necessarily, everything that instantiates G at a given time also instantiates F at that time. Put less formally, **A**-properties strongly supervene on **B**-properties just in case any instantiation of an **A**-property has to be accompanied by an instantiation of some **B**-property, which in turn necessitates that the **A**-property is instantiated whenever it is itself instantiated. We have already used the example of dot-matrix pictures and their symmetry properties. Those symmetry properties strongly supervene on the arrangement of the dots in the picture's matrix. That is, any symmetry property of a dot-matrix picture has to be accompanied by the picture's instantiating some arrangement of dots or other, and any such arrangement that can underlie the symmetry of a picture necessitates its symmetry.

Now if a set of properties **A** strongly supervenes on a set of properties **B**, then the following is true: for each **A**-property F there is a subset of the **B**-properties – call this subset the *realizers* of F – such that, first, the instantiation of F necessitates the instantiation of a realizer of F and, second, the instantiation of a realizer of F necessitates the instantiation of F (at the same time and by the same object).[2] Take, for instance, the property of being point-symmetric for 3×3 dot-matrix pictures. By the supervenience of symmetry properties on dot arrangements, any point-symmetric

---

[2] For a similar result, see Kim 1984. Sometimes realization is taken to be a notion that is different from the one defined here. Advocates of such a notion of realization can simply substitute another term for what I have called a realizer. For a recent discussion of various notions of realization in the context of mental causation, see Walter 2010.

Mental Causation by Counterfactual Dependence 63

picture (actual or merely possible) has some dot arrangement that underlies this symmetry. Take all the possible dot arrangements that can underlie point-symmetry: ∴, ∵, ⦂ ⦂, etc. We have already established that, by the supervenience of symmetry properties on dot arrangements, any point-symmetric picture has to have one of the arrangements ∴, ∵, ⦂ ⦂, etc. It also follows from the supervenience – more precisely, from the second 'necessarily' in the definition – that any picture (actual or merely possible) that has one of the arrangements ∴, ∵, ⦂ ⦂, etc. is point-symmetric. Thus, the set {∴, ∵, ⦂ ⦂, etc.} is the set of realizers of point-symmetry for 3×3 dot-matrix pictures.

Let us return to the general case and expand the notation. If we are dealing with supervenient **A**-properties, let $\mathbf{P}_F$ be the set of realizers for each **A**-property F ('**P**' for 'physical', as we shall be dealing exclusively with physical realizers). For a set of properties **S**, let $\cup\mathbf{S}$ be the proposition that some member of **S** is instantiated. Let a roman capital letter stand for the proposition that the property referred to by the corresponding italicized capital letter is instantiated. Then we can formulate the consequence of **A**'s strong supervenience on **B** as follows: for each property F in **A**, there is a set of realizers $\mathbf{P}_F$ (where $\mathbf{P}_F$ is a subset of **B**) such that

- (i)   necessarily, if F is instantiated, then a realizer of F is instantiated ($\Box[\mathrm{F} \supset \cup\mathbf{P}_F]$); and
- (ii) necessarily, if a realizer of F is instantiated, then F is instantiated ($\Box[\cup\mathbf{P}_F \supset \mathrm{F}]$).

We can express the consequence of **A**'s supervenience on **B** more concisely by turning (i) and (ii) into a strict biconditional: for each property F in **A**, there is a set of realizers $\mathbf{P}_F$ (where $\mathbf{P}_F$ is a subset of **B**) such that

- (iii) necessarily, F is instantiated if and only if a realizer of F is instantiated. ($\Box[\mathrm{F} \equiv \cup\mathbf{P}_F]$)

Applied to the strong supervenience of mental properties on physical properties, (iii) says that, necessarily, a given mental property is instantiated if and only if one of its realizers is instantiated. For instance, that someone is in pain is strictly equivalent to her instantiating a realizer of pain. Thus, that someone is in pain is strictly equivalent to her having firing c-fibres or having firing x-fibres or having an active semiconductor network of a certain kind in her head, etc. The strict equivalence of the instantiation of a mental property with the instantiation of one of its realizers is an important ingredient of the argument for mental causation under non-reductive physicalism, which we can now state.

64 Mental Causation

According to non-reductive physicalism, mental properties strongly supervene on physical properties. We just saw that the instantiation of a property that strongly supervenes is strictly equivalent to the instantiation of one of its realizers. Let M be a specific mental property. Given that mental properties strongly supervene on physical properties, we have:

(1) Necessarily, M is instantiated if and only if a realizer of M is instantiated. ($\Box[M \equiv \cup\mathbf{P}_M]$)

Unless M is instantiated at the last moment of history, some physical properties are instantiated later than M. Plausibly, some of them would not have been instantiated if M's actual realizer had not been instantiated. Even more plausibly, some of them would not have been instantiated if none of M's realizers had been instantiated. The asymmetry-by-fiat approach says so too. In the closest worlds where no realizer of M is instantiated, things are exactly as they actually are until just before the time at which M's actual realizer is actually instantiated; then the non-occurrence of any realizer of M is brought about with minimal difference to the actual world; then things evolve lawfully again. It is hard to see how the absence of any realizer of M could leave no physical trace whatsoever. Indeed, we should expect many later physical events that actually occur not to occur in the closest worlds where no realizer of M is instantiated. Let P^* be a corresponding physical property that is instantiated later than M and that would not have been instantiated if none of M's realizers had been instantiated:

(2) If none of M's realizers had been instantiated, then P^* would not have been instantiated. ($\sim\cup\mathbf{P}_M \Box\!\!\!\rightarrow \sim P^*$)

We saw in Section 1.4 that Lewis's truth-conditions for counterfactuals allow us to replace the antecedent of a counterfactual with a strictly equivalent proposition. Thus, from (1) and (2) it follows logically that the P^*-instance counterfactually depends on the M-instance:

(3) If M had not been instantiated, then P^* would not have been instantiated. ($\sim M \Box\!\!\!\rightarrow \sim P^*$)

We saw that counterfactual dependence is sufficient for causation that is forward in time. Applied to our case, this yields:

(4) If P^* is instantiated later than M, and P^* would not have been instantiated if M had not been instantiated, then the instance of M causes the instance of P^*.

Mental Causation by Counterfactual Dependence

We have assumed that

(5) P^* is instantiated later than M.

From (3), (4), and (5) it follows logically that

(6) The instance of M causes the instance of P^*.

It follows, in other words, that there is causation of physical events by mental events.[3]

As it stands, the argument merely makes an existence claim, namely that there is some physical effect or other of a given mental property. We can also run the argument with reference to a specific physical event. I have a headache and reach for an aspirin. Having a headache is strictly equivalent to instantiating one of the realizers of having a headache. If I had instantiated none of these realizers, my hand would not have moved towards the aspirin. It follows that my hand's moving towards the aspirin counterfactually depends on my headache. Given our sufficient condition for causation,[4] it follows that my headache causes my hand's moving towards the aspirin.[5]

This is not to say, of course, that the argument can show an arbitrary physical event to be caused by a given mental event. And some physical events that have a good claim to be caused by a given mental event may not counterfactually depend on that mental event. (Thus, counterfactual dependence fails to be necessary for mental causation, just as it fails to be necessary for causation in general.) Perhaps a hospital patient has a headache and takes an aspirin, but if she had not had the headache, an overzealous nurse would have moved her hand towards the aspirin anyway. Cases like that of the hospital patient are the exception rather than the rule,

---

[3] If causation itself is non-hyperintensional (that is, if causal claims allow the substitution *salva veritate* of events whose occurrence is strictly equivalent), one could formulate an even easier argument for the causal efficacy of the M-instance. Assuming that the instance of the disjunctive property that some member of $\mathbf{P}_M$ is instantiated causes the instance of P^*, it would follow by the strict equivalence of M and $\cup\mathbf{P}_M$ that the instance of M causes the instance of P^*. The assumption that the instance of the disjunctive property is a cause is not without problems, however; see Sections 2.4 and 4.4 for further discussion.

[4] If I continue to have a headache after I have started reaching, let 'my headache' refer to the earlier temporal part of the continuing headache.

[5] We can also run the argument for (occurrent) propositional attitudes. If externalism about mental content is true, the realizers of those attitudes are at least partly extrinsic, but this does not threaten the efficacy of the attitudes, for the argument does not require the realizers themselves to be causes (see Sections 2.4 and 4.4). It seems to me that the account of mental causation presented here by itself neither solves nor exacerbates the problem of the efficacy of content. For discussion of that problem in the context of counterfactual accounts of causation, see Yablo 1997.

Mental Causation

however, and in a wide range of cases the argument can show specific mental events to have specific physical effects.

The argument, both in its general and in its specific variety, assumes non-reductive physicalism about mental properties, but uses only the strong supervenience of mental properties on physical properties that non-reductive physicalism claims and no other specific assumptions about mental properties. Thus, the argument easily generalizes. Indeed, it can be used to show that virtually any instance of a property that strongly supervenes on physical properties has physical effects. For any such property F, it seems, we can find a physical property P^* that is instantiated later than F and that would not have been instantiated if none of F's realizers had been instantiated. It follows from the argument that the instance of F causes the instance of P^*. Thus, it follows that there is downward causation of physical property-instances by virtually any supervenient property-instance.

Before assessing this result, we need a clarification. It does *not* follow from the argument that the instances of any property that is necessitated by a property with certain physical effects inherit all those physical effects. Suppose that an instance of a physical property P^* counterfactually depends on, and hence is caused by, an earlier instance of property F, which in turn necessitates the instantiation of property H. These suppositions do not entail that the instance of P^* counterfactually depends on, and hence is caused by, the instance of H, for the inference from $\sim F \; \square\!\!\rightarrow \sim P^*$ and $\square[F \supset H]$ (contrapositively, $\square[\sim H \supset \sim F]$) to $\sim H \; \square\!\!\rightarrow \sim P^*$ is invalid (see Section 1.4 and Lewis 1973b: 32). Thus, we do not get the result that every higher-level property-instance takes on all the effects of any lower-level property-instance that necessitates it. But of course it is consistent with the argument that sometimes higher-level property-instances do take on such effects.

Higher-level causes are not in general objectionable. Assume, as many do, that moral and aesthetic properties strongly supervene on physical properties.[6] Then our argument yields that they have some physical effects, for the absence of all physical realizers of a moral or aesthetic property would have made a difference to the physical future. Sometimes the argument can even be employed to show that they have certain specific effects. By the supervenience of aesthetic properties on physical properties,

---

[6] Even moral particularists like Dancy (1993) can accept the strong supervenience of moral properties on physical properties and the corresponding corollaries of forms (i)–(iii), for the realizers of moral properties are likely to be so complex that the supervenience claim does not yield any action-guiding principles.

Mental Causation by Counterfactual Dependence   67

beauty has certain physical realizers. If Helen of Troy had not instantiated any of those realizers while at Sparta, the arrowhead would not have moved towards Achilles' heel some nine years later. Hence the arrowhead's movement counterfactually depends on, and is caused by, the instance of beauty.

Cases like this are interesting corollaries of the argument for downward causation rather than problems for it. At least, I think so. The more cautious may simply restrict our principle about causation so that instances of moral and aesthetic properties are no longer allowed. As we saw in Section 1.5, some restrictions to rule out properties whose instances are generally ill-suited to enter into causal relations – restrictions to properties that are sufficiently intrinsic and temporally intrinsic, for instance – need to be imposed anyway, so this manoeuvre would not be *ad hoc* (or at least no more *ad hoc* than the original restrictions). Besides, other accounts of causation have to do the same, so our argument faces no special difficulty.[7] Restricting the sufficient condition for causation is unlikely to pose a threat to the efficacy of mental property-instances, for it is a desideratum of common sense that they can be causes. That they cannot, after all, be causes should be the conclusion of an argument, not a premise.

The argument I have presented in this section shows that, given non-reductive physicalism, particular mental events have physical effects. One might have lingering doubts about the efficacy not of particular mental events, but of mental events *qua* mental. Such doubts can easily be dispelled, however. For we have assumed the strong Kimian account of events, according to which events are not merely constituted by a property, an object, and a time, but have these constituents essentially. Given the combination of the strong Kimian account of events and non-reductive physicalism about the mind, mental events (that is, events that are constituted, *inter alia*, by mental properties) are not identical to physical events (that is, events that are constituted, *inter alia*, by physical properties) because of the distinctness of mental and physical properties that non-reductive physicalism claims. Thus, mental events do not have physical effects *qua* physical. One might still be worried that they have physical effects *qua* nothing, but this possibility can be ruled out, too. For clearly it is the mental properties that constitute, *inter alia*, mental events that are relevant for their causal efficacy. Unlike Quinean events or tropes, these mental properties are general features of the mental events, not particulars.

---

[7] For instance, a view on which event *c* causes event *e* if the occurrence of *c* and the actual laws of nature entail the occurrence of *e* also needs to be restricted to properties that are sufficiently temporally intrinsic. Otherwise, properties such as the property of shattering-in-a-minute yield counterexamples. The relation between causation and nomological sufficiency will be discussed in Section 4.5.

The mental properties are causally relevant because they do the work in the counterfactual dependence that implies the causal relation: if a given mental property had not been instantiated, then the later physical property would not have been instantiated.

2.3 The Problem of Overlapping Realizers

The argument for mental causation under non-reductive physicalism from the previous section shows that instances of supervenient mental as well as non-mental properties have physical effects. We saw in the Helen of Troy example that it can also be used to show that a supervenient non-mental property-instance has a specific physical effect. Sometimes, however, the argument seems to ascribe the wrong effects to supervenient property-instances. In particular, we seem to get the result that sometimes a supervenient property-instance has an effect that really is due to the instance of a different supervenient property that shares realizers with the first supervenient property. This section discusses that problem and explores several responses to it.

The problem arises as follows. I hold an aluminium ladder against a power line and subsequently get electrocuted.[8] Being made of aluminium, the ladder is an electrical conductor. Conductivity supervenes on physical properties and can be realized in different ways. If the ladder had not instantiated any realizer of conductivity, I would not have been electrocuted. It follows from the argument for downward causation that the instance of conductivity causes my electrocution. So far, so good. But being made of aluminium, the ladder is also opaque. Opacity too supervenes on physical properties and can be realized in different ways. The realizers of opacity are closely related to the realizers of conductivity. Almost all conductors are opaque. Some conductors are transparent (see Ginley et al. 2010), but they are not used to make ladders. Thus, it seems that if the ladder had not instantiated any realizer of opacity, I would not have been electrocuted either. It follows from the argument for downward causation that the instance of opacity causes my electrocution. That, however, does not seem very plausible, at least at first sight.[9]

---

[8] I borrow this example from Menzies (1988), with slight modifications. Jackson and Pettit (1990) also use the example, albeit in a different context.

[9] If artefacts such as ladders have their origin essentially, as Kripke (1980) holds, the ladder could not have been made of a different material from the one it is actually made of. If that is the case, the problem can be reformulated by taking the relevant events to be constituted by (i) the spatial region that is occupied by the ladder, (ii) the property of containing a ladder that is made of such-and-such a material, and (iii) the time in question.

Mental Causation by Counterfactual Dependence 69

Let us formulate the argument for the implausible conclusion along the lines of the argument from the previous section by using the following abbreviations:

C: being an electrical conductor
O: being opaque
E: being electrocuted

(In the example the object that instantiates property E (that is, myself) is distinct from the object that instantiates properties C and O (the ladder). In the original argument, property P^* might or might not be instantiated by the same object as M.) By the supervenience of opacity, we have:

(1-O)   Necessarily, opacity is instantiated if and only if a realizer of opacity is instantiated. ($\Box[O \equiv \cup \mathbf{P}_O]$)

The close relation between the opacity-realizers and the conductivity-realizers seems to give us:

(2-O)   If no opacity-realizer had been instantiated, then I would not have been electrocuted. ($\sim\cup\mathbf{P}_O \,\Box\!\!\rightarrow \sim E$)

From (1-O) and (2-O) it follows logically that

(3-O)   If opacity had not been instantiated, then I would not have been electrocuted. ($\sim O \,\Box\!\!\rightarrow \sim E$)

By the sufficiency of counterfactual dependence for (forward-in-time) causation, from (3-O) we get the implausible conclusion:

(4-O)   The opacity-instance causes my electrocution.

In the following I shall discuss several responses to the argument for this conclusion. We shall see that it is possible to deny the conclusion, but that this denial comes at a price. Ultimately, the best response will turn out to be the acceptance of the conclusion, coupled with an explanation of why it seems implausible.

The first response follows a strategy analogous to the strategy for dealing with backtracking counterfactuals that was discussed in Section 1.5 and denies the counterfactual that expresses the counterfactual dependence of my electrocution on the opacity-instance, (3-O).[10] Since (3-O) follows logically from (1-O) and (2-O), denying (3-O) requires denying either (1-O) or (2-O). Statement (1-O) seems unassailable, so one has to deny

---

[10] Menzies (1988: 573) denies this counterfactual dependence, but does not give an argument against it.

70 Mental Causation

(2-O). One has to deny, that is, that I would not have been electrocuted if no opacity-realizer had been instantiated. To see what denying (2-O) amounts to, consider the following argument *for* (2-O):

(5-O) If no opacity-realizer had been instantiated, then no conductivity-realizer would have been instantiated. ($\sim\!\cup\mathbf{P}_O \,\square\!\!\!\rightarrow \sim\!\cup\mathbf{P}_C$)

(6-O) If no opacity-realizer had been instantiated and no conductivity-realizer had been instantiated, then I would not have been electrocuted. ($\sim\!\cup\mathbf{P}_O \,\&\, \sim\!\cup\mathbf{P}_C \,\square\!\!\!\rightarrow \sim\!E$)

(2-O) If no opacity-realizer had been instantiated, then I would not have been electrocuted. ($\sim\!\cup\mathbf{P}_O \,\square\!\!\!\rightarrow \sim\!E$)

The argument from (5-O) and (6-O) to (2-O) has the form of the restricted transitivity inference, which is valid (see Section 1.4 and see Lewis 1973b: 35). Given the validity of the argument, denying (2-O) requires denying either (5-O) or (6-O). Statement (6-O) looks very plausible. If all conductivity-realizers had been absent, I certainly would not have been electrocuted. It would be strange if the additional absence of all opacity-realizers were to bring back my electrocution.[11]

So denying (3-O), that is, denying the counterfactual dependence of the electrocution on the opacity-instance, ultimately requires denying (5-O). Denying (5-O) comes at a price, however. It is natural to think that if the ladder had not instantiated any opacity-realizer, then it would have been made of some middle-of-the-road transparent material (glass or transparent plastic, say), which would not have been conductive. This natural thought must be given up if (5-O) is denied. Instead, worlds where the ladder is made of some exotic transparent conductive material[12] have to be taken to be just as close to the actual world as worlds where the ladder is made of some middle-of-the-road transparent non-conductive material.

The second response is to drop the strong Kimian account of events in favour of a conception that allows for more flexibility in the modal relation between the event and the property that is instantiated, like the weak Kimian account or the Lewisian account. It does not matter for our

---

[11] Which is not to say that (6-O) follows logically from $\sim\!\cup\mathbf{P}_C \,\square\!\!\!\rightarrow \sim\!E$, for it does not, owing to the invalidity of antecedent-strengthening for counterfactuals (see Section 1.4 and Lewis 1973b: 31).

[12] These days, transparent conductors are not exotic *per se*. They are used in smartphone screens and solar panels, for example (see Ginley *et al.* 2010). But they are certainly exotic in the context of ladders.

Mental Causation by Counterfactual Dependence

purposes which of these two alternatives we accept. (As we saw in Section 1.3, they are very similar in any case.) In order to spell out the response, we merely need an account of events that allows for a more relaxed connection between events and properties than the strong Kimian account does. Given such an account, it seems promising, at least *prima facie*, to proceed as follows: let o be the event of the ladder's being opaque. Event o should essentially involve the instantiation of opacity by the ladder. Otherwise we would have to say that the ladder's being opaque could have occurred while the ladder was not opaque, which seems strange.[13] Thus, we have:

(9) Necessarily, if o occurs, then opacity is instantiated. ($\Box[Oc(o) \supset O]$)

(In this addition to the notation, '$Oc(x)$' stands for the proposition that event x occurs.) By itself, (9) does not relax the connection between events and their constituent properties, because (9) is also true on the strong Kimian account, according to which events have their constituent properties essentially, too. The converse of (9) is the claim that, necessarily, if opacity is instantiated, then o occurs; equivalently, that, necessarily, if opacity is not instantiated, then o does not occur. The converse of (9) is true on the strong Kimian account as well (assuming, as we tacitly do, that we are holding the constituent object and time fixed). We can relax the connection between events and their constituent properties by assuming not the converse of (9), which is a strict conditional, but the following counterfactual, which is logically weaker:

(10) If o had not occurred, then opacity would not have been instantiated. ($\sim Oc(o) \Box\!\!\rightarrow \sim O$)

Lastly, we should demand that it is not the case that if o had not occurred, then the ladder would not have been conductive:

(11) It is not the case that if o had not occurred, then conductivity would not have been instantiated. ($\sim[\sim Oc(o) \Box\!\!\rightarrow \sim C]$)

Claim (11) allows us to deny that event o causes my electrocution: if o had not occurred, I might still have been electrocuted because the ladder might still have been conductive.

The trouble with this response is that it is at least as problematic as the previous response, which sought to deny the claim that my electrocution

---

[13] At least it sounds strange in our case. In general, properties that feature in the description of a weak Kimian or Lewisian event do not have to be essential to that event. See Lewis 1986b: 247–254 for discussion.

Mental Causation

counterfactually depends on the opacity-instance. By contraposition, claim (9) is equivalent to the claim that

> (12) Necessarily, if opacity is not instantiated, then o does not occur. $(\Box[\sim\!O \supset \sim\!Oc(o)])$

Since strict conditionals logically imply the corresponding counterfactual conditionals, from (12) we get:

> (13) If opacity had not been instantiated, then o would not have occurred. $(\sim\!O \;\Box\!\!\longrightarrow \sim\!Oc(o))$

Claims (10), (11), and (13) logically imply:[14]

> (14) It is not the case that if opacity had not been instantiated, then conductivity would not have been instantiated. $(\sim\![\sim\!O \;\Box\!\!\longrightarrow \sim\!C])$

By our earlier assumption (1-O), the instantiation of opacity is strictly equivalent to the instantiation of a realizer of opacity. Similarly, the instantiation of conductivity is strictly equivalent to the instantiation of a realizer of conductivity:

> (1-C) Necessarily, conductivity is instantiated if and only if a realizer of conductivity is instantiated. $(\Box[C \equiv \cup\mathbf{P}_C])$

Given (1-O) and (1-C), (14) is equivalent to:

> (15) It is not the case that if no opacity-realizer had been instantiated, then no conductivity-realizer would have been instantiated. $(\sim\![\sim\!\cup\mathbf{P}_O \;\Box\!\!\longrightarrow \sim\!\cup\mathbf{P}_C])$[15]

Claim (15) is the negation of claim (5-O). We saw earlier that denying (5-O) is problematic because it requires giving up the natural thought that the ladder would have been made of some middle-of-the-road transparent material if it had not instantiated any opacity-realizer. Thus, the response that adopts a more coarse-grained conception of events instead of the strong Kimian account is at least as costly as the first response.

---

[14] The inference has the form of an inference from $\phi\;\Box\!\!\longrightarrow\chi$, $\chi\;\Box\!\!\longrightarrow\phi$, and $\sim\![\chi\;\Box\!\!\longrightarrow\psi]$ to $\sim\![\phi\;\Box\!\!\longrightarrow\psi]$, which is valid if and only if the inference from $\phi\;\Box\!\!\longrightarrow\chi$, $\chi\;\Box\!\!\longrightarrow\phi$, and $\phi\;\Box\!\!\longrightarrow\psi$ to $\chi\;\Box\!\!\longrightarrow\psi$ is, which we saw to be valid in Section 1.4; see also Lewis 1973b: 33.

[15] We saw in Section 1.4 that we may substitute necessarily equivalent antecedents in counterfactuals. The substitution of necessarily equivalent consequents is likewise allowed – if two propositions are true at exactly the same worlds, then they are either both true or both false at the closest worlds where a given antecedent is true.

The third response is to refine the sufficient condition for causation by taking into account counterfactuals with more complex antecedents. If opacity had not been instantiated, then I would not have been electrocuted. But if opacity had not been instantiated *while conductivity had still been instantiated*, then I would still have been electrocuted. On the other hand, if conductivity had not been instantiated *while opacity had still been instantiated*, then I would not have been electrocuted. More generally, the idea is that one event causes another if the first event makes a difference to the occurrence of the second event if we hold the occurrence of certain other events fixed.

What other events should we hold fixed? This is not an easy question to answer. For virtually any pair of events that are related by counterfactual dependence, we can find other events that actually occur and for which holding them fixed makes no difference to the occurrence or non-occurrence of the dependent event. Take the example of my throwing a dart at a balloon. I throw the dart; the balloon bursts. If I had not thrown the dart, then the balloon would not have burst. If I had not thrown the dart and there had been just as many grains of sand on Mars as there actually are, then the balloon would not have burst either. On the other hand, for virtually any pair of events that are related by counterfactual dependence, we can also find other events that actually occur and for which holding them fixed does make a difference to the occurrence or non-occurrence of the dependent event. For instance, if I had not thrown the dart and the dart had been on its actual trajectory a second later (somehow materializing there despite not having been thrown), then the balloon would still have burst. Why should we hold fixed the ladder's being conductive when assessing whether the ladder's being opaque causes the electrocution, but not hold fixed the dart's being on its later trajectory when assessing whether my throw causes the balloon's bursting? Intuitively, the difference is that the dart's being on its later trajectory is on the causal path from my throw to the bursting, while the ladder's being conductive is not on a causal path – if such there be – from the ladder's being opaque to the electrocution. (Nor, for that matter, is the sand event on Mars on a causal path from my throw to the balloon's bursting.) Only off-path events, it seems, should be held fixed.

As it stands, this suggestion is rather vague. It also smacks of circularity. How can we identify causal paths without making prior assumptions about what causes what? So-called causal modelling theories of causation can be used to make the suggestion more precise and to avoid the apparent circularity. I will elaborate in Section 3.5, but one difficulty with the solution can be outlined here without going into details. Causal modelling theories of causation use causal models (unsurprisingly), which consist, *inter alia*, of a set of variables that represent the occurrence of events. In order to spell out the idea that counterfactual dependence is sufficient for causation if the dependence persists when all off-path events are held fixed, it is not enough to demand that there be *some* causal model where the dependence thus persists. If this were enough, we could take a simple model that merely contained variables for the putative cause and the putative effect and for no other events. In that simple model, it would be trivially true that the counterfactual dependence between the putative cause and the putative effect persists if all off-path events are held fixed, for there are no off-path events in the model. Instead of merely stating an existential condition for models of a certain kind, it seems that we should demand that the counterfactual dependence persists in an appropriate model. This requires spelling out what an appropriate model is, however. As we shall see, that is no easy task.

If the responses discussed so far all seem unsatisfactory, we have two more options, which are more radical. The fourth response is to deny that counterfactual dependence is sufficient for causation without attempting to replace it with a modified sufficient condition (such as the sufficient condition in terms of holding off-path events fixed). The fifth response is to maintain the original sufficient condition and accept that the opacity-instance causes the electrocution. Denying that counterfactual dependence is sufficient for causation is simple. But so is the idea that what makes a difference is a cause. It seems premature to give that idea up unless all alternatives turn out to be untenable. The other radical option, namely accepting that the opacity-instance causes the electrocution, might initially seem like excessive bullet-biting. But a closer look reveals it to be not so unattractive. If we choose that option, we can hold on to our original simple and elegant sufficient condition for causation. We shall have to accept the result that the opacity-instance causes the electrocution, but we can try to explain away the implausibility of this result. It is because of the intimate relation between the realizers of conductivity and the realizers of opacity that the electrocution counterfactually depends on the opacity-instance. This intimate relation may well eventuate in the opacity-instance's causing the electrocution. We might still hesitate to call the opacity-instance a cause of the electrocution, but we hesitate because the opacity-instance is a cause that has little explanatory relevance in our context, not because it is not a cause at all.[16] (Recall the example from Section 1.5 of my bumping into Albert as an explanatorily irrelevant cause of Berta's death.)

---

[16] It might seem promising to apply Swanson's (2010) account of the context-sensitivity of causal talk to our case. Unfortunately, there are some *prima facie* difficulties with this application. Swanson

Mental Causation by Counterfactual Dependence

This defence of the fifth response, which holds on to our principle about causation but denies that the opacity-instance is a cause that is explanatorily relevant in our context, does not threaten the status of mental causes. For mental events do typically count as explanatorily relevant. And the argument from the previous section showed that they can cause physical events. Thus, it is clearly appropriate to say that they cause those physical events. For instance, it is clearly appropriate to name my headache as a cause of my hand's moving towards the aspirin, because the headache is not merely a cause of my hand's moving (because my hand's moving counterfactually depends on it), but a cause that we would cite in an explanation of my hand's moving. That mental events are explanatorily relevant seems obvious (see Burge 1993). It can also be established through argument. As we shall see in Section 3.5, causal modelling theories allow us to formulate a criterion for explanatory relevance within the counterfactual approach to causation.

2.4 Comparison with Zhong's Argument

Lei Zhong has suggested an argument that is similar to the argument for mental causation under non-reductive physicalism that I have presented. He argues as follows.[17] Assume non-reductive physicalism. Assume further that an instance of a mental property M causes an instance of a mental property M^* that is realized by a physical property P^*. By the realization of M^* by P^*, that P^* is instantiated entails that M^* is instantiated ($\Box[P^* \supset M^*]$). Contrapositively, that M^* is not instantiated entails that P^* is not instantiated ($\Box[\sim M^* \supset \sim P^*]$). Thus, the P^*-instance counterfactually depends on whatever the M^*-instance counterfactually depends on, since

---

appeals to the principle that when ascribing causal responsibility for a given effect to a causal path, one should use good representatives of that path (2010: 225). One cannot use this principle to show that the conductivity-instance is a better representative of a path that contains both the conductivity-instance and the opacity-instance than the opacity-instance is, for both by Swanson's definition and by the causal modelling definition (which will be presented in more detail in Section 3.4) the two property-instances are on different paths. Perhaps it could be shown that the opacity-instance is a poor representative of a path that contains it but does not contain the conductivity-instance. But showing this would not be straightforward either, since one of Swanson's principal criteria for an event's being a *good* representative, the effect's counterfactually depending on the representative, does apply to the opacity-instance and the electrocution.

[17] See Zhong 2011: 141–143; 2012: 80–81. I follow the 2012 version of the argument here, which Zhong prefers (2012: 81 n. 7). Zhong uses his argument in the context of a strategy that is different from the one I pursue. Instead of arguing that non-reductive physicalism can accommodate mental causation, he uses his argument to strengthen the exclusion problem for non-reductive physicalism. Zhong's argument is also discussed in Pernu 2016.

76 Mental Causation

$\sim$X $\square\!\!\!\rightarrow$ $\sim$P* follows logically from $\sim$X $\square\!\!\!\rightarrow$ $\sim$M* and $\square[\sim$M* $\supset \sim$P*].[18] Now if the M-instance causes the M*-instance, then either

(i)   the M*-instance counterfactually depends on the M-instance; or
(ii) there is an intermediary, namely an instance of a mental property M' which is caused by the M-instance and on which the M*-instance counterfactually depends.

In case (i), it follows that the P*-instance counterfactually depends on the M-instance; hence the M-instance causes the P*-instance. In case (ii), it follows that the P*-instance counterfactually depends on the M'-instance; hence the M'-instance causes the P*-instance; hence, by the transitivity of causation, the M-instance causes the P*-instance. In sum, if some instances of mental properties cause instances of other mental properties, then they also cause instances of the realizers of these mental properties.

Zhong's conclusion is weaker than mine. He concludes that a mental property-instance causes the instance of the realizer of another mental property *if* the first mental property-instance causes the second mental property-instance. I conclude that some mental property-instances cause physical property-instances *tout court*. That some mental property-instances cause other mental property-instances is not very controversial, however,[19] so the fact that Zhong's conclusion is a conditional one while mine is not does not make for a substantial difference between our arguments.

Zhong's argument is more specific than mine. My argument can easily be generalized to supervenient properties besides mental properties as conceived of by non-reductive physicalism. All that is required for this generalization is that the absence of all realizers of the supervenient property in question would have made a difference to the physical future. In order to generalize Zhong's argument to other supervenient properties, we would first have to identify a future instance of another supervenient property that is caused by the instance of the original supervenient property. It might not always be straightforward to find such a future instance. We saw in the previous section that the ease with which my argument can be generalized is a mixed blessing. It might therefore be taken to be an advantage of Zhong's argument that it does not generalize so easily. His argument has a number of disadvantages, however.

---

[18] This valid inference should not be confused with the similar but invalid inference from $\sim\psi$ $\square\!\!\!\rightarrow$ $\sim\chi$ and $\square[\psi \supset \phi]$ (contrapositively, $\square[\sim\phi \supset \sim\psi]$) to $\sim\phi$ $\square\!\!\!\rightarrow$ $\sim\chi$; see Section 1.4.

[19] Proponents of the so-called autonomy approach such as Gibbons (2006) accept mental-to-mental causation while denying mental-to-physical causation.

Mental Causation by Counterfactual Dependence

Zhong's assumptions about causation are stronger than mine. He assumes that counterfactual dependence is sufficient for causation and that counterfactual dependence – or counterfactual dependence via a caused intermediary – is necessary for causation. I merely assume that counterfactual dependence is sufficient for causation. (Strictly speaking, I assume even less: that counterfactual dependence between property-instances is sufficient for causation that is forward in time. But Zhong could do so as well without jeopardizing the validity of his argument, so we are on a par here.) In spite of the worries we have discussed in previous sections, the sufficiency of counterfactual dependence for causation is very plausible. The necessity of counterfactual dependence – or counterfactual dependence via a caused intermediary – is not very plausible. Consider a case of late pre-emption, such as Billy and Suzy throwing rocks at a bottle. Billy's rock arrives at the bottle first and causes it to shatter. We saw in Section 1.4 that this is a case of causation without counterfactual dependence: it is not the case that the bottle would not have shattered had Billy not thrown, because in this case Suzy's rock would have shattered it. It is also a case of causation without counterfactual dependence on a caused intermediary. Whatever intermediate event we choose that is caused by Billy's throw, the shattering does not counterfactually depend on it. For instance, the event of Billy's rock being on its actual trajectory a split-second after the throw is caused by Billy's throw, but the shattering would still have occurred if that event had not occurred, because in that case, too, Suzy's rock would have shattered the bottle. Cases of overdetermination, such as deaths by firing squad, also yield counterexamples not only to the necessity of counterfactual dependence for causation, but also to the necessity of counterfactual dependence via a caused intermediary for causation.[20]

Another controversial assumption about causation that Zhong makes is that causation is transitive. He assumes, that is, that if a first event causes a second event and the second event causes a third event, then the first event causes the third event. The transitivity of causation is subject to various counterexamples. Here is one of them.[21] I throw a railway switch, diverting a train to a side track. The side track later rejoins the main track. Further down on the main track someone left a cart, which is run over by the train. My throwing the switch causes the train to be on the side track a moment later. The train's being on the side track at that moment causes it to run over the cart later on. But my throwing the switch does not seem to cause the train

---

[20] On a similar issue, see Lewis 1986d: 193–212.
[21] So-called switching cases like this one are due to McDermott (1995: 532). For further discussion of the transitivity of causation, see Paul 2000 and Paul and Hall 2013: 215–244.

to run over the cart. (The case is *not* also a counterexample to the sufficiency of counterfactual dependence for causation, for the running over of the cart does not counterfactually depend on my throwing the switch to start with: if I had not thrown the switch, the train would simply have stayed on the main track and would still have run over the cart later on.)

Perhaps Zhong's argument would still be valid if the controversial assumptions about causation were appropriately weakened. He could assume, for instance, that counterfactual dependence – or counterfactual dependence via a caused intermediary – is necessary for causation *in the absence of redundancy* and that causation is transitive *in standard cases*. The weakened assumptions would be less controversial. But controversy might arise over whether they can be applied in particular cases. If we can give them up completely, so much the better.

Zhong's argument is open to an objection to which my argument is immune. Jonas Christensen and Jesper Kallestrup (2012) object to Zhong's argument as follows. The necessitation of M^* by its realizer P^*, which is required to establish that the P^*-instance counterfactually depends on the M-instance or the M'-instance, holds only if P^* is a 'total realizer' of M^* (2012: 515). That is, P^* has to be a conjunctive property that includes various 'background properties' such as 'properties pertaining to pertinent causal laws of nature' besides its 'core realizer' properties, which are more narrowly circumscribed (2012: 514). The background properties, however, are not themselves 'causal properties' that could feature as causes or effects (2012: 515). Given that P^* includes those background properties, the claim that the instance of P^* is an effect becomes problematic. Moreover, the background properties are shared between P^* and the actual realizer of M. Thus, Christensen and Kallestrup claim, M and P^* are no longer sufficiently distinct to be causally related (2012: 516).

Whatever the success of Christensen and Kallestrup's objection to Zhong's argument, their objection does not touch mine.[22] Granted, I would have to restrict the sufficient condition for causation to causal properties if the objection were sound, for otherwise background properties would yield counterexamples. (As we have seen, we need to impose some restrictions along these lines in any case.) Granted, the realizers of M that featured in claims (1) and (2) from Section 2.2 would have to be read as total realizers if the objection were sound, for otherwise the instantiation of M would no longer be strictly equivalent to the instantiation of one of its realizers, as (1) claims.

---

[22] Zhong (2015) addresses the objection by Christensen and Kallestrup. We shall return to the issue of whether the instances of realizers can be causes in Section 4.4.

Mental Causation by Counterfactual Dependence 79

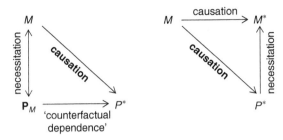

Figure 2.1. Zhong's argument (right) vs mine (left)

But these concessions would not threaten the causal relation between our M-instance and our P^*-instance. Zhong's argument is open to the Christensen–Kallestrup objection because there is a realizer (namely the realizer of M^*) whose instance is claimed to be an effect. In my argument no realizers need to have instances that are causes or effects. The set of M's realizers (as represented by proposition $\cup\mathbf{P}_M$ in (1) and (2)) is merely a logical intermediary, not a causal one. And our property P^* can be as causal as one likes, since it need not realize anything.

What is the role of the actual realizer of M (call it P)? One might object that I cannot avoid treating at least the instance of P as a causal intermediary, since it follows from M's being necessitated by P that P would not have been instantiated if M had not been instantiated, wherefore the M-instance causes the P-instance. I have to concede only the first half of this reasoning, however. It does follow that the P-instance counterfactually depends on the M-instance. But the sufficient condition for causation I have used remains silent on whether or not the M-instance causes the P-instance, because the two instances are simultaneous. Further, given that we restrict the sufficient condition for causation to causal properties, it would remain silent on whether or not the P-instance causes the P^*-instance should it turn out that our P^*-instance counterfactually depends on the P-instance while P is not a causal property. So it neither follows that the P-instance is an effect of the M-instance nor that the P-instance is a cause of the P^*-instance. Nonetheless it still follows that the M-instance is a cause of the P^*-instance.

Figure 2.1 summarizes the structure of Zhong's argument and mine. Zhong's argument proceeds from causation on the mental level and concludes that the realizer of the mental effect (more precisely: the instance of the realizer of the property of which the mental effect is an instance) has the same mental cause as the mental effect. My argument does not proceed from causation on the mental level. Nor does it proceed from causation on the physical level. Nor does it proceed from counterfactual dependence on the physical level, strictly speaking. In a loose sense, the P^*-instance counterfactually depends on the set of M's realizers, $\mathbf{P}_M$ (namely in the sense that P^* would not have been instantiated had no member of $\mathbf{P}_M$ been instantiated). Together with the strict equivalence of the instantiation of M with the instantiation of a member of $\mathbf{P}_M$, it follows that the P^*-instance counterfactually depends on the M-instance (in the strict sense) and hence is caused by it. On the level of realizers, Zhong's argument merely takes into account the actual realizer P^* of the mental effect M^*; hence the relation of necessitation is merely one-way, unlike the relation between M and the set of realizers $\mathbf{P}_M$.

2.5   Dualism

Of all positions about the nature of mind, dualism has been considered the one for which mental causation spells most trouble. The interaction problem is particularly severe for dualism. If the mental is neither identical to nor necessitated by the physical, how can it interact with the physical at all? The exclusion problem, too, is particularly severe for dualism. Even if the mental can interact with the physical in principle, how can it do so without making it the case that physical effects are caused twice over, like in a firing squad? This section deals with the interaction problem for dualism. (The exclusion problem will be discussed in Chapter 4.) It will turn out that dualists can solve the interaction problem provided they make certain assumptions about the status of the psychophysical relation.

I will not discuss varieties of dualism that do not even assume that the relation between mental and physical properties is a matter of natural law. Those varieties cannot avail themselves of the solution I am going to suggest, and I doubt that there is an alternative solution for them. Let us assume, then, that what we called 'naturalistic dualism' in Section 1.2 is true:

Naturalistic dualism: Each mental property is distinct from all physical properties. No subset of mental properties strongly supervenes on physical properties, but mental properties nomologically supervene on physical properties.

Recall that the notion of nomological supervenience was in turn defined as follows:

Nomological supervenience: A set of properties **A** *nomologically supervenes* on a set of properties **B** if and only if it is nomologically necessary that if anything instantiates some property F in **A** at a given time, then there is a property G in **B** such that that thing instantiates G at that time, and it is nomologically necessary that everything that instantiates G at a given time also instantiates F at that time.

Applied to the case of mental and physical properties, we get the following claim of nomological supervenience:

Nomological psychophysical supervenience: It is nomologically necessary that if anything instantiates some mental property at a given time, then there is a physical property such that that thing instantiates the physical property at that time, and it is nomologically necessary that everything that instantiates the physical property at a given time also instantiates the mental property at that time.

According to nomological psychophysical supervenience, it is a matter of nomological necessity that a mental property is accompanied by some physical property whenever it is instantiated, and it is also a matter of nomological necessity that the mental property is instantiated whenever one of the physical properties that can underlie its instantiation is instantiated.

As was the case with strong supervenience, nomological supervenience allows us to correlate each supervenient property with a disjunction of subvening properties, although, unlike in the case of strong supervenience, this correlation holds only with nomological necessity, not with metaphysical necessity. In the case of nomologically supervenient mental properties, for each mental property M, there is a set $\mathbf{P}_M$ of physical properties – call them the *bases* of M – such that

(i) it is nomologically necessary that if M is instantiated, then a base of M is instantiated; and

(ii) it is nomologically necessary that if a base of M is instantiated, then M is instantiated.[23]

(For simplicity, I am again leaving reference to times and to the things that instantiate the properties in question implicit.) We can turn (i) and (ii) into a biconditional that holds with nomological necessity:

---

[23] Alternatively, one could call the members of $\mathbf{P}_M$ *realizers*, as in the non-reductive physicalist case. But, since talk of realization invokes a relation of metaphysical necessitation, it seems preferable to use a different term.

(iii) It is nomologically necessary that M is instantiated if and only if a base of M is instantiated.

For example, according to nomological psychophysical supervenience, it is nomologically necessary that someone is in pain if and only if they have firing c-fibres or they have firing x-fibres or an active semiconductor network of a certain kind in their head etc. Thus, the properties of having firing c-fibres, of having firing x-fibres, of having an active semiconductor network of a certain kind in one's head, etc. are the bases of pain.

Let us assume that the nomological necessity of the fact that a mental property is instantiated just in case one of its bases is instantiated is due to a psychophysical law that has the status of a fundamental law of nature.[24] Thus, the psychophysical laws are nomologically necessary, which they should be, for nomological necessity is truth in all worlds where all the actual laws of nature hold (see Section 1.2), and in any worlds where all the actual laws of nature hold, *a fortiori* the actual psychophysical laws hold. The converse, that all the actual laws hold in any worlds where the actual psychophysical laws hold, does not follow. There might be worlds where the actual psychophysical laws hold, but some of the other actual laws of nature do not hold. If this is the case, then the actual psychophysical laws are in a sense 'more necessary' than the remaining actual laws of nature, while still being nomologically necessary. As we shall see, it is worth taking this possibility seriously.

The psychophysical laws cannot be metaphysically necessary as well as nomologically necessary, at least by dualists' lights, for if they were metaphysically necessary, mental properties would strongly supervene on physical properties, and dualism does not allow this.[25] Given the failure of mental properties strongly to supervene, we can no longer use claim (1) from Section 2.2, according to which the instantiation of a mental property is strictly equivalent to the instantiation of a realizer of that property, as a starting-point for an argument for mental causation. We can, however, use the weaker claim that the instantiation of a mental property is, as it were, counterfactually equivalent to the instantiation of a physical base of that property: if the mental property had not been instantiated, then none of its bases would have been instantiated, and if none of its bases had been

[24] On such laws, see Chalmers 1996: 127.
[25] If one included irreducible psychophysical laws in the subvening properties and also stipulated that the subvening properties include physical properties and perhaps physical laws, the result would be that mental properties strongly supervene. This result would not vindicate physicalism, however, for physicalism requires that the mental supervene on the physical alone; thus, physicalism cannot allow irreducible *psycho*physical laws in the subvening properties.

Mental Causation by Counterfactual Dependence   83

instantiated, then the mental property would not have been instantiated. As before, we can combine this with the claim that the absence of all physical bases would have made a difference to the physical future. Thus, we get the following argument (where M is a specific mental property and P^* is a physical property that is instantiated later than M and that would not have been instantiated if none of M's bases had been instantiated):

(16) If none of M's bases had been instantiated, then M would not have been instantiated. ($\sim\cup\mathbf{P}_M \square\!\!\!\rightarrow \sim M$)

(17) If M had not been instantiated, then none of M's bases would have been instantiated. ($\sim M \square\!\!\!\rightarrow \sim\cup\mathbf{P}_M$)

(18) If none of M's bases had been instantiated, then P^* would not have been instantiated. ($\sim\cup\mathbf{P}_M \square\!\!\!\rightarrow \sim P^*$)

---

(19) If M had not been instantiated, then P^* would not have been instantiated. ($\sim M \square\!\!\!\rightarrow \sim P^*$)

Claim (19) says that the P^*-instance counterfactually depends on the M-instance. Once this is established, we can continue as we did in the case of non-reductive physicalism. Applied to the case of M and P^*, our sufficient condition for causation yields:

(4) If P^* is instantiated later than M, and P^* would not have been instantiated if M had not been instantiated, then the instance of M causes the instance of P^*.

We have assumed that

(5) P^* is instantiated later than M.

From (4), (5), and (19) it follows logically that

(6) The instance of M causes the instance of P^*.

The argument from (16)–(18) to (19) is the most controversial part of this reasoning for the causal claim, (6). The validity of the argument, however, is beyond reproach. We saw in Section 1.4 that inferences of the form of the present inference are valid, in spite of the general failure of transitivity for counterfactuals. Given this failure, (19) does not follow from (17) and (18) alone, but (19) does follow if we add premise (16). Together with premise (16), (17) guarantees that the closest worlds where M is not instantiated coincide with the closest worlds where none of M's physical bases is

84   Mental Causation

instantiated. Since by (18) the latter are worlds where P^* is not instantiated, so are the former.[26]

What about the premises, claims (16)–(18)? Let us consider them in reverse order. I take it that premise (18) – more precisely, the existence of a physical property P^* that is instantiated later than M and that makes (18) true – is as plausible as it was in the case of non-reductive physicalism. Taking away the actual physical base of a mental event and not replacing it by an alternative base certainly makes a difference to the physical future.

Premise (17), by contrast, looks problematic. Let us try to apply the asymmetry-by-fiat approach. According to this approach, the closest worlds where M is not instantiated are exactly like the actual world until just before the time at which M is actually instantiated. Then the instantiation of M is prevented with minimal difference to the actual world; then things evolve lawfully again. What does it mean to prevent the instantiation of M with minimal difference to the actual world? We could prevent the instantiation of M by not having any of M's physical bases instantiated. If this makes for a minimal difference to the actual world, (17) comes out true. Or we could prevent the instantiation of M by eliminating its instantiation while leaving everything as it is in the physical world; given dualism, this is a metaphysical possibility since the instantiation of a base of M does not metaphysically necessitate the instantiation of M. If the second option makes for a minimal difference to the actual world, (17) comes out false. It is not entirely clear which way of preventing M's instantiation is the way of minimal difference to the actual world, but one might suspect that it is the way that leaves the physical world as it is, for this way differs from actuality merely with respect to one event (namely the M-instance) and not with respect to two events (the M-instance and the instance of its actual physical base).

The problem looks even worse if we consider the verdict of the miracles approach to closeness or overall similarity. Recall Lewis's criteria for overall similarity to the actual world:

(1)   It is of the first importance to avoid big, widespread, diverse violations of law.

(2)   It is of the second importance to maximize the spatiotemporal region throughout which perfect match of particular fact prevails.

---

[26] The inference would still be valid if (17) were replaced with the corresponding 'might' conditional (see Lewis 1973c: 433).

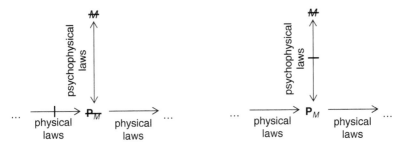

Figure 2.2. Type-1 worlds (left) vs type-2 worlds (right) as candidate antecedent-worlds for premise (17)

(3) It is of the third importance to avoid even small, localized, simple violations of law.
(4) It is of little or no importance to secure approximate similarity of particular fact, even in matters that concern us greatly. (Lewis 1979: 472)

Compare the following two types of antecedent-worlds of (17) for closeness to the actual world (see Figure 2.2): worlds of type 1 match the actual world perfectly in particular fact until just before the time at which M is instantiated; then the physical laws are violated while the psychophysical laws are not, such that M's failure to be instantiated implies the failure of any of its physical bases to be instantiated. Worlds of type 2 match the actual world perfectly in particular fact until just before the time at which M is instantiated too; then the psychophysical laws are violated while the physical laws are not, such that M's actual physical base is still instantiated, but M is not. By Lewis's criteria, type-2 worlds are closer to the actual world than type-1 worlds. While worlds of the respective types are on a par as far as violations of law are concerned, there is vastly more match of particular fact to the actual world in the type-2 worlds, for type-2 worlds match the actual world perfectly at all times after M's actual instantiation. Type-1 worlds, by contrast, cannot equal this match; owing to the failure of any of M's physical bases to be instantiated, they lawfully evolve into a different future.[27] In type-2 worlds, the antecedent of (17) is true while its consequent is false; in type-1 worlds, both are true. Thus, if Lewis's similarity criteria apply, (17) is false.

Naturalistic dualists can avoid this result, however. They hold that the relation between mental events and physical events is contingent owing to

---

[27] See Loewer 2001a: 51–52 for an argument along these lines.

86   Mental Causation

the failure of mental properties strongly to supervene on physical properties. Specifically, they hold that it is contingent that the instantiation of a physical base of M implies the instantiation of M. The psychophysical laws that entail such contingent implications must be contingent as well. But nothing forces dualists to accept that psychophysical laws are modally on a par with ordinary laws of nature, such as the laws of physics. They are within their rights to claim that psychophysical laws could not have failed so easily as the other laws. They can claim, in other words, that worlds where the psychophysical laws are violated are further from actuality than any worlds where only the ordinary laws are violated. (One might object that this claim is *ad hoc*. This objection is addressed at the end of this section.) Lewis's account of the similarity relation does not make provisions for a special status of the psychophysical laws. This is not surprising, since Lewis himself was a materialist (see Lewis 1994b). His account can easily be modified to accommodate the distinction, however.[28] Then the new principal criterion for overall similarity to the actual world is that none of the actual psychophysical laws be broken. (Call a violation of the actual psychophysical laws a *psychophysical miracle*.) The new principal criterion can be grafted onto Lewis's original criteria:

(1*)   It is of the first importance to avoid violations of psychophysical laws.

(2*)   It is of the second importance to avoid big, widespread, diverse violations of ordinary laws of nature.

(3*)   It is of the third importance to maximize the spatiotemporal region throughout which perfect match of particular fact prevails.

(4*)   It is of the fourth importance to avoid even small, localized, simple violations of ordinary laws of nature.

(5*)   It is of little or no importance to secure approximate similarity of particular fact, even in matters that concern us greatly.

According to the new set of criteria, a world where a violation of the actual psychophysical laws occurs is always less similar overall to our world than a world without such violations; among worlds that are on a par with respect to violations of the actual psychophysical laws, a world where a large-scale violation of the ordinary actual laws of nature occurs is always less similar overall to our world than a world without such large-scale violations; and so on. According to the new set of criteria, type-1 worlds

---

[28] A number of authors have suggested different modifications of Lewis's account of similarity recently, including Woodward (2003: 133–145) Kment (2006a), Williams (2008), and Dunn (2011).

Mental Causation by Counterfactual Dependence 87

come out more similar overall to the actual world than type-2 worlds since they involve no violation of the psychophysical laws. Hence, on the modified account, (17) is true.

Given the new similarity criteria, premise (16) comes out true too. Worlds where the antecedent of (16) holds in the absence of a psychophysical miracle are closer to the actual world than any worlds where such a miracle takes place. But if the actual psychophysical laws are intact in a world where none of M's physical bases is instantiated, M is not instantiated there either. So in the closest worlds where none of M's physical bases is instantiated, M is not instantiated either. Hence, (16) is true.[29]

The new similarity criteria (1*)–(5*) do not commit us to backtracking evaluations of counterfactuals, at least not any more than the original criteria (1)–(4) do. Our psychophysical laws are synchronic, so holding them fixed by itself never requires changing the past. Even if the new similarity criteria sometimes yield backtracking evaluations because the old criteria sometimes do, the argument for dualist mental causation emerges unscathed. None of its counterfactual premises involves such a backtracking reading. The instantiation of a base of M can be prevented by a small miracle just before the time at which M's actual base is actually instantiated. Thus, the closest worlds where no base of M is instantiated match the actual world perfectly in particular fact until just before the time at which M is instantiated in the actual world. By (16) and (17), the closest worlds where no base of M is instantiated coincide with the closest worlds where M is not instantiated. Thus, the closest worlds where M is not instantiated match the actual world perfectly in particular fact until just before the time at which M is instantiated in the actual world too. Hence, no backtracking ensues under the counterfactual supposition that M is not instantiated.[30] In particular, the truth of counterfactual (19), which expresses the counterfactual dependence of the P^*-instance on the M-instance, is not due to a backtracking evaluation. We saw in Section 1.5 that we can restrict our principle about causation to cases of counterfactual dependence that are not due to backtracking evaluations of the relevant counterfactuals. This restricted principle can be applied here, so the conclusion that the M-instance causes the P^*-instance still follows.[31]

---

[29] For a discussion of (16), albeit in the context of non-reductive physicalism, see Kallestrup 2006: 473.
[30] Except perhaps into the very near past, as was the case for the original criteria (1)–(4).
[31] Instead of modifying the similarity criteria of the miracles approach in order to make room for dualist mental causation, one could try to modify the asymmetry-by-fiat approach. Instead of requiring that the antecedent be made true with minimal difference to the actual world, one

So far the argument merely establishes that mental events cause some physical events or other, because the absence of their physical bases would have made some difference to the physical future. But, as in the case of non-reductive physicalism, we can easily apply the argument to specific pairs of mental and physical events, such as my headache and my hand's moving towards the aspirin. For a specific physical effect, the relevant premise, (18), is just as plausible as the corresponding premise (2) was in the non-reductive physicalism case.

We have seen that, assuming naturalistic dualism, the critical condition for establishing that behavioural events counterfactually depend on, and hence are caused by, mental events is that worlds where the actual psycho-physical laws are violated are always less similar overall to our world than worlds without such violations, irrespective of violations of ordinary laws of nature. Call the conjunction of this condition and the position of naturalistic dualism as it was defined earlier *super-nomological dualism*. Put less technically, the position of the super-nomological dualist is that the relation between the mental and the physical is a matter of law, but that the relevant laws are 'more necessary' than ordinary laws of nature.[32] The upshot so far is this: while other varieties of dualism may struggle at the task, super-nomological dualism can show that mental events have physical effects. Thus, super-nomological dualism can solve the interaction problem.

The argument for mental causation under super-nomological dualism can be illustrated geometrically. Imagine the modal universe spread out on a plane, with the actual world (@) at the centre. In this framework, Figure 2.3 represents a typical way for a counterfactual $\phi \; \square\!\!\!\rightarrow \psi$ to be non-vacuously true (see Lewis 1973b: 17). Applied to our case, we may represent the truth of premise (18) similarly (see Figure 2.4). What premises (16) and (17) add to this picture is a sphere of worlds **S** in which M is instantiated just in case a base of M is instantiated and which contains a world w where neither M nor a base of M is instantiated (see Figure 2.5). (Intuitively, we

---

could require that it be made true with minimal difference to the actual world *provided that this does not involve a psychophysical miracle*. As it stands, this suggestion is incomplete, however. It does not say, for instance, how the truth of the antecedent is to be brought about if the antecedent can only be made true at the cost of a psychophysical miracle. The modified miracles approach provides a neater solution.

[32] Super-nomological dualism is incompatible with Armstrong's (1983) theory of laws of nature, for Armstrong's theory involves a single universal of necessitation that is responsible for lawhood. By contrast, super-nomological dualism is compatible in principle with Lewis's (1973b, 1983, 1994a) 'best system' theory of laws of nature, for Lewis's theory is merely about what the laws of a given world are, not about how easily they could have failed.

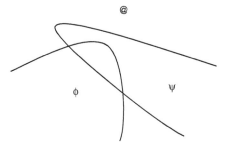

Figure 2.3. $\phi \;\square\!\!\rightarrow\; \psi$ true

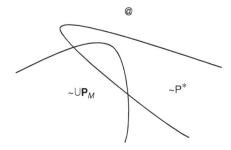

Figure 2.4. (18) ($\sim\!\cup P_M \;\square\!\!\rightarrow\; \sim\!P^*$) true

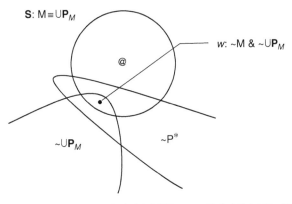

Figure 2.5. (16) ($\sim\!\cup P_M \;\square\!\!\rightarrow\; \sim\!M$), (17) ($\sim\!M \;\square\!\!\rightarrow\; \sim\!\cup P_M$), (18) ($\sim\!\cup P_M \;\square\!\!\rightarrow\; \sim\!P^*$) true

can think of a sphere of worlds as a set of worlds that resemble the actual world at least to a certain degree. More formally, we can define a sphere as a set of worlds that are closer to the actual world than all the worlds that

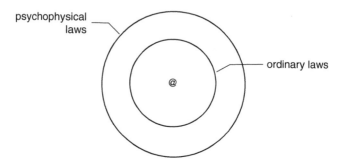

Figure 2.6. A misleading picture of super-nomological necessity

are not in the set (see Lewis 1973b: 4–19). When talking about a proposition being *true in a sphere*, I mean that the proposition is true in all worlds in that sphere.) In the situation represented in Figure 2.5, claim (19) is true, that is, it is true that P^* would not have been instantiated if M had not been instantiated. (The details are explained in Appendix 1.)

Thus, from (16), (17), and (18) we get the existence of a sphere **S** in which M is instantiated just in case a base of M is instantiated and which contains a world w where neither M nor a base of M (nor P^*) is instantiated. In **S**, the psychophysical laws that govern the relation between M and its bases hold. This is not the case for the physical laws. The physical laws are violated at w, where a small miracle prevents the instantiation of a base of M. We need to depart further from actuality to find worlds where the psychophysical laws are broken than we do to find worlds where the ordinary laws of nature are broken. This is of course just what super-nomological dualism says.

It is tempting to generalize Figure 2.5 to a spherical model of nomological and, as it were, super-nomological necessity. According to this model, all worlds where the ordinary laws of nature hold are contained in a sphere, and all worlds where the psychophysical laws hold are contained in a larger sphere (see Figure 2.6).

While there is a certain elegance to this model, super-nomological dualists should not endorse it. If the model is correct, there are no worlds where the psychophysical laws are violated while the ordinary laws of nature are not, because worlds outside of the sphere where the psychophysical laws hold are *ipso facto* outside of the sphere where the ordinary laws of nature hold. Like other dualists, however, super-nomological dualists are likely to hold that there are zombie worlds that are physically like our world but where the psychophysical laws are violated. In zombie worlds, not just the particular physical facts, but also the ordinary laws of nature, are supposed to be like they are in our

Mental Causation by Counterfactual Dependence 91

world. If there are zombie worlds, we cannot have the picture of super-nomological necessity that is depicted in Figure 2.6. For super-nomological dualists, modal space is less orderly than the spherical model has it.[33]

There is an obvious objection to the account of dualist mental causation presented in this section. The account assumed on behalf of the dualist that the psychophysical laws have a privileged status in the similarity criteria for worlds. Correspondingly, it assumed that these laws could not have failed so easily as the ordinary laws of nature. Assuming such a special modal status for psychophysical laws, however, seems distinctly *ad hoc*.

I offer two replies. First, assuming a distinct modal status for psychophysical laws might be more congenial to dualism than it initially seems. Dualists hold that the mind is special, so they may well hold that the mind is modally special. More specifically, they may hold that a special modal status of the psychophysical laws has independent epistemological virtues. Perhaps it is easier to imagine electricity without magnetism than it is to imagine my body without my mind. If so, this could be straightforwardly explained if the physical laws that link magnetism to electricity could have failed more easily than the psychophysical laws that link my mind to my body.

Second, even if the assumption that the psychophysical laws have a special modal status is made without independent motivation, it may be worthwhile in order to save mental causation, at least for those independently convinced of the truth of dualism. If astrophysicists are allowed to posit dark matter to save their convictions about gravity, why should dualists not be allowed to posit a special modal status for the psychophysical laws to save their conviction that there is mental causation? Jaegwon Kim has argued for reductive physicalism from the existence of mental causation (see, e.g., Kim 1998, 2005). Proponents and detractors of the trope identity theory agree that it is legitimate to make substantial metaphysical assumptions in order to fit the mind into the causal order of the physical world (see Robb 1997, Nordhoof 1998, and Robb 2001). If this general kind of argument is acceptable, it should likewise be acceptable for dualists to fine-tune their metaphysics of mind and adopt super-nomological dualism in order to accommodate mental causation.

---

[33] Kment endorses a spherical model of different kinds of necessity, but does not discuss the possibility of psychophysical laws that have a special modal status. The context of his discussion also differs from ours in that he allows laws to have exceptions. See Kment 2006a, 2006b, 2014.

2.6 Agency, Transference, and Physical Causes

The arguments for mental causation under non-reductive physicalism and dualism that I have presented in this chapter have drawn on the sufficiency of counterfactual dependence for causation. It might be objected that, even if these arguments solve the interaction problem in the sense that they show that physical events have mental causes, they do not, in the end, give us all we expect of mental causation. In this vein, Kim claims that agency requires more than counterfactual dependence. He holds that agency requires causal processes between mental causes and bodily movements. 'These causal processes', Kim holds,

> all involve *real connectedness* between cause and effect, and the connection is constituted by phenomena such as energy flow and momentum transfer, an actual movement of some (conserved) physical quantity.[34]

We saw in Section 1.6 that it is doubtful that causation generally requires the transfer of some physical quantity because of cases of double prevention. One might still claim that at least mental causation requires such a transfer if it is to yield genuine agency. That claim, however, runs into difficulties that arise from empirical facts about human physiology. The causal processes from mental events to bodily movements involve muscle contractions. As Jonathan Schaffer points out, muscle contractions work by double prevention and thus do not involve the transfer of a physical quantity.[35] In the muscle, myosin proteins are tense. They would bind to actin filaments, move them forward and thus make the muscle contract if it weren't for the obstruction of the binding sites by tropomyosin molecules. If the muscle receives a nerve signal, calcium is released at the neuromuscular junction, which causes the tropomyosin to move away from the binding sites. Muscle contraction works like the examples of the spring and the pillar that were discussed in Section 1.6: an event (here the calcium release) prevents something from happening (the obstruction of the binding sites) which, unless prevented, prevents the another event (the muscle contraction) from happening. Figures 2.7 and 2.8 are neuron diagram representations of the case. Figure 2.7 shows the actual situation; Figure 2.8 shows the situation where no nerve signal is received.[36]

Whatever the exact nature of the causation of a bodily movement by a mental cause, it seems that the mental cause has to operate via the calcium

---

[34] Kim 2007: 236. Esfeld (2007) advances a similar objection.
[35] See Schaffer 2000a and 2004a. For the physiological details, see Guyton and Hall 2006: 72–84. For another example from biology that involves double prevention, see Woodward 2002.
[36] I borrow these diagrams from Schaffer 2000a: 288 and 2004a: 200 with slight variations.

Mental Causation by Counterfactual Dependence

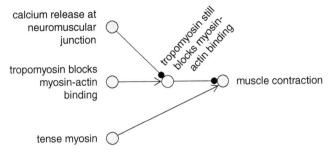

Figure 2.7. Double prevention in muscle contraction

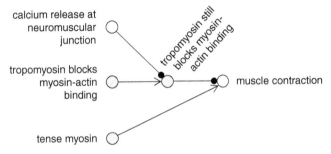

Figure 2.8. If no calcium had been released ...

release at the neuromuscular junction. (Indeed, it seems that the mental cause already has to operate via intermediate events that are further upstream in the nervous system, for the calcium release takes place quite some time after the mental event does – at least by physiological standards.) If the mental cause transfers something to the bodily movement, it seems that this transfer, too, has to go through the calcium release. But given the facts about human physiology, there is no such transfer because of the double-prevention structure of the case.[37] Thus, if human agency requires there to be a transfer of a conserved physical quantity from mental causes of bodily movements to those bodily movements, then there is no human agency. If we believe that there is human agency, we should conclude that, contra Kim, agency does not require the transfer of a physical quantity from the

---

[37] This is not to say that no energy is ever transferred on the muscle, of course, but the energy does not come from the nervous system. We shall discuss energy-transferring causes of muscle contractions in Section 4.5.

mental causes to the bodily movements after all.[38] We can still have counterfactual dependence of bodily movements on mental events, however. While this might not give us 'real connectedness' in Kim's sense, it still allows our minds to make a difference to what we do (see Loewer 2007: 255).

(Do the physiological facts about muscle contraction not also have ramifications about the *physical* causes of bodily movements if causation is understood in terms of transfer? They do. We will take up this issue in the context of the exclusion problem in Section 4.5.)

It might seem that the argument against Kim's claim about agency, causal processes, and transfer is somehow parasitic on the assumption that double prevention is causation, which some might not find convincing, despite the strong case that we saw can be made for it. But in fact the issue of whether double prevention is causation is a red herring here. Anyone who agrees with Kim's claim and the assumption that the mental cause operates via the calcium release at the neuromuscular junction will also agree with the following modified claim: in human agency, a physical quantity is transferred to bodily movements from earlier events via the calcium release at the neuromuscular junction. The modified claim does not talk about causation; it merely talks about transfer. The modified claim is still false because of the facts about human physiology. Thus, the Kimian approach to agency is flawed for reasons that are independent of whether double prevention is causation.

So far, I have followed Kim in talking about the transfer (or lack thereof) of a physical quantity in muscle contraction. The arguments generalize to the transfer (or lack thereof) of powers. Appealing to powers has become popular not just in the philosophy of causation in general, but also in attempts to solve the problems of mental causation.[39] We saw in Section 1.6 that powers theories that take the shape of powers transference views have the same trouble with double prevention as standard transference views, because no power is passed from the double preventer to the event that would have been prevented but for the occurrence of the double preventer. Given the mechanism of muscle contraction, no power is transferred from the calcium release at the neuromuscular junction to the movement of the muscle, just as no physical quantity

---

[38] The applicability of the double-prevention structure of muscle contraction to Kim's claim about agency was discovered independently by Russo (2016). Schaffer (2000a, 2004a, 2012) makes similar points about the kind of causation involved in human agency.

[39] Recent discussions of mental causation that explicitly appeal to powers theories of causation include Heil 2012: 133–134, Gibb 2013 and 2015a, Lowe 2013, Hornsby 2015, Robb 2015, and Mayr 2017. Gibb advocates a powers-based solution to the exclusion problem according to which certain mental events are double preventers that do *not* cause the physical events that would have been prevented but for the occurrence of the mental events. Her suggestion is not motivated by purely physical cases of double prevention like the muscle contraction case, however.

Mental Causation by Counterfactual Dependence 95

is transferred. Thus, proponents of powers transference views cannot endorse an analogue of Kim's claim that talks about a transfer of powers, any more than proponents of standard transference views can endorse Kim's original claim. Likewise for a modified claim that does not talk about causation, but merely demands a transfer of powers to bodily movements via the calcium release at the neuromuscular junction: the modified claim is empirically false too.

In sum, Kim's 'real connectedness' is not to be had, either as a transfer of a physical quantity or as a transfer of powers. It is more sensible if we do not endorse it in the first place and satisfy ourselves with the result that, as agents, we can make a difference in the physical world because our bodily movements counterfactually depend on what is going on in our minds.

Let me briefly address a question of intra-physical causation before concluding this chapter. So far, I have mostly talked about the causal relation between the instance of a mental property M and the later instance of a physical property P^*. What I have said about the actual base or realizer of M, P, has been negative. In the context of non-reductive physicalism, I said in Section 2.4 that the argument for the causation of the P^*-instance by the M-instance commits us neither to claiming that the M-instance causes the P-instance nor to claiming that the P-instance causes the P^*-instance. The argument for mental causation under dualism yields no such commitments either. There, too, the set of M's physical bases functions merely as a logical intermediary between the M-instance and the P^*-instance, not as a causal one, and nothing follows about the role of the actual physical base of M.

While no commitment to the P-instance's being a cause or effect follows from the arguments I have presented, our sufficient condition for causation can be used independently to make a case for the claim that the P-instance causes the P^*-instance. Assume that the P-instance is a c-fibre firing and the P^*-instance is my hand's moving towards the aspirin. We may assume that there are no redundant additional physical causes of my hand's moving. We may also assume that there are no pre-empted alternative physical causes of my hand's moving, such as the intervention of the overzealous nurse who would move my hand towards the aspirin if I were not to do it myself. Given these assumptions, it seems that my hand would not have moved if my c-fibres had not fired.[40] The movement occurs later than the c-fibre firing.[41] Therefore, by our sufficient condition for causation, the c-fibre firing causes my hand to move.

---

[40] For further discussion of this counterfactual, see Lowe 2008: 103–107 and Paprzycka 2014.
[41] Once more, we might have to take a suitable temporal part of the c-fibre firing in order to avoid temporal overlap between the putative cause and the putative effect.

96 Mental Causation

This sounds like a commonsensical result, but besides putting the exclusion problem on the agenda, it conjures up the issues from Section 2.4 about whether realizers can be causes or effects, for we are now committed to the claim that the instances of certain realizers or bases of mental properties are causes. We will return to this issue in Section 4.4.

2.7 Conclusion

This chapter has presented arguments for the existence of mental causation under non-reductive physicalism and dualism. Both views allow us to establish that physical events counterfactually depend on, and hence are caused by, mental events. For non-reductive physicalists, showing that physical events counterfactually depend on mental events is straightforward. For dualists, showing this is less straightforward, but it can still be done if one endorses the super-nomological variety of dualism that assigns a special modal status to the psychophysical laws. Like counterfactual dependence in general, mental causation by counterfactual dependence falls short of showing that mental causes transfer a physical quantity or a power to their physical effects. But that there be such a transfer should not be a requirement for agency, for it is an empirical fact that in humans bodily movements are caused by double prevention and hence do not involve a transfer of a physical quantity from cause to effect.

On the face of it, having accommodated mental causation looks like good news for non-reductive physicalists and super-nomological dualists. This result can be employed in different ways, however, depending on how serious one takes the exclusion problem to be. One could read the result as a *reductio* of non-reductive physicalism and super-nomological dualism: the physical effect has a physical cause that is simultaneous with its mental cause (namely the instance of the realizer or base of the relevant mental property). Thus, the physical effect is overdetermined, like a death by firing squad. But the physical effects of mental causes are not thus overdetermined. Contradiction! Non-reductive physicalism and super-nomological dualism have to go. Alternatively, my argument can be read in favour of non-reductive physicalism and super-nomological dualism: it brings the good news that these positions allow the mental to have physical effects. Granted, a physical effect of a mental cause has a physical cause simultaneous with its mental cause. Depending on what we mean by overdetermination, we might or might not have to call the physical effect overdetermined. But even if we call it overdetermined, there is nothing objectionable or particularly firing-squad-like about the situation. Far from being a coincidence, the fact that the physical effect has a mental cause in addition to its physical cause is explained by the relation of strong supervenience and nomological supervenience that non-reductive physicalism and super-nomological dualism posit. I prefer the second use of our result, but discussion will have to wait until Chapter 4.

CHAPTER 3

Mental Causation by Causal Modelling

3.1 Introduction

The world of modelling is glamorous. This holds even within philosophy, where for the past two decades or so causal modelling has been one of the most successful approaches to the study of causation. In particular, causal modelling theories of token causation[1] (that is, causation between token events) have been able to solve numerous problems that had plagued earlier theories.

Causal modelling theories of token causation can be regarded as descendants of earlier counterfactual theories such as Lewis's (1973a). Their central tools are causal models, that is (roughly), structures that represent events and counterfactuals about these events. The advantage of causal modelling theories is that they can represent more complex counterfactual structures than those earlier theories could. The earlier theories were limited to counterfactuals whose antecedents and consequents talked about the occurrence or non-occurrence (typically the non-occurrence) of individual events, such as 'If I had not thrown the dart, the balloon would not have burst.'[2] Causal modelling theorists, by contrast, can invoke counterfactuals about what would have been the case if a certain event had or had not occurred while such-and-such other events had or had not occurred.

To illustrate the approach of taking into account more complex antecedents, consider a case of so-called early pre-emption.[3] An apprentice

---

[1] Among such theories that have been advanced following Pearl 2000 and Spirtes *et al.* 2000 are Hitchcock 2001, Woodward 2003, Halpern and Pearl 2005, Hall 2007, Hitchcock 2007a, Halpern and Hitchcock 2010, and Halpern and Hitchcock 2015.

[2] The earlier theories could achieve more complexity by formulating conditions on causation in terms of chains of such counterfactuals (see Lewis 1973a; compare also Section 2.4).

[3] The following is a simplified version of a case from Hitchcock 2004b. The difference from late pre-emption that was introduced in Chapter 1 is that in early pre-emption the backup cause is pre-empted before the chain from the actual cause to the effect is completed.

98

assassin, called Apprentice, shoots the victim, called Victim, who dies. There was a risk that Apprentice would lose his nerve and fail to fire. To complete the assassination in that case, an expert assassin, called Expert, was present as a back-up: if Apprentice had not fired, Expert would have fired instead. We would like to say that the firing of Apprentice causes Victim to die, but Victim's death does not counterfactually depend on Apprentice's firing, for if Apprentice had not fired, Expert would have fired instead, in which case Victim would have died anyway. If Apprentice had not fired *and Expert had not fired either*, however, then Victim would not have died. Causal modelling theorists can capitalize on this insight. They can claim that what matters for causation is that one event depends on another if we hold certain other facts fixed (in our example, the fact that Expert did not fire). This seems to be an intuitive diagnosis of why Apprentice's firing causes Victim to die. The diagnosis can in turn be formulated neatly in terms of causal models.[4]

On the face of it, causal modelling theories of causation, and the counterfactuals with complex antecedents that they employ, are ideally suited for being applied to (putative) cases of mental causation, where not only a mental event and its (putative) effect are in play, but also the physical realizer of the mental event and earlier physical goings-on. It is thus somewhat surprising that the application to mental causation has only been investigated for one causal modelling theory in the literature so far, namely the interventionist theory by James Woodward (2003). Whether interventionism can accommodate mental causation has turned out to be controversial, so there is reason to be suspicious about the ability of other causal modelling theories to do so.[5]

This chapter applies causal modelling theories to the case of putative mental causes and argues that these theories can, after all, explain mental causation. We shall see that this holds for other causal modelling theories as well as for interventionism. These different causal modelling theories can explain mental causation, I will argue, although this requires some unorthodoxy in how the relevant causal models are built. The chapter does not merely provide a vindication of mental causation by causal modelling, however. It also uses causal modelling to provide a solution

---

[4] Lewis's theory offers a diagnosis too, by claiming that there is chain of counterfactual dependence from the apprentice assassin's firing to the victim's death, but this diagnosis seems less intuitive.

[5] Gebharter (2017) investigates the applicability to mental causation both for certain probabilistic causal modelling theories and for Woodward's interventionism. His results are negative in both cases, however, which strengthens the suspicion that causal modelling theories in general cannot accommodate mental causation.

to the problem of overlapping realizers from Section 2.3. Recall that the problem was that our principle about causation in terms of counterfactuals commits us to the claim that an aluminium ladder's opacity causes my electrocution when I hold it against a power line, because the realizers of opacity overlap with the realizers of conductivity. It will turn out that conditions on causation in terms of causal modelling that avoid the commitment to the ladder's opacity being a cause are problematic. But causal modelling will allow us to formulate a criterion for explanatory relevance that can solve the problem.

One can be more or less ambitious in using causal modelling, trying to find necessary and sufficient or merely sufficient conditions for causation. As in the previous chapter, in this chapter I will consider only sufficient conditions for causation, not necessary and sufficient conditions. Another respect in which one can be ambitious in causal modelling is to aim not merely at formulating conditions on causation in terms of causal models, but also at providing new foundations for counterfactuals in terms of causal models.[6] In this respect, too, I choose the modest side, because this will allow us to continue working with the account of counterfactuals that was established in Chapter 1.[7]

The plan for this chapter is as follows. Section 3.2 introduces the causal modelling framework. Section 3.3 presents a causal model that represents the counterfactual structure involving a mental event and various physical events. The design of the model is somewhat unorthodox, but it satisfies a simple sufficient condition for causation in terms of causal models. Section 3.4 shows that mental causation survives possible refinements of this simple sufficient condition for causation. Section 3.4 applies the causal modelling framework to the problem of overlapping realizers. Section 3.5 addresses several objections according to which the model for mental causation is in some respect inappropriate. Section 3.7 discusses how interventionism fares vis-à-vis mental causation and argues that it can accommodate mental causation in a similar way to other causal modelling theories.

3.2 Causal Models

The point of causal models is to represent complex patterns of counter-factuals about events, from which conclusions about causal relations

---

[6] This approach is advocated in Galles and Pearl 1998, Halpern 2000, and Hiddleston 2005.
[7] Briggs (2012) argues that accounts of counterfactuals in terms of causal models face significant formal limitations. See also Halpern 2013 and Huber 2013.

Mental Causation by Causal Modelling 101

between those events may be drawn. In this section I will introduce causal models by way of an example which does not involve mental events. I will follow the framework presented by Christopher Hitchcock (2001, 2007a). This framework deals with counterfactuals about, and causation between, token events; Section 3.7 will discuss interventionism, which uses a slightly different framework.

The example I will use is this:

> *Lightning Strike.* Lightning strikes my house, which subsequently catches fire. The sprinkler system is activated and extinguishes the fire. If the lightning had not struck, then the sprinkler system would not have been activated. If the sprinkler system had not been activated, then the house would have burnt down.

The counterfactuals that are true in *Lightning Strike* can be captured by a causal model. Formally, a *causal model* is an ordered pair $\langle \mathbf{V}, \mathbf{E} \rangle$ of a set of variables $\mathbf{V}$ and a set of equations $\mathbf{E}$ (also known as *structural equations*) that involve these variables. In causal modelling theories of token causation, the variables represent the occurrence or non-occurrence of token events, or different ways in which a token event can occur. In the *Lightning Strike* example it suffices to use binary variables that represent whether or not a given event occurs. In a given case there are typically various options for the choice of the variables. In our example, it seems reasonable to use the variables L, S, and B with the following interpretation:

$L = 1$ if the lightning strikes, 0 otherwise
$S = 1$ if the sprinkler system is activated, 0 otherwise
$B = 1$ if the house burns down, 0 otherwise

(In this chapter, italic capital letters, which were used for properties in previous chapters, stand for variables. Some letters double as variables and as names for properties.) Let us also introduce a further variable, U, to represent the initial conditions before the lightning strike:

$U = 0$ or $U = 1$ depending on the initial conditions

The purpose of U is to determine whether or not the lightning strike takes place. Introducing a variable like U is not mandatory in our example, but it will prove useful when modelling mental causation (see also Halpern and Pearl 2005: 856).

The equations in $\mathbf{E}$ represent counterfactuals about how the values of the variables in $\mathbf{V}$ depend on one another. As in previous chapters, I will

Mental Causation

assume Lewis's truth-conditions for counterfactuals. I stipulate that all the counterfactuals that we are dealing with be read in a non-backtracking way and I will continue to assume determinism. Some of the counterfactuals that are relevant for our example are already contained in the description of *Lightning Strike*, for instance, the claim that if the lightning had not struck, then the sprinkler system would not have been activated. Other counterfactuals are true in the example without being mentioned in the description, for instance, the claim that if the lightning had not struck while the sprinkler system had been activated anyway, then the house would not have burned down.

The equations of a causal model represent the counterfactuals that are true in a given case as follows. Each variable appears on the left-hand side of exactly one equation, which is called the equation *for* that variable. The equations are read from right to left: for any assignment of values to the variables on the right-hand side, the equation says that if the variables on the right-hand side had assumed those values, the variable on the left-hand side would have assumed the value that results from the function on the right-hand side.[8] This function may simply be identity, or it may be more complex, as in the equation for B below. The equations must not contain any redundant elements. If the value of a given variable does not make a difference to the value of the target variable over and above other variables, it must be eliminated from the equation of the target variable.

In the *Lightning Strike* example, the equations are as follows:

$$
\begin{aligned}
LS \quad U &\Leftarrow 1 \\
L &\Leftarrow U \\
S &\Leftarrow L \\
B &\Leftarrow L \cdot (1 - S)
\end{aligned}
$$

(In what follows, I will use names such as 'LS' to refer both to a causal model as a whole and to the model's equations.) U is the only variable whose value is given and not determined by any other variables. Such variables are called *exogenous*; the variables that are not exogenous (in our example, L, S, and B) are called *endogenous*. Typically, the equations for the exogenous variables specify the actual values of variables. This is what the equation for U (that is, the first equation) does here, which says that (the value of) U is 1. But, as we shall see shortly, when a modification of

---

[8] Some authors, including Hitchcock, use the identity sign to write the equations of a model instead of an arrow, but even when they are thus written, the equations do not express identities, but the non-symmetric relation described here.

an original causal model is used to evaluate a counterfactual in the original model, the equations for exogenous variables can have the role of counterfactual suppositions.

I said earlier that the equations in a causal model represent counterfactuals. Admittedly, it is somewhat idiosyncratic to say that the equation for U, which merely sets U to 1, represents a counterfactual, but at any rate the equations for the endogenous variables represent genuine counterfactuals. The equation for L (that is, the second equation) represents two counterfactuals: if U had been 0, then L would have been 0; and if U had been 1, then L would have been 1. Similarly, the equation for S (that is, the third equation) represents two counterfactuals: if L had been 0, then S would have been 0; and if L had been 1, then S would have been 1. The equation for B represents four counterfactuals: if both L and S had been 1, then B would have been 0; if L had been 1 while S had been 0, then B would have been 1; if L had been 0 while S had been 1, then B would have been 0; lastly, if both L and S had been 0, then B would have been 0. We can of course translate these counterfactuals back into natural language. For instance, the penultimate counterfactual represented by the equation for B is the counterfactual mentioned three paragraphs back that is among those not contained in the description of *Lightning Strike*, namely the claim that if lightning had not struck while the sprinkler system had been activated anyway, then the house would not have burned down.

A set of equations can represent counterfactuals besides those that are represented by the individual equations. For instance, the equations in LS represent that if the sprinkler system had not been activated, then the house would have burned down. This is so, roughly, because if we set S to 0, the equations for the remaining variables yield that B is 1. More formally, we can define the truth of a counterfactual in a causal model as follows. Let X_1, $X_2, \ldots, Y$ be variables in a causal model $\langle \mathbf{V}, \mathbf{E} \rangle$. Then the *counterfactual* 'If X_1 had been x_1, X_2 had been $x_2, \ldots$, then Y would have been y' is *true in* $\langle \mathbf{V}, \mathbf{E} \rangle$ if and only if, in the new causal model $\langle \mathbf{V}, \mathbf{E}' \rangle$ that we get by replacing the equations for $X_1, X_2, \ldots$ with the equations $X_1 \Leftarrow x_1, X_2 \Leftarrow x_2, \ldots, Y$ assumes value y. (This definition subsumes the truth of counterfactuals that are represented by individual equations.)

To see how the formal definition applies to the example of the claim that if the sprinkler system had not been activated, then the house would have burned down, the claim first needs to be rephrased in terms of variables. Thus rephrased, it says that if S had been 0, then B would have been 1. In order to evaluate the claim in our model LS, we need to replace the equation for S in that model, which reads '$S \Leftarrow L$', with an equation that

104   Mental Causation

reads '$S \Leftarrow 0$'. In other words, we need to replace the original equation for
S with an equation that sets S to the value specified in the antecedent of our
counterfactual. This change of the equation of S yields the following new
model:

$$
\begin{aligned}
LS' \quad U &\Leftarrow 1 \\
L &\Leftarrow U \\
S &\Leftarrow 0 \\
B &\Leftarrow L \cdot (1 - S)
\end{aligned}
$$

In the new model LS', we can calculate the value of B by successively
substituting specific values for variables: the equation for U sets U to 1;
substituting '1' for 'U' in the equation for L sets L to 1 as well; the new
equation for S sets S to 0; which, together with the other specific values
gathered to far, allows us to substitute '$1 \cdot (1 - 0)$' for the right-hand-side of
the equation for B. Thus, in LS', B assumes value $1 \cdot (1 - 0)$, that is, value 1,
which is what the consequent of our counterfactual says; therefore, the
counterfactual is true in our original model LS.

The procedure of determining the value of a given variable from the
equations might not succeed if we get stuck in a circle. Therefore, it is
common to impose the requirement that the sets of equations be
acyclic, that is, that the equations can be ordered such that no variable
appears on the right-hand side of any equation after it has appeared on
the left-hand side. The equations in LS, for instance, are acyclic, since
we can thus order them (in the reverse order of their listing). Non-
acyclic sets of equations may still allow the procedure for evaluating
counterfactuals to work, however; we will return to this issue in the
following section.

Recall the standard definition of counterfactual dependence between
events from Section 1.4: an actually occurring event e counterfactually
depends on an actually occurring event c if and only if e would not have
occurred if c had not occurred. A notion of counterfactual dependence
between *variables* can be defined in the causal modelling framework. Thus,
for variables X and Y in a causal model $\langle \mathbf{V}, \mathbf{E} \rangle$ that have the actual values
x and y respectively, let us say that Y *counterfactually depends on X* in $\langle \mathbf{V}, \mathbf{E} \rangle$
if and only if there are non-actual values x' and y' of X and Y, respectively,
such that the counterfactual 'If X had been x', then Y would have been y'' is
true in $\langle \mathbf{V}, \mathbf{E} \rangle$.

In LS, for example, the variable for the sprinkler system's being activated, S, counterfactually depends on the variable for the lightning strike,

Mental Causation by Causal Modelling 105

L, since the actual values of S and L are both 1 and the counterfactual 'If L had been 0, then S would have been 0' is true in our causal model. By contrast, the variable for the house's burning down, B, does not counter-factually depend on L, for the counterfactual 'If L had been 0, then B would have been 1' is not true in our model, and no other counterfactuals with non-actual values of both L and B are available in it.

What is the relation between counterfactual dependence between variables in a causal model and counterfactual dependence between events? If variables X and Y are binary and their actual values stand for the occurrence of events (as opposed to the occurrence of omissions), we get standard counterfactual dependence between events from the counterfactual dependence between variables X and Y. More precisely, if X and Y are binary and their actual values – let x and y be these actual values – stand for the occurrence of events, then it follows from the counterfactual dependence of variable Y on variable X that the event represented by $Y = y$ counterfactually depends on the event represented by $X = x$ in the standard sense. For example, in LS, variable S counterfactually depends on variable L; both variables are binary; and their actual values stand for the occurrence of events, namely $L = 1$ for the lightning strike and $S = 1$ for the activation of the sprinkler system. It follows that the activation of the sprinkler system counterfactually depends on the lightning strike in the standard sense of counterfactual dependence between events.

In cases of multi-valued variables and omissions, we might have counterfactual dependence between variables without counterfactual dependence between events. For instance, suppose that a multi-valued variable Y counterfactually depends on a multi-valued variable X. It is consistent with this counterfactual dependence of Y on X that it is merely the case that the event represented by Y would have occurred slightly differently if the event represented by X had occurred slightly differently while the event represented by Y would still have occurred (albeit perhaps slightly differently) if the event represented by X had not occurred. Or suppose that variables X and Y are binary, Y counterfactually depends on X, and the actual value of X stands for an omission: if omissions are not events, no counterfactual dependence between events follows.

In previous chapters, we took counterfactual dependence to suffice for causation between events. (At least where the dependent event occurs later than the event it depends on – I suppress that qualification until Section 3.6.) We may continue to do so without further ado by taking counterfactual dependence between variables in corresponding cases to suffice for causation. When putative mental causes are concerned, the new task will be to establish the counterfactual dependence claims in the framework of causal modelling.

Cases of counterfactual dependence between variables that might not correspond to cases of counterfactual dependence between events have to be treated with a bit of caution. I will set aside until Section 3.4 cases of counterfactual dependence between variables whose actual values stand for omissions. As for counterfactual dependence involving multi-valued variables, we should distinguish cases where the variable for the putative effect remains binary from cases where the variable for the putative effect is itself multi-valued. If the variable for the putative effect is binary and it counterfactually depends on a multi-valued variable that stands for the putative cause, it seems straightforward to infer a causal relation. Consider the following non-technical analogue: irrespective of what would have happened had I not thrown the dart, if the balloon would not have burst had I thrown the dart differently, we can still infer that my (actual) throw caused the bursting. If the variable for the putative effect is multi-valued, things are not quite so straightforward. Consider again a non-technical analogue: suppose that event e would merely have occurred slightly differently if event c had not occurred or if event c had occurred slightly differently. Should we infer that c caused e? A positive answer seems plausible, but it is not obvious.[9] Fortunately, we need not settle the issue here. The important cases of multi-valued variables for putative causes in this chapter will be cases where the variable for the putative effect is still binary. For simplicity, I will ignore the potential complication from multi-valued effect variables and assume that counterfactual dependence between variables (multi-valued or not) is sufficient for causation, at least when their actual values do not stand for omissions.

Let us return to the tools of causal modelling. The equations from a causal model can be used to construct a *causal graph*. The causal graph of a given model contains all the variables of that model. An arrow is drawn from a variable to another if and only if the first variable appears on the right-hand side of the equation for the second variable. Figure 3.1 shows the causal graph of the *Lightning Strike* example.

While causal graphs often make the structure of the equations in a causal model easier to grasp, we should not overestimate the amount of information it carries. There can be arrows that do not correspond to counterfactual dependence. In our example, there is an arrow from L to B although, as we

---

[9] The issue is closely related to Lewis's (2004) theory of causation as influence. For critical discussion of this theory, see Collins 2000 and Kvart 2001.

Mental Causation by Causal Modelling

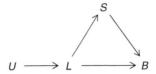

Figure 3.1. The causal graph of *LS*

saw, *B* does not counterfactually depend on *L*.[10] We have not pronounced any verdicts about which events in our example fail to stand in a causal relation. But it seems at least doubtful that the lightning strike causes the house *not* to burn down.[11] If there turns out to be no causal relation between what is represented by the actual values of *L* and *B*,[12] our case also illustrates that there can be an arrow in a causal graph without a corresponding causal relation.

We can define a graph as *acyclic* if and only if one can never double back on the same variable by following a path along the direction of the arrows. A graph is acyclic if and only if the corresponding equations are acyclic.

For further illustration of the causal modelling framework, let us model the assassination example from the previous section. This example will also allow us to anticipate the strategy for formulating conditions on causation in causal models that will be employed later in this chapter. In the example, Apprentice fires and kills Victim. If Apprentice had not fired, Expert would have fired and killed Victim instead. If neither Apprentice nor Expert had fired, Victim would not have died. In order to model the example, we need three binary variables that represent the actions of Apprentice and Expert and the fate of Victim. Let us use the variables *A*, *E*, and *D* with the following interpretations:

A = 1 if Assassin fires, 0 otherwise
E = 1 if Expert fires, 0 otherwise
D = 1 if Victim dies, 0 otherwise

---

[10] Variable *B potentially* counterfactually depends on variable *L*, however, for *B* would counterfactually depend on *L* if *S* were held fixed at value 0.

[11] Strictly speaking, the house's not burning down is an omission, but this is inessential, for we would reach the same verdict if we replaced *B* with a variable that stands for the *bona fide* event of the house's (still) standing at a later time: it seems at least doubtful that the lightning strike causes that event.

[12] The case is similar to the counterexample to the transitivity of causation that was discussed in Section 1.4. It is even more similar to an example by Hartry Field from an unpublished lecture, which is also often cited as a counterexample to the transitivity of causation. In Field's example, someone places a bomb outside Smith's door; Smith sees the bomb, disarms it and survives. For a discussion of the case, see Paul and Hall 2013: 215–231.

108 Mental Causation

(One could add an exogenous variable U, as in the model for *Lightning Strike*, but I omit such a variable here for simplicity.) The counterfactual claims that are true in the example include the following: if A had been 0, then E would have been 1 (if Apprentice had not fired, then Expert would have fired instead); if A had been 0, then D would have been 1 (if Apprentice had not fired, then Victim would still have died); if A had been 0 and E had been 0, then D would have been 0 (if neither Apprentice nor Expert had fired, then Victim would not have died). The equations for the case are as follows:

$$AS \quad A \Leftarrow 1$$
$$E \Leftarrow 1 - A$$
$$D \Leftarrow \text{Max}\{A, E\}$$

It can easily be verified that the equations in AS represent the above counterfactuals (and further true counterfactuals about the case). For instance, we can verify the truth of 'If A had been 0 and E had been 0, then D would have been 0' as follows: replace the equation for A with the equation '$A \Leftarrow 0$', which sets A to the value specified in the antecedent. Similarly, replace the equation for E with the equation '$E \Leftarrow 0$'. In the resulting model, substitute the values of A and E in the equation for D. Thus, D assumes value $\text{Max}\{0, 0\}$, that is, value 0. This is the value specified in the consequent of our counterfactual, so the counterfactual is true in our original model AS.

The counterfactual 'If A had been 0, then D would have been 0' is false in our model AS, because Victim would still have died if Apprentice had not fired. Thus, variable D does not counterfactually depend on variable A, for the only non-actual value that variables A and D can assume is 0. Apprentice's firing (that is, the event represented by $A = 1$), causes Victim's death (the event represented by $D = 1$). Since D does not counterfactually depend on A, this causal relation cannot obtain because of counterfactual dependence between the two variables. We saw in the previous section, however, that it seems plausible that what underlies the causal relation in this case is that Victim would not have died if neither Apprentice nor Expert had fired. In variable-talk, what underlies the causal relation seems to be the truth of the counterfactual 'If A had been 0 and E had been 0, then D would have been 0.' The causal graph of our model, which is shown in Figure 3.2, suggests a reason for the relevance of this counterfactual. There are two ways of travelling from A to D by following the direction of the arrows in the graph. One can travel from A to D directly, or one can

Mental Causation by Causal Modelling

Figure 3.2. The causal graph of AS

travel via E. One of these routes, the direct route, yields dependence of D on A if we hold the variable that is not on this route, E, fixed at its actual value. To say that there is dependence between two variables when certain other variables are held fixed at their actual values is simply to say that a certain counterfactual with a complex antecedent is true. In our case, that counterfactual is 'If A had been 0 and E had been 0, then D would have been 0.'

The strategy behind this kind of reasoning is that the causal graph of a model provides information about routes or paths in the model, which in turn allows us to formulate conditions on causation in the form of counterfactuals with complex antecedents; these antecedents say that, first, the variable for the candidate cause assumes a different value while, second, certain off-path variables are held fixed at their actual values. In Section 3.5, I will investigate how this strategy can be used to deal with the problem of overlapping realizers. First, however, let us turn to mental causation.

3.3 A Model for Mental Causes

This section applies the causal modelling framework to mental causation. The case of non-reductive physicalism will be considered first; at the end of this section we will turn to super-nomological dualism. The plan for the non-reductive physicalist case is to start by selecting the variables for a causal model for mental causation. Then we will draw up an inventory of various true counterfactuals involving those variables. A set of equations that represents these counterfactuals will complete the causal model for mental causation. The model will be shown to have the consequence that there is mental causation because a simple sufficient condition for causation in terms of causal models is satisfied. We shall see that, *mutatis mutandis*, the results from the non-reductive physicalist case also hold for the dualist case.

Assume that we are dealing with a specific instance of a mental property and a later physical event that is the (putative) effect of the mental property-instance. Without loss of generality, let my headache be the instance of the mental property, and let my hand's moving towards the aspirin be the later physical event. For modelling the case, we need a binary variable M that represents the instantiation or non-instantiation of the property of having a headache (equivalently, the occurrence or non-occurrence of the corresponding strong Kimian event that is constituted, *inter alia*, by the property of having a headache). We need a variable P that represents the instantiation or non-instantiation of the various realizers of headaches. Variable P should be multi-valued, so that it can represent the instantiation of the actual realizer of the mental property, the instantiation of alternative realizers, and the non-instantiation of all realizers. (In Section 3.6 I will address objections to modelling the mental event and its realizers in the way I have just suggested.) We need a binary variable P^* that represents the occurrence or non-occurrence of my hand's moving towards the aspirin, the putative physical effect of the headache. Lastly, let us use an exogenous variable U to represent initial conditions again. We can think of U as representing the physical goings-on in my body and perhaps in my immediate environment just before the mental event occurs. The purpose of U is to at least partially determine the value of P; it should therefore be multi-valued as well. We can specify what the different values of the variables represent as follows:

U = 0 or 1 or 2 . . . depending on the initial conditions
P = 0 if no realizer of headaches is instantiated, 1 or 2 or . . . otherwise, depending on which realizer is instantiated
M = 1 if the property of having a headache is instantiated, 0 otherwise
P^*= 1 if my hand moves towards the aspirin, 0 otherwise

If one would like to flesh out the different positive values of P, one can let $P = 1$ represent my having firing c-fibres, let $P = 2$ represent my having firing x-fibres, let $P = 3$ represent my having an active semiconductor network of a certain kind in my head, etc. Correspondingly, we can think of $U = 1$ as representing a state of my body and perhaps my immediate environment that is standardly followed by a c-fibre firing of mine, $U = 2$ as representing a state that is standardly followed by an x-fibre firing of mine, $U = 3$ as representing a state that is standardly followed by semiconductor activity of a certain kind in my head, etc. Since $P = 0$ represents that no realizer of headaches is instantiated, we can think of $U = 0$ as representing a state that is standardly followed by no instantiation of a realizer of headaches. For our purposes, however, all that is matters is that the positive values of P represent instantiations of the different

Mental Causation by Causal Modelling

realizers of headaches and that the positive values of U represent corresponding earlier states that standardly lead up to them.

What are the counterfactual relationships between the different values of our variables that our causal model should capture? Let us start with the relationship between P and P^*. Part of this relationship is straightforward. As we saw in the previous chapter, if I had not instantiated any realizer of headaches, my hand would not have moved towards the aspirin. Expressed in terms of variables, this counterfactual reads:

(1)   If P had been 0, then P^* would have been 0.

It is also straightforward that if I had had firing c-fibres, my hand would have moved towards the aspirin. Indeed, this counterfactual is automatically true given that in fact I have firing c-fibres and my hand moves towards the aspirin. (I'll present a counterfactual in terms of variables that subsumes this counterfactual in a moment.)

What is not so straightforward is what would have been the case if I had instantiated the alternative realizers of headaches. At first sight, it might seem that my hand would still have moved towards the aspirin if I had instantiated any such realizer. But a moment's reflection shows that the latter claim is dubious at best. Many of the alternative realizers are rather exotic. Implanting them in my body is likely to be a pretty disruptive procedure that yields behavioural effects (or a lack thereof) of the alternative realizers that differ drastically from the behavioural effects of firing c-fibres. In other words, it seems likely that the instantiations of many alternative realizers would not be followed by my hand's moving towards the aspirin. It will turn out in the next chapter that this result has some positive repercussions for solving the exclusion problem, but it would complicate our task of model-building considerably (not least because the list of alternative realizers is open-ended). In this chapter, I will therefore assume, for simplicity, that all the alternative realizers have uniform behavioural consequences. I will assume, that is, that the instantiation of any alternative realizer of headaches would have been followed by my hand's moving towards the aspirin. If we combine this assumption with the straightforward claim that the actual realizer of headaches would be (indeed, is) followed by hand's moving towards the aspirin, we get the following claim in terms of variables:

(2)   If P had been p, with $p \neq 0$, then P^* would have been 1.[13]

---

[13] Strictly speaking, (2) is not a counterfactual but a schema, or perhaps a counterfactual that is in the scope of a universal quantifier that ranges over the possible values of P. For simplicity I will treat (2)

Mental Causation

Claim (2) says that, for any non-zero value of P, if P had assumed that value, then P^* would have assumed value 1. Without the assumption of (2) for simplicity, the arguments from this chapter would still go through, at least *mutatis mutandis*.[14]

Let us consider the relationship between the realizer-variable, P, and the variable for the headache, M. A number of counterfactuals about how the values of M and P are related can be read off from the relation between the mental property and its realizing properties. Recall that, according to non-reductive physicalism, mental properties strongly supervene on physical properties. Recall that from this strong supervenience it follows that the instantiation of a mental property strictly implies, and is strictly implied by, the instantiation of a realizer of that mental property. Applied to our case, we get the following two strict conditionals:

(i) Necessarily, if the property of having a headache is instantiated, then a realizer of headaches is instantiated.
(ii) Necessarily, if a realizer of headaches is instantiated, then the property of having a headache is instantiated.

Claims (i) and (ii) express the consequence of strong supervenience in terms of properties. If we rephrase these claims in terms of variables, we get:

(3) Necessarily, if M is 1, then P is not 0.
(4) Necessarily, if P is p, with $p \neq 0$, then M is 1.

By contraposition and the assumption that, necessarily, M is either 1 or 0, we get:

---

as a counterfactual, however (similarly for claim (8) below). As an alternative to (2), we could formulate a separate counterfactual for each possible value of the antecedent-variable: we could use the claims $P = 1 \;\square\!\!\rightarrow P^* = 1$, $P = 2 \;\square\!\!\rightarrow P^* = 1$, etc. instead. This would make our set of equations rather cumbersome, although the excess complexity would not be as bad as in the case of the alternative model MC^* that will be discussed in Section 3.6.

[14] It is an option to change the framework and to let variable P^* be multi-valued, with different non-zero values of P^* standing for different variations of my post-headache behaviour, instead of assuming (2) with binary P^*. A problem with this option is that, for all we know, different alternative realizers result in exactly the same variation from my actual behaviour, though we do not know which of the many realizers do. In response, one could try to err on the side of proliferation of values, give P^* as many values as P has, and stipulate that, for any value x of P, if P had been x, then P^* would have been x too. But then P^* would have to assume the different values that correspond to a given specific behavioural variation at once, which is impossible (on constraints on the values of variables; see Hitchcock 2007a: 502 and Halpern and Hitchcock 2010, §4.3).

Mental Causation by Causal Modelling

(5) Necessarily, if P is 0, then M is 0.

(6) Necessarily, if M is 0, then P is 0.[15]

Strict conditionals entail the corresponding counterfactuals (see Section 1.4). Thus, (3)–(6) entail, respectively, the following counterfactuals:

(7) If M had been 1, then P would not have been 0.[16]

(8) If P had been p, with $p \neq 0$, then M would have been 1.

(9) If P had been 0, then M would have been 0.

(10) If M had been 0, then P would have been 0.

Note that these counterfactuals do not backtrack, since the mental event and its possible realizers occur at the same time. (Whether any causal relation between the mental event and its realizers follows from such counterfactuals will be discussed in Section 3.6.)

Variable U was introduced to represent initial conditions that should at least contribute to determining the value of P. On the face of it, it might seem that we can simply say that which realizer (if any) is instantiated depends merely on the initial conditions, such that P would assume whatever value U had. But things are more complicated, since, by (7) and (10), whether a realizer occurs also depends on whether or not the mental event occurs. Moreover, since the dependence expressed by (7) and (10) derives from a metaphysically necessary connection between the mental property and its realizers that is expressed by (3) and (6) respectively, this connection should trump any contingent connection between the initial conditions and the instantiation of a realizer.

For the case in which U and M are both 0, claim (6) and the idea that P assumes the value of U pull in the same direction; in this case P would be 0 too:

(11) If U had been 0 and M had been 0, then P would have been 0.

Put less technically, (11) says that if I had been in a state that is standardly followed by no instantiation of a realizer of headaches

---

[15] I have not defined the truth of claims about metaphysical modality such as (3)–(6) in a causal model; indeed, these claims are not supposed to be true *in* the causal model that we are about to construct in the strict sense. I am using variables in these claims merely to facilitate the derivation of certain counterfactuals which, in contrast to (3)–(6), will be true in our model in the strict sense.

[16] Counterfactuals like (7) that are not about variables' assuming specific values are not covered by our definition of the truth of a counterfactual in a causal model. The definition can easily be extended, however; see Halpern and Pearl 2005: 851–852. For a discussion of counterfactuals with disjunctive antecedents, see Briggs 2012.

and I had not had a headache, then I would not have instantiated any realizer of headaches. Similarly, in a case in which U and M are both not 0 (such that M is 1), claim (3) and the idea that P assumes the value of U agree in predicting that P would assume the value of U:

> (12)   If U had been u, with $u \neq 0$, and M had been 1, then P would have been u.

In intuitive terms, (12) says that if I had been in a state that is standardly followed by the instantiation of a certain realizer of headaches and I had had a headache, then I would have instantiated the realizer.

If one of U and M had been 0 while the other had not been 0, however, there is a conflict between the idea that P assumes the value of U on the one hand, and (3) and (6) on the other, which must be resolved in favour of (3) and (6). Thus, we get:

> (13)   If U had not been 0 and M had been 0, then P would have been 0.

The intuitive gloss of (13) says that if I had been in a state that is standardly followed by the instantiation of a realizer of headaches, but I had not had a headache, then I would not have instantiated a realizer of headaches. Parallel reasoning yields:

> (14)   If U had been 0 and M had been 1, then P would not have been 0.

Intuitively, (14) says that if I had been in a state that is standardly followed by no instantiation of a realizer of headaches, but had had a headache, then I would have instantiated a realizer of headaches. For definiteness, let us assume that P would have been 1 if U had been 0 and M had been 1:

> (14′)   If U had been 0 and M had been 1, then P would have been 1.

Given the suggestion about how to flesh out the different positive values of the realizer-variable P, (14′) says that if I had been in a state that is standardly followed by no instantiation of a realizer of headaches, but had had a headache, then I would have had firing c-fibres. The assumption of (14′) will facilitate constructing our causal model, but nothing hinges on it.

Here is a set of equations that represents the counterfactuals we have established so far:

Mental Causation by Causal Modelling

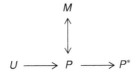

Figure 3.3. The causal graph of *MC*

$$MC \quad U \Leftarrow 1$$
$$P \Leftarrow 1 \text{ if } U \text{ is } 0 \text{ and } M \text{ is } 1, M \cdot U \text{ otherwise}$$
$$M \Leftarrow \text{Min}\{P, 1\}$$
$$P^* \Leftarrow \text{Min}\{P, 1\}$$

Figure 3.3 shows the causal graph corresponding to *MC*.

The graph of *MC* is not acyclic, since we can go back and forth on the double-arrow between *P* and *M*. Correspondingly, the equations in *MC* are not acyclic either. Generally, a set of equations that fails to be acyclic may have no solutions or more than one solution. It can easily be verified that the equations in *MC* have two solutions. On one solution, *U*, *P*, *M*, and *P** are all 1; on the other solution, *U* is 1 while *P*, *M*, and *P** are 0.

That the equations in our causal model fail to be acyclic does not preclude us from evaluating counterfactuals in this model, however. At least it does not preclude us from evaluating the counterfactuals that are most interesting for our purposes, namely those that are about the relation between *M* and *P**. This is so because the truth-conditions for a counterfactual in a given causal model that were given in the previous section draw on what is the case in a certain modification of that model. In our case, this modification has a unique solution even though the original model does not.[17]

The following counterfactual is the most interesting one for our purposes:

(15) If *M* had been 0, then *P** would have been 0.

Counterfactual (15) says that my hand would not have moved towards the aspirin if I had not had a headache. In order to evaluate counterfactual (15) in our model *MC*, we have to consider the new model we get from *MC* by

---

[17] It is also possible to give a general definition for the truth of counterfactuals for non-acyclic equations; see Halpern and Pearl 2005: 883–884.

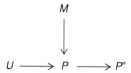

Figure 3.4. The causal graph of MC'

replacing the equation for M with an equation that sets M to the value specified in the antecedent of (15), that is, to 0. Here is this new model:

MC' $U \Leftarrow 1$
        $P \Leftarrow$ if U is 0 and M is 1, $M \cdot U$ otherwise
        $M \Leftarrow 0$
        $P^* \Leftarrow \text{Min}\{P, 1\}$

Figure 3.4 shows the causal graph corresponding to the new model MC'.

The equations in MC' and the corresponding graph are acyclic. This can easily be seen from the graph of MC', where one cannot trace a path that contains a variable twice by following the direction of the arrows. Since the equations in MC' are acyclic, they have a unique solution. According to this solution, M, P, and P^* are all 0, while U is 1. Since P^* is 0 according to this solution, counterfactual (15) is true in our original model MC. (By parallel reasoning we get that 'If M had been 1, then P^* would have been 1' is true in our original model MC.)

We took certain counterfactuals as a starting-point and constructed a causal model, MC, whose individual equations represented those counterfactuals. It turned out that counterfactual (15) is also true in MC. While it will be seen that this is good news for the project of accommodating mental causation in the causal modelling framework (a project we will resume in a moment), I should forestall a possible misunderstanding of the result. Equations that individually represent true counterfactuals may well collectively represent false counterfactuals. It may happen, in other words, that the individual equations of a model represent counterfactuals that are in fact true while a counterfactual that is in fact false is also true in that model.[18] So the mere fact that our model MC was constructed to yield

---

[18] Take, for instance, a model (call it TR) that consists in the set of binary variables $\{X, Y, Z\}$ and the set of equations $\{X \Leftarrow 1, Y \Leftarrow X, Z \Leftarrow Y\}$. The second equation represents (*inter alia*) the counterfactual (i) 'If X had been 0, then Y would have been 0'; the third equation represents (ii) 'If Y had been 0, then Z would have been 0.' The counterfactual (iii) 'If X had been 0, then Z would have been 0' is

Mental Causation by Causal Modelling

certain true counterfactuals and that (15), too, is true in MC should not be taken to demonstrate that (15) is in fact true. But we can make a stronger case for (15). Counterfactual (15) follows logically from the counterfactuals that we built into our model. Specifically, (15) follows from (1), (9), and (10). (The inference has the same form as the inference from (16)–(18) to (19) in Section 2.5 had.) Thus, our model does not by itself prove (15), but since (15) can be established independently, it is a virtue of the model that (15) is true in it.[19]

The two solutions to the equations in MC leave it open whether the mental event, a realizer-instance, and the later physical event actually occur – according to one solution, they do; according to the other, they do not.[20] But we may stipulate that they do all actually occur, such that U, M, P, and P^* are all 1.[21] We may stipulate, in other words, that I am in a state that is standardly followed by a c-fibre firing, that later I have a headache and firing c-fibres, and that later still my hand moves towards the aspirin. Then it follows from (15), by the definition of counterfactual dependence between variables from the previous section, that variable P^* counterfactually depends on variable M. As for the relation between P^* and P, counterfactual (1) says that if P had been 0, then P^* would have been 0 (if I had not instantiated a realizer of headaches, then my hand would not have moved towards the aspirin). That (1) is true was built into our model MC. Given that the actual values of U, M, P, and P^* are all 1, by (1) P^* counterfactually depends on P in addition to counterfactually depending on M.

We saw in the previous section that we may draw causal conclusions from counterfactual dependence between variables, provided their actual values do not correspond to omissions. The actual values of M, P, and P^* do not correspond to omissions. Thus, we may infer from the

---

true in TR without being represented by an individual equation. Since counterfactuals are not generally transitive (see Section 1.4) it might be that in fact (i) and (ii) are true while (iii) is false.

[19] Hitchcock (2001: 287, 2007a: 502–503) takes the requirement that no counterfactuals be true in a given model that are in fact false to be a criterion for the appropriateness of that causal model. Another requirement he imposes, namely that the variables correspond to events that are sufficiently independent, will be discussed in Section 3.6.

[20] This is consistent with our assumption of determinism. It may well be that the initial conditions represented by U are rich enough for it to follow from the actual laws of nature and the assumption that U is 1 that P, M, and P^* are all 1. That there are two solutions to our equations that involve the same value of U while differing in the values of P, M, and P^* merely shows that the lawful connection between U and the variables that represent later events can be broken in a counterfactual situation where M's being 0 forces P's being 0.

[21] Instead of this stipulation, we could build the actual values of all our variables into the model; see Briggs 2012: 144.

counterfactual dependence of variable P^* on variable M that (the event represented by) $M = 1$ causes (the event represented by) $P^* = 1$. Similarly, from the counterfactual dependence of P^* on P we may infer that $P = 1$ causes $P^* = 1$. We may infer, that is, that my headache causes my hand to move towards the aspirin and that my c-fibres' firing causes my hand to move towards the aspirin.

Thus, causal models can capture the patterns of counterfactual dependence and causation that hold in cases involving supervenient mental properties. This is good news for those who are sceptical about the ability of causal modelling theories to accommodate mental causation in light of the controversy about interventionism (which will be discussed in Section 3.7). To the disinterested, it may seem that causal models have not given us anything that we did not already have. Our simple argument in Section 2.2 establishes the same as the comparatively complicated model MC does, namely that some actually occurring physical events counterfactually depend on actually occurring mental events. We can feed this result into our old sufficient condition for causation in terms of counterfactual dependence between events irrespective of how we arrived at the result. This is true, but causal modelling can do more. First, some theorists have suggested replacing simple counterfactual dependence as a sufficient condition for causation with more sophisticated sufficient conditions that are not entailed by simple counterfactual dependence. We shall see in the following section that these more sophisticated conditions still apply in cases involving mental events like the one discussed in this section. Thus, causal modelling theories can still accommodate mental causation when they move beyond the simple conditions for causation that were used by standard counterfactual theories. Second, we saw in Section 2.3 that one option to solve the problem of overlapping realizers is to qualify the simple sufficient condition for causation within the causal modelling framework. We shall see that, eventually, causal modelling is better suited to formulating a sufficient condition for explanatory relevance than to formulating a sufficient causation for causation in order to solve the problem of overlapping realizers. But the condition for explanatory relevance, too, essentially involves the resources of the framework, especially the structure of a causal model, which can be read off from the model's graph.

Before turning to the refinements of our sufficient condition for causation, let me note that our causal model MC can be used by super-nomological dualists as well as non-reductive physicalists. We took as a starting-point the strict conditionals (3)–(6), which are false if dualism is true, but we might equally well have started from the corresponding counterfactuals (7)–(10), which are true if super-nomological dualism is. According to super-

Mental Causation by Causal Modelling 119

nomological dualism, the psychophysical laws could not have failed so easily as the ordinary laws of nature. The relation between the mental property and its physical bases is a matter of psychophysical laws, whereas the relation between physical goings-on at different times is a matter of ordinary laws of nature. Thus, as in the case of non-reductive physicalism, the relation between variable P and variable M trumps that between variable U and variable P in case there is a conflict. As a result, we get counterfactuals (11)–(14)/(14'), the model MC and the corresponding causal results, just as we did in the non-reductive physicalism case.

3.4 Defaults and Normality

Our old counterfactual principle about causation from Section 1.4 said that if an actually occurring event e counterfactually depends on an actually occurring event c, then c causes e. (As I said earlier, the temporal qualification that e occurs later than c will be suppressed until Section 3.6.) An analogous principle in terms of causal modelling says that if, in a causal model, variable X is x, variable Y is y, and Y counterfactually depends on X, then (the event represented by) $X = x$ causes (the event represented by) $Y = y$. One might endorse the old principle without endorsing the causal modelling principle if one thinks that omissions are not events or that omissions cannot be causes or effects. In this case, a refinement of the causal modelling principle is called for. I will not pronounce a verdict on whether there really is a need for such a refinement. It will suffice for our purposes to show that, if there is, the resulting principle about causation can still accommodate mental causation.

I will illustrate the refinements of the causal modelling principle with the following case:[22]

> *Omission.* Assassin poisons Victim's drink. Bodyguard possesses an antidote that would neutralize the poison, but does not administer it. Victim dies of poisoning, but would not have died if the drink had not been poisoned or if the antidote had been administered.

We can model *Omission* by using variables A, G, and D with the following interpretation:

$A = 1$ if Assassin poisons Victim's drink, 0 otherwise
$G = 1$ if Bodyguard administers the antidote, 0 otherwise
$D = 1$ if Victim dies, 0 otherwise

---

[22] My presentation of the case follows Hitchcock 2007a: 504–505.

Figure 3.5. The causal graph of *OM*.

The description of *Omission* tells us that the actual value of A is 1, and that the actual value of G is 0. It also tells us that D would have been 0 if A had been 0 (Victim would not have died had Assassin not poisoned the drink), and that D would have been 0 if A and G had both been 1 (Victim would not have died if the drink had been poisoned and the antidote administered). Thus, we get the following equations:

$$OM \quad A \Leftarrow 1 \\ G \Leftarrow 0 \\ D \Leftarrow \text{Min}\{A, 1 - G\}$$

Figure 3.5 shows the causal graph corresponding to *OM*.

Variable D counterfactually depends on variable G in the model *OM*, for if we replace the equation for G with one that sets G to the non-actual value 1, the equations yield that D assumes the non-actual value 0. That is, the equations tell us that Victim would not have died if Bodyguard had administered the antidote. If we take counterfactual dependence between variables to suffice for causation, it follows that $G = 0$ causes $D = 1$. It follows, in other words, that Bodyguard's failure to administer the antidote causes Victim's death.

If one finds this result implausible,[23] one can pursue different strategies for qualifying the sufficiency of counterfactual dependence for causation within the causal modelling framework. This section discusses two such strategies. The first strategy adds the qualification that the causal model in which counterfactual dependence obtains be of a certain kind. The second strategy instead adds the qualification that only counterfactuals with certain features should be regarded as indicative of causation.[24] In what follows, I shall present both strategies and argue that either strategy still

---

[23] For a recent discussion of causation and responsibility in cases of omission, see Moore 2009.
[24] The first strategy is pursued in Hitchcock 2007a, the second in Halpern and Pearl 2005, Hall 2007, Halpern 2008, Halpern and Hitchcock 2010, and Halpern and Hitchcock 2015. For critical discussion of the first strategy, see Wolff 2016.

Mental Causation by Causal Modelling

allows mental causation, or at any rate accommodates mental causation at least as well as physical-to-physical causation.

Following Hitchcock (2007a), we can formulate a new sufficient condition according to which counterfactual dependence is sufficient for causation in causal models where the connection between the putative cause and the putative effect is of a certain kind. Hitchcock introduces the distinction between *default* and *deviant* values of variables. Roughly, default values are those that correspond to states of a system that persist in the absence of outside influence, while deviant values are those that correspond to states that do not thus persist. According to the present suggestion, we may take counterfactual dependence to suffice for causation in a given model if in that model the connection between the putative cause and the putative effect is such that default values of previous variables always yield default values of later variables.

This idea can be made more precise by using the following terminology.[25] Let a *predecessor* of a variable be a variable that occurs on the right-hand side of the equation for that variable, and let a *path* be a sequence of variables such that the first variable is a predecessor of the second variable, the second variable is a predecessor of the third variable, ..., and the penultimate variable is a predecessor of the last variable. Let a *path from X to Y* be a path that contains X and Y as first and last elements of such a sequence, respectively. Let a path be *acyclic* if and only if it does not contain any variables twice, *cyclic* otherwise. In a causal graph, the predecessors of a variable X are those variables that have an arrow pointing towards X, and a path from X to Y can be traced by following the direction of arrowheads. Let the *network* connecting variable X to variable Y be the set of variables that are on some path or other between X and Y. We can now define the notion of a self-contained network as follows: a network connecting X and Y is *self-contained* if and only if each variable Z in this network takes its default value if all its predecessors in the network (if any) take their default value while all its predecessors outside of the network (if any) assume their actual values. Following Hitchcock, one might claim that the counterfactual dependence of variable Y on variable X is sufficient for $X = x$ to cause $Y = y$ in a given causal model if the network connecting X to Y is self-contained.[26] (In case variables have multiple default values, 'its

---

[25] My terminology differs slightly from Hitchcock's in order to be applicable to sets of equations that are not acyclic.

[26] Hitchcock (2007a: 511–512) takes counterfactual dependence to be necessary as well as sufficient for causation for the values of variables that are connected by a self-contained network, or at least

default value' and 'their default value' should be replaced by 'a default value' in the definition.)

This sufficient condition for causation no longer implies that in *Omission* Bodyguard's inaction causes Victim's death. We may assume that the default state of Assassin is not to poison Victim's drink, that the default state of Bodyguard is not to administer the antidote, and that the default state of Victim is not to die. Correspondingly, the default values of A, G, and D are all 0. The network connecting G to D contains just these two variables themselves. This network is not self-contained, for if G assumes its default value 0 while A assumes its actual value 1, then D assumes value 1, which is not its default. By contrast, the network connecting A to D is self-contained, for if A assumes its default value 0 while G assumes its actual value 0, then D assumes its default value 0. Thus, the new sufficient condition for causation rules that Assassin's poisoning the drink causes Victim to die, but it remains silent on whether Bodyguard's failure to administer the antidote causes the death.

The new sufficient condition also remains silent on whether there is causation in the cases of double prevention that we discussed in Sections 1.6 and 2.6.[27] Take our neuron example of double prevention, where the firing of c prevents the firing of d, which, had it not been prevented, would have prevented the firing of e (see Figure 1.1 on p. 51).

To model the example, let us use the variables A, B, C, D, and E, where $A = 1$ if neuron a fires, 0 otherwise; $B = 1$ if neuron b fires, 0 otherwise; etc. The following equations give us the counterfactuals that are true in the example:

$$
\begin{aligned}
DP \quad A &\Leftarrow 1 \\
B &\Leftarrow 1 \\
C &\Leftarrow 1 \\
D &\Leftarrow B \cdot (1 - C) \\
E &\Leftarrow A \cdot (1 - D)
\end{aligned}
$$

Figure 3.6 shows the causal graph corresponding to DP.

In the model DP, the counterfactual 'If C had been 0, then E would have been 0', the technical equivalent of 'If neuron c had not fired, then neuron e would not have fired', is true. This can easily be verified by replacing the equation for C by the equation '$C \Leftarrow 0$', which sets C to the value specified

---

necessary and sufficient for us to be inclined to judge that there is causation. For our purposes only the sufficiency for causation is relevant.

[27] Hitchcock alludes to this result at 2007a: 513.

Mental Causation by Causal Modelling

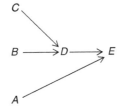

Figure 3.6. The causal graph of *DP*

in the antecedent of the counterfactual; substituting the specific values of A, B, and C in the remaining equations yields value 1 for D and, eventually, value 0 for E, which is the value specified in the consequent. Hence, in the model *DP*, variable E counterfactually depends on variable C. But the new qualification, namely that the network connecting the putative cause to the putative effect be self-contained, is not met. The network connecting C to E is the set $\{C, D, E\}$. This network fails to be self-contained irrespective of whether 0 or 1 is the default value for our variables, that is, irrespective of whether non-firing or firing is the default state of our neurons. Suppose that A and B, which are outside of the network connecting C and E, assume their actual values. Suppose further that the default value for our variables is 0. Then if C assumes the default value 0, D assumes the deviant value 1, so $\{C, D, E\}$ is not self-contained. Suppose, on the other hand, that the default value for our variables is 1. Then, given that A and B both have their actual value 1, if C assumes the default value 1, D assumes the deviant value 0, so again $\{C, D, E\}$ is not self-contained.

While the new principle about causation no longer implies that omissions and double preventers are causes, it still yields the verdict that, in our model *MC*, the headache is a cause of my hand's movement. What are the default and deviant values of the variables in that model? It turns out that we can leave this question open as long as we assume some degree of uniformity in what counts as a default and deviant value for our variables. Whether or not the default state for my headache, which is represented by variable M, is one where it occurs, it seems reasonable that occurrence is the default state for the headache if and only if the default states for its realizers, which are represented by variable P, are such that some realizer is instantiated. Similarly, it seems reasonable that occurrence is the default state for the movement of my hand, which is represented by variable P^*, if and only if the default state for the realizers is one where some realizer is instantiated.

Thus, we get two cases: in case (i), the default values of P, M, and P^* are all 0; in case (ii), the default values of P, M, and P^* are all not 0; more precisely, any non-zero value of P is a default value, and the default values of M and P^* are both 1.[28]

The network connecting M to P^* is the set $\{M, P, P^*\}$.[29] Assume that the default and deviant values of our variables are as specified in case (i). Variable P^* has only one predecessor, namely P, which is in the network. By the equation for P^*, if P assumes its default value 0, then P^* assumes its default value 0. Variable P has one predecessor in the network, namely M, and one predecessor outside of the network, namely U. By the equation for P, if M assumes its default value 0, then P assumes its default value 0 regardless of the value of U; *a fortiori*, P assumes its default value 0 if M assumes its default value 0 while U assumes its actual value 1. Variable M has one predecessor, namely P, which is in the network. By the equation for M, if P assumes its default value 0, then M assumes its default value 0. Thus, in case (i), the network connecting M to P^* is self-contained.

Assume now that the default and deviant values of our variables are as specified in case (ii). In this case, if P assumes a default value, that is, a non-zero value, then P^* assumes its default value 1. If M assumes its default value 1, then P assumes a default value, that is, P is not 0, regardless of the value of U; *a fortiori*, P assumes a default value if M assumes its default value while U assumes its actual value 1. If P assumes a default value, that is, a non-zero value, then M assumes its default value 1. Thus, in case (ii) the network connecting M to P^* is self-contained as well.

In sum, the network connecting M to P^* is self-contained irrespective of how we assign default and deviant values to our variables (provided that we do it uniformly). Hence, if we do not simply take counterfactual dependence between variables to suffice for causation but restrict this sufficient condition for causation to cases where the network between the variable for the putative cause and the variable for the putative effect is self-contained, it still follows that $M = 1$ causes $P^* = 1$. Since the network that connects P to P^* is a subset of the network that connects M to P^*, it is self-contained as well. Therefore, $P = 1$ also still counts as a cause of $P^* = 1$.

---

[28] In case (i) P has multiple deviant values (namely all non-zero values), and in case (ii) P has multiple default values.

[29] Since M is a predecessor of P while P is also a predecessor of M in our causal model, there are many paths from M to P^* besides the path $\langle M, P, P^* \rangle$, for instance, $\langle M, P, M, P, P^* \rangle$, $\langle M, P, M, P, M, P, P^* \rangle$, etc. Still, the network connecting P to P^* just is the set $\{P, M, P^*\}$; multiple occurrences of M and P on cyclic paths do not make a difference to the identity of the network.

The second strategy of qualifying the sufficient condition for causation in terms of counterfactual dependence imposes no restriction on the network between the putative cause and the putative effect within a causal model, but instead restricts the conditions under which a counterfactual that expresses counterfactual dependence may be taken to entail causation. The idea is that, in order to entail causation, such a counterfactual must not take us to situations that are too abnormal.

To make this idea more precise, say that a setting of values of all the variables of a given model *manifests* the counterfactual dependence of variable Y on variable X if and only if this setting is a setting of variables we get in a model that is the result of replacing the equation for X with '$X \Leftarrow x'$', where x' is a non-actual value of X, and Y assumes a non-actual value in that model. Intuitively, a setting of variables that manifests the counterfactual dependence of Y on X represents a situation that would have been the case if Y had differed along with X.[30]

For instance, in the *Omission* example, there is one setting of the variables in the corresponding model OM that manifests the counterfactual dependence of D on G. In this setting A is 1, G is 1, and D is 0: Assassin poisons the drink; Bodyguard administers the antidote; and Victim survives. One might think that actions are always less normal than omissions. Since the variable setting that manifests the counterfactual dependence of D on G involves two actions (namely Assassin's and Bodyguard's) while the actual setting involves merely one (Assassin's), one might take this to show that the setting is too abnormal for Bodyguard's omission to be a cause of Victim's death (see Halpern and Hitchcock 2015: 439–441).

While it no longer seems to follow that Bodyguard's omission causes Victim's death, the new sufficient condition for causation in terms of counterfactual dependence plus normality, unlike the new condition in terms of self-contained networks, still seems to rule that double preventers are causes. If actions are less normal than omissions, presumably firings of neurons are less normal than non-firings. In the model for the double-prevention case, DP, the counterfactual dependence of E on C is manifested by a setting where C and E are 0 while A, B, and D are 1. In the actual situation, all variables except D are 1. In other words, if c had not fired, there would have been three firings and two non-firings, while there are four firings and one non-firing in the actual situation. Cumulatively, the situation that would have been the case if c had not fired is more normal

---

[30] Manifestation as defined here is a simplified version of what Halpern and Hitchcock (2015: 436) call being a 'witness' for a causal relation.

126 Mental Causation

than the actual situation, which *prima facie* seems pretty normal itself. Since the counterfactual dependence of E on C is manifested by a comparatively normal situation, we may infer that $C = 1$ causes $E = 1$.

Admittedly, more can be said about the notion of normality and how it depends on the default or deviant values of individual variables.[31] The details of how normality is assessed need not concern us for the purposes of assessing the efficacy of mental events in the model MC, however. We shall see that the variable settings that manifest the counterfactual dependence of my hand's moving on my headache coincide with those that manifest the counterfactual dependence of the hand's moving on the actual realizer-instance. Thus, the headache is on a par with its actual realizer as far as normality considerations are concerned. Since the realizer seems to be a *bona fide* cause of the later physical event,[32] mental causation remains unscathed.

We saw in the previous section that P^*, the variable for my hand's moving towards the aspirin, counterfactually depends both on M, the variable for my headache, and on P, the variable for the realizers of headaches, because the following counterfactuals are true:

(15) If M had been 0, then P^* would have been 0.
(1)   If P had been 0, then P^* would have been 0.

Counterfactuals (15) and (1) represent the only ways in which these counterfactual dependences can come about in our model. For (15), this is clear since M and P^* are binary and (we assumed) both have the actual value 1. While P is not binary, the only non-actual value that P can assume such that the value of P^* varies along with P is 0. Thus, the variable settings that manifest the counterfactual dependence of P^* on M and on P are both unique. Moreover, these settings are identical. The setting that manifests the counterfactual dependence of P^* on M can be calculated by replacing the equation for M with '$M \Leftarrow 0$' in MC (which yields the equations of model MC'); then the remaining equations yield that P and P^* are both 0. The setting that manifests the counterfactual dependence of P^* on P can be calculated by replacing the equation for P with '$P \Leftarrow 0$' in MC; then the

---

[31] See Halpern and Hitchcock 2010, §5; 2015: 433–436 for further discussion. One aspect that we will briefly return to in the following section is that of statistical normality. Notice that the normality dimension is standardly taken to be different from the dimension of overall similarity between worlds that is in play in Lewis's (1973b, 1979) semantics for counterfactuals. In particular, that the actual world is most similar overall to itself is standardly taken to be consistent with there being worlds that are more normal than the actual world.

[32] In the previous chapter, we saw that one might doubt that instances of realizers can in principle be causes or effects. These doubts will be addressed in Section 4.4.

Mental Causation by Causal Modelling

remaining equations yield that M and P^* are both 0.[33] Thus, the setting where M, P, and P^* are all 0 is the one setting that manifests both the counterfactual dependence of P^* on M and the counterfactual dependence of P^* on P.[34] Since the causation of $P^* = 1$ by $P = 1$ does not seem problematic, this setting should be regarded sufficiently normal to license the inference that $P = 1$ causes $P^* = 1$. Consequently, the same setting should be regarded as sufficiently normal to license the inference that $M = 1$ causes $P^* = 1$. So the strategy of qualifying the sufficiency of counterfactual dependence for causation by requiring that the counterfactual dependence not take us to situations that are too abnormal poses no threat to my account of mental causation.

In this section we have considered two qualifications to the principle that counterfactual dependence between variables in a causal model suffices for a causal relation between (what is represented by) the values of these variables. One qualification is that the network between the variables in question be self-contained. The other qualification is that the counterfactual dependence be manifested in worlds that are not too abnormal. The unqualified principle rules certain omissions to be causes. With either qualification, this result no longer follows. The unqualified principle also rules certain cases of double prevention to be causes. With the self-containment qualification, this result no longer follows; with the normality qualification, it still follows. The most important result for our purposes is that either qualification still yields the result that mental events can have physical effects. Thus, mental causation can be robustly accommodated within the causal modelling framework.

---

[33] It might be objected that it is an artefact of our definition of manifestation that M assumes the value specified by its equation, despite being in an intuitive sense off the path from P to P^*. If we allowed a setting where M is 1 while P and P^* are 0 to manifest the counterfactual dependence of P^* on P, however, this setting is unlikely to count as more normal than one where M, P, and P^* are all 0. Non-reductive physicalists would deem such a setting metaphysically impossible. It would seem dubious if metaphysically impossible settings could be more normal than metaphysically possible ones even if we allowed the normality dimension of worlds to differ from the overall similarity dimension. Dualists would deem the setting metaphysically possible. But they might follow the lead of those theorists who take inactions to make for increased normality and actions to make for decreased normality by claiming that the non-occurrence of an event makes for increased normality and that the occurrence of an event makes for decreased normality. In sum, the occurrence of the mental event that is represented by a setting where M is 1 while P and P^* are 0 makes that setting *less* normal, or at any rate not more normal, than one where all three variables are 0.

[34] In this setting, variable U assumes its actual value 1, but even if we allowed U to vary, yielding different settings that manifest our counterfactual dependences, the set of such settings that manifest the counterfactual dependence of P^* on P would coincide with the set of settings that manifest the counterfactual dependence of P^* on M.

What lesson should we draw from the different verdicts about double prevention that the two qualifications of the sufficient condition for causation yield? We saw in Section 1.6 that a good case can be made for the claim that double preventers are causes. And we saw that, if there is no causation by double prevention, there is no human agency, because if there is no causation by double prevention, then there is no causation of muscle contraction by neural impulses. Friends of the self-containment qualification could try to argue that the default and deviant states of muscle fibres are somehow different from those of the idealized neurons of our double-prevention case. Or they could use a different sufficient condition for causation to accommodate the causation involved in muscle physiology. But they are not forced to pursue either strategy. Having advocated merely a sufficient condition for causation, they are not committed to denying a causal relation in cases of double prevention.

3.5 Overlapping Realizers Redux

This section investigates how causal modelling can help us solve the problem of overlapping realizers from Section 2.3. Recall the example that made trouble for the unqualified sufficient condition for causation in terms of counterfactual dependence between events: I hold an aluminium ladder against a power line and subsequently get electrocuted. Being made of aluminium, the ladder is both conductive and opaque. If the ladder had not been conductive, I would not have been electrocuted. But if the ladder had not been opaque, I would not have been electrocuted either. For if the ladder had not been opaque, presumably it would have been made of some standard transparent material that would have been non-conductive, in which case I would not have been electrocuted. Thus, by the unqualified sufficient condition for causation, the opacity-instance causes my electrocution. This result seems implausible. In this section I shall elaborate on two suggestions from Section 2.3 about how to respond to the problem of overlapping realizers. The first suggestion is to replace the unqualified sufficient condition for causation with a condition in terms of causal models that allows us to draw causal conclusions only if the actual values of certain variables are held fixed. We shall see that this suggestion is initially attractive, but ultimately problematic, because of difficulties in selecting an appropriate causal model. The second suggestion is to use the condition from the first suggestion not as a condition for causation, but as a condition for explanatory relevance. Used as a condition for explanatory relevance, the condition will allow us to formulate what seems, overall, the best response to the problem of overlapping realizers, namely that the opacity-instance is a cause of the electrocution, but not one that is typically considered explanatorily relevant.

Both suggestions exploit the asymmetry between what would have been the case if the ladder had been opaque but not conductive and what would have been the case if the ladder had been conductive but not opaque that we observed in Section 2.3: if the ladder had been opaque but not conductive, then I would not have been electrocuted, whereas, if the ladder had been conductive but not opaque, then I would still have been electrocuted. We saw that, in order to elaborate this idea, we need a rationale for identifying the events to be held fixed in these comparisons. Such a rationale is needed because, for virtually any pair of events that are related by counterfactual dependence, we can find other events that actually occur and whose holding fixed makes no difference to the occurrence or non-occurrence of the dependent event, while we can also find other events that actually occur and whose holding fixed does make a difference to the occurrence or non-occurrence of the dependent event. For instance, if I had not thrown the dart and there had been just as many grains of sand on Mars as there actually are, then the balloon would not have burst, but if I had not thrown the dart and the dart had been on its actual trajectory a second later, then the balloon would still have burst. Intuitively, the relevant events to be held fixed seemed to be those that are not on a causal path between the putative cause and the putative effect; the dart's being on its actual trajectory a second after the time at which I actually threw it seems to lie on such a causal path from my throw to the balloon's bursting. We shall see that the causal modelling apparatus enables us to spell this idea out by using the definition of a path from the previous section.

But, first, let us construct a causal model for the electrocution example; call this model EL. Let C, O, and E be binary variables that stand for the ladder's being conductive, the ladder's being opaque, and my being electrocuted, respectively. Let P be a multi-valued variable that represents the microphysical makeup of the ladder. As in our model for mental causation, let us introduce an exogenous variable U that contributes to determining the value of P by representing initial conditions. Like P, U should be multi-valued. Let us use the following interpretation of the variables:

$U = 0$ or 1 or 2 or 3, depending on the initial conditions
$P = 0$ if the ladder instantiates a realizer of both conductivity and opacity (e.g., aluminium), 1 if the ladder instantiates a realizer of

conductivity that is not also a realizer of opacity (that is, an exotic transparent conductor), 2 if the ladder instantiates a realizer of opacity that is not also a realizer of conductivity (e.g., wood), 3 if the ladder instantiates neither a realizer of conductivity nor a realizer of opacity (e.g., if the ladder is made of transparent plastic)

C = 1 if the ladder is conductive, 0 otherwise
O = 1 if the ladder is opaque, 0 otherwise
E = 1 if I am electrocuted, 0 otherwise

Given that my electrocution counterfactually depends both on the ladder's conductivity and on the ladder's opacity, the following counterfactuals should be true in our causal model for the case:

(16) If C had been 0, then E would have been 0.
(17) If O had been 0, then E would have been 0.

As we saw, the case is not symmetric between C and O. If the ladder had been conductive but not opaque, then I would still have been electrocuted:

(18) If C had been 1 and O had been 0, then E would have been 1.

On the other hand, if the ladder had been opaque but not conductive, then I would not have been electrocuted:

(19) If O had been 1 and C had been 0, then E would have been 0.

What is the counterfactual relation between C and O on the one hand, and P on the other? From the way in which P was characterized, we can easily read off the values that C and O would have assumed if P had assumed a specific value. For instance, C would have been 0, but O would have been 1 if P had been 2 (that is, the ladder would have been opaque but not transparent if it had been made of a material like wood). Conversely, specific values of C and O rule out certain values of P. For instance, if O had been 0, then P would not have been 0 or 2 (that is, if the ladder had not been opaque, then it would not have been made out of a material like aluminium or a material like wood). Indeed, in light of the results from Section 2.3, we can be more specific. We saw that it seems plausible that if the ladder had not been opaque, it would have been made out of a middle-of-the-road, non-conductive transparent material like transparent plastic rather than an exotic transparent conductor. Thus, we have:

(20) If O had been 0, then P would have been 3.

Mental Causation by Causal Modelling

Similarly, it seems plausible that if the ladder had not been conductive, it would have been made out of a material like wood rather than a material like transparent plastic:

(21) If C had been 0, then P would have been 2.

As in the model MC, the value of U should set the value of P, provided there would be no conflict with the values of C and O. Thus, we can think of $U = 0$ as representing a state that is standardly followed by the ladder's being made of aluminium, of $U = 1$ as representing a state that is standardly followed by the ladder's being made of an exotic transparent conductor, etc. If there is a conflict between U on the one hand and C and O on the other, it must be resolved in favour of C and O. For instance, if U had been 1, then P would have been 1, but if U had been 1 and C had been 0, then P would have been 2. That is, if the initial state had been one that is standardly followed by the ladder's being made out of an exotic transparent conductor, then the ladder would have been made out of an exotic transparent conductor, but if the initial state had been one that is standardly followed by the ladder's being made out of an exotic transparent conductor and the ladder had failed to be conductive, then the ladder would have been made out of a material like wood.

For our purposes, we need not write down the equations of EL; drawing the graph will suffice. The graph looks like this: there is an arrow to E from P, but from no other variable, since the value of P makes a difference to the value of E, but no other variable makes a difference to E over and above the difference made by P.[35] There is an arrow from P to C. There is also an arrow from C to P, owing to the truth of (21).[36] Similarly, there is an arrow from P to O, and there is an arrow from O to P, owing to the truth of (20). In sum, we get the graph depicted in Figure 3.7.

The graph of EL shows that there is one acyclic path from C to E, which does not include O (namely the path $\langle C, P, E \rangle$), and one acyclic path from O to E, which does not include C (namely the path $\langle O, P, E \rangle$).[37]

---

[35] Difference-making is supposed to be captured by counterfactuals that are non-vacuously true. The fact that, say, $P = 0 \& C = 0 \:\square\!\!\!\rightarrow E = 0$ is vacuously true while $P = 0 \:\square\!\!\!\rightarrow E = 0$ is false is not a reason for including C in the equation for E.

[36] If one finds (21) implausible, one could still justify the inclusion of C in the equation for P, and hence the arrow from C to P in the causal graph, from the truth of the counterfactual $C = 0 \:\square\!\!\!\rightarrow P = 2 \vee P = 3$.

[37] These acyclic paths overlap with various cyclic paths with the same starting-points and ends. For instance, the acyclic path $\langle C, P, E \rangle$ overlaps with the cyclic path $\langle C, P, C, P, E \rangle$.

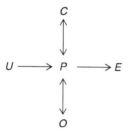

Figure 3.7. The causal graph of *EL*

The counterfactual dependence of *E* on *O* as well as the counterfactual dependence of *E* on *C* was built into our model *EL*, because we stipulated that counterfactuals (17) and (16) be true in the model. The actual values of *C*, *O*, and *E* all stand for the occurrence of genuine events that are not omissions, namely the ladder's being opaque, the ladder's being conductive, and my electrocution. Thus, it follows from the simple sufficient condition for causation in terms of counterfactual dependence between variables that the opacity-instance as well as the conductivity-instance causes the electrocution. This result does not come as a surprise, of course, but merely mirrors the situation outside of the causal modelling context that we investigated in Section 2.3. The question is whether we can use the resources of the causal modelling framework in order to avoid the result that the opacity-instance causes the electrocution. The graph of *EL* and its path-structure corroborates the idea that what matters is not counterfactual dependence as such, but counterfactual dependence when off-path variables are held fixed at their actual values. However, before discussing in detail a qualification for our sufficient condition for causation along these lines, let us briefly investigate how the qualifications discussed in the previous section deal with the electrocution example.

The first qualification was that counterfactual dependence is sufficient for causation only in a self-contained network. Variable *E* counterfactually depends both on *C* and on *O*. The network connecting *C* to *E* is the same as the network connecting *O* to *E*, namely the set $\{C, P, O, E\}$. If this network is self-contained, the suggestion yields that both $C = 1$ and $O = 1$ are causes of $E = 1$. If the network is not self-contained, the suggestion remains neutral with respect to either putative cause. Thus, the suggestion does not help us to discriminate between *C* and *O*.[38]

---

[38] It seems that in fact the network $\{C, P, O, E\}$ is not self-contained. It is a bit unclear how to assign default and deviant values to the variables, but presumably 1 is the deviant value for *E*, while the

The second qualification was that counterfactual dependence suffices for causation only if the situations that manifest the counterfactual dependence do not take us to worlds that are too abnormal. If the ladder had not been conductive, then (i) it would have been made out of a material like wood, in which case it would still have been opaque and I would not have been electrocuted. If the ladder had not been opaque then (ii) it would have been made out of a material like transparent plastic, in which case it would not have been conductive and I would not have been electrocuted. Given that there are few transparent plastic ladders while wooden ladders abound, case (ii) counts as less normal than case (i), at least statistically speaking. This might explain why we take the conductivity-instance to be a 'better' cause than the opacity-instance.

Given the normality qualification, the opacity-instance still qualifies as a good enough cause, however. We saw in the discussion of the *Omission* example that the normality qualification takes actions to be less normal than omissions. Although it might sound a bit odd to say that my electrocution is an action, it seems that my electrocution should similarly count as less normal than my non-electrocution. If so, the aspect of case (ii) in which it is less normal than the actual situation, namely the ladder's being made out of a material like transparent plastic, would be offset by the aspect in which it is more normal than the actual situation, namely my failure to be electrocuted. Overall, case (ii) should come out about as normal as the actual situation, so nothing prevents us from taking the opacity-instance to be a cause of the electrocution. Moreover, there are cases where an opacity-instance is a *bona fide* cause of a later event, so the situation that would have obtained if the ladder had not been opaque cannot by itself be too abnormal. Suppose that, in our set-up, the ladder casts a shadow. Had it not been opaque, it would not have cast a shadow; hence, the ladder's being opaque causes the shadow. There seems to be nothing wrong with this reasoning, but here too the counterfactual dependence is manifested in a situation where the ladder is made out of a material like transparent plastic.

Let us turn to the suggestion of formulating a sufficient condition for causation in terms of paths. While E counterfactually depends both on C and on O, C still makes a difference to E if we hold O fixed at its actual value, but O does not make a difference to E if we hold C fixed at its actual value. The causal graph of EL suggests a rationale for taking these counterfactuals to indicate that the conductivity-instance causes the electrocution,

---

actual values are (among the) default values of C, P, and O. Thus, the actual distribution of values in the network is a counterexample to its being self-contained.

while not taking them to indicate that the opacity-instance causes the electrocution: E varies along with C if we hold the variables that are off the acyclic path from C to E fixed at their actual values, while E does not vary along with O if we hold the variables that are off the acyclic path from O to E fixed at their actual values. What matters is whether a variable makes a difference to another if we hold the off-path variables fixed at their actual values; if it does, we may infer a causal relation.

Thus, we can formulate a new sufficient condition for causation as follows: let X and Y be binary variables in an appropriate causal model and let the actual values of X and Y (assume they are both 1) represent the occurrence of property-instances such that the property-instance represented by '$Y = 1$' occurs later than the property-instance represented by '$X = 1$'. Let both '$Y = 1$' and '$X = 1$' represent (strong Kimian) events that are not omissions. If '$X = 0 \, \square\!\!\rightarrow Y = 0$' is true in that model and '$X = 0$ & FIX $\square\!\!\rightarrow Y = 0$' is true in that model,[39] where FIX stands for the claim that all variables that are not on any acyclic path from X to Y are held fixed at their actual values, then the property-instance represented by '$X = 1$' causes the property-instance represented by '$Y = 1$'.[40] (Henceforth, when talking about off-path variables, I shall mean variables that are not on any *acyclic* path between the variables in question.)

The new sufficient condition for causation not only seems to handle the electrocution example well, it also still allows us to establish mental causation in the model MC. In that model, there is one acyclic path from the variable for my headache, M, to the variable for my hand's moving towards the aspirin, P^*, namely the path $\langle M, P, P^* \rangle$. The only variable in the model that is not on this path is variable U, which represents the initial conditions. The actual values of the variables in the model are all 1. Thus, when we apply the condition, FIX is the claim that U has value 1. It is true in the model that if M were 0, then P^* would be 0; this is just the counterfactual

---

[39] Since ϕ & $\chi \, \square\!\!\rightarrow \psi$ does not logically imply $\chi \, \square\!\!\rightarrow \psi$ (because ψ can be true in the closest ϕ-&-χ-worlds without being true in the closest χ-worlds *simpliciter*), '$X = 0$ & FIX $\square\!\!\rightarrow Y = 0$' can be true while '$X = 0 \, \square\!\!\rightarrow Y = 0$' is false; hence '$X = 0 \, \square\!\!\rightarrow Y = 0$' is not redundant here.

[40] Hitchcock 2001 defends the view that it is a necessary and sufficient condition for causation that there is an *active causal route* between the putative cause variable and the putative effect variable. In our terminology a route is a kind of path. For there to be an active causal route between variables X and Y it is necessary and sufficient that the value of X makes a difference to the value of Y if all variables that are on other paths between X and Y are held fixed at their actual values (Hitchcock 2001: 286–287). Hitchcock's condition is different from the new sufficient condition for causation under discussion, for the latter does not require variables on alternative paths from X to Y to be held fixed, and the former does not require variables that are *not* on any path from X to Y to be held fixed. Hitchcock's condition is similar to the spirit behind our informal diagnosis of the example involving the apprentice and expert assassins in Section 3.2, however.

Mental Causation by Causal Modelling

dependence of variable P^* on variable M. It is also true in the model that if M were 0 and FIX were the case, then P^* would be 0. Thus, it follows from the new sufficient condition that $M = 1$ causes $P^* = 1$; less technically, it follows that my headache causes my hand to move towards the aspirin.

Unfortunately, the new sufficient condition for causation has a number of disadvantages. First, although it delivers the verdict that the conductivity-instance and the mental property-instance are causes while not delivering the verdict that the opacity-instance is a cause, it no longer delivers the verdict that the realizer-instance is a cause of the electrocution and the later physical event. There are several reasons for this. To start with, the realizer-variable P in MC and EL fails to be binary, but the new sufficient condition can be applied only to binary variables for the putative causes and effects. Technically, this can easily be rectified: we can allow multi-valued cause and effect variables X and Y and simply demand that there be *some* non-actual value of X which would have yielded *some* non-actual value of Y, holding the off-path variables fixed at their actual values. Now, in EL, we cannot vary P at all while holding the off-path variables fixed at their actual values. The only acyclic path from P to E is $\langle P, E \rangle$. By the characterization of P, it is metaphysically impossible for P to vary while C and O are held fixed at their actual values. The counterfactual '$P = p$ & FIX $\square\!\!\!\rightarrow E = 0$' is *vacuously* true for some non-actual value p of P, but taking this to imply a causal relation is certainly not in the spirit of the present suggestion. In MC, the only acyclic path from P to P^* is $\langle P, P^* \rangle$. Holding M fixed at its actual value 1 while varying P is metaphysically possible for some variations of P, but those variations do not yield a change in the value of P^*. Setting P to 0 would change P^* to 0, but again we run up against a metaphysical impossibility, namely that of P's being 0 while M is 1.

We can modify the new sufficient condition so that these metaphysical impossibilities no longer bar the efficacy of the realizer-instance of O/C and M. We can stipulate that off-path variables need to be held fixed only if their values are not necessitated by the value of the (putative) cause-variable.[41] Then $P = 1$ still comes out as a cause of $P^* = 1$ in MC, and $P = 1$ still comes out as a cause of $E = 1$ in EL. But even if we did not make this modification, the situation would at most be unfortunate, not untenable. Our new condition that requires off-path variables to be held fixed still is merely a sufficient condition for causation. It may remain silent on whether a case involves causation as long as it does not

---

[41] See Woodward 2015 for a similar suggestion. Alternatively, one could let P^* be multi-valued, but, even setting the problem from note 14 aside, this would have the desired result only in MC, not in EL.

Mental Causation

$$O \longrightarrow E$$

Figure 3.8. The causal graph of EL'

diagnose causation where there is none. That the realizer-instances of the mental property and of conductivity/opacity are causes is plausible in any case and does not require a principled argument.

The second and more pressing problem with the new sufficient condition is that it uses the notion of an *appropriate* causal model. By itself, this is not an unusual requirement. Causal models are standardly required to be appropriate in the sense of satisfying certain minimal standards of model-building. In the new sufficient condition, however, the notion of appropriateness carries a lot of weight – indeed, too much weight.

There are several alternative causal models of the electrocution case where, by the new sufficient condition, the opacity-instance causes the electrocution. For instance, take a simple model, call it EL', that includes only the variables O and E. Figure 3.8 shows the causal graph of EL'.

In EL', there are no variables that are off the path from O to E. Hence it is trivially true that the value of O makes a difference with respect to the value of E if all off-path variables are held fixed at their actual values. Similarly for a model, call it EL'', that is like the original model EL but does not contain C. As Figure 3.9 shows, there is an off-path variable in EL'', namely U, but E still varies along with O if that off-path variable is held fixed.

It might seem that the result that the opacity-instance causes the electrocution can be avoided as soon as we include a variable for the ladder's conductivity in our model, but this is not the case. Take a model, call it EL''', that is just like the original model EL but does not contain a variable for the physical realizer. In EL''' the value of O makes a difference to the value of E, but this difference is nothing over and above the difference made by the value of C. So C is on the path from O to E (see Figure 3.10), and again E varies along with O if the off-path variable U is held fixed.[42]

---

[42] The double-arrow between C and O in the causal graph of EL''' comes about as follows. Given the truth of (20), we have $O = 0 \; \square\!\!\rightarrow P = 3$. By the characterization of variable P, we have $\square[P = 3 \supset C = 0]$. From these two claims, $O = 0 \; \square\!\!\rightarrow C = 0$ follows logically (see Section 1.4). Similarly, given the truth of (21), we have $C = 0 \; \square\!\!\rightarrow P = 2$. Together with $\square[P = 2 \supset O = 1]$ we get $C = 0 \; \square\!\!\rightarrow O = 1$. Thus, O occurs in the equation for C and vice versa. The derivations of

Mental Causation by Causal Modelling

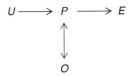

Figure 3.9. The causal graph of EL''

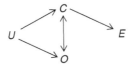

Figure 3.10. The causal graph of EL'''

Thus, in order to avoid the result that the opacity-instance causes the electrocution, we have to read the requirement that the causal model be appropriate such that a causal model for the case it not appropriate unless it includes a variable for the realizer-instance *and* a variable for the conductivity-instance.

These are very strong requirements of appropriateness for our case, and they smack of being *ad hoc*, of being tailored to avoiding the result that the opacity-instance causes the electrocution. (To avoid misunderstanding: I think that it *is* appropriate to include a variable for the realizers of supervenient properties. Indeed, I will defend this claim in the following section. What strikes me as too strong is the claim that it is *in*appropriate *not* to represent the realizers or, for that matter, the conductivity.)

Could we formulate the new sufficient condition for causation without invoking this overly strong notion of an appropriate causal model? We could say that it suffices for causation that the value of one variable makes a difference to the value of another if we hold fixed all off-path variables in *some* model. This suggestion is clearly a non-starter, for it would still yield the result that the opacity-instance causes the electrocution owing to the condition's being satisfied by $O = 1$ and

---

$O = 0 \:\square\!\!\!\rightarrow C = 0$ and $C = 0 \:\square\!\!\!\rightarrow O = 1$ that I just gave used variable P, which is not contained in EL''', as a logical intermediary. This is harmless, because the realizers of conductivity and opacity can play a role in deriving certain true counterfactuals which do not themselves talk about those realizers. Among these counterfactuals, those that talk about the relation between C and O should be true in EL'''. An alternative way of establishing $O = 0 \:\square\!\!\!\rightarrow C = 0$ is via claim (5-O) from Section 2.3.

$E = 1$ in simple alternative models like EL'. Alternatively, we could say that it suffices for causation that the value of X makes a difference to the value of Y if we hold fixed all off-path variables in *all* models with variables corresponding to X and Y. Then it would no longer follow that the opacity-instance causes the electrocution-instance, because the condition fails to be satisfied by $O = 1$ and $E = 1$ in the original model *EL*. It would, however, be virtually impossible to apply the condition in practice. So far, causal modelling theorists have constructed *a* model for a given case and investigated what is true in it. Investigating what is true in *all* models that contain a certain pair of variables is a task of a very different kind, and *prima facie* it does not look very promising. Lastly, we could say that it suffices for causation *in a given model* if the value of one variable makes a difference to the value of another if we hold fixed all off-path variables *in that model*. Then, however, causation would be model-relative and, it seems, cease to be an objective feature of the world. This seems to be too high a price to pay for solving the problem of overlapping realizers.[43]

Owing to its troublesome model-relativity, the condition of dependence while holding off-path variables fixed fails to solve the problem of overlapping realizers when it is used as a sufficient condition for causation. It can be used in a different and more promising way, however. Recall the final suggestion for solving the problem of overlapping realizers from Section 2.3: according to this suggestion, the opacity-instance is a cause of the electrocution, but one that, unlike the conductivity-instance, has little explanatory relevance in our context. The causal modelling framework allows us to spell out this suggestion in more detail by formulating principles about explanatory relevance. As was the case with causation, these principles will fall short of constituting a full-blown theory of explanatory relevance, but we shall see that together they are still strong enough to solve our problem. The basic idea, which I will elaborate in the remainder of this section, is that standard counterfactual dependence is a defeasible sufficient condition for explanatory relevance among whose defeaters is the failure to satisfy the condition of dependence while holding off-path variables fixed.[44]

---

[43] Van Fraassen (1980: Ch. 5) holds that causation is a context-dependent relation. Newen and Čuplinskas (2002) advocate an account of (mental) causation that draws on an interest-relative notion of *events*. Hitchcock (2003) holds that causation is an objective matter, but that there is no unique causal relation. Menzies (2004) holds that causation is relative to a causal model, but he uses 'causal model' in a sense that is different from the present one. For further discussion, see Price and Corry 2007 and Ismael 2016.

[44] The same general strategy, viz. that of distinguishing causation from explanatory relevance in a causal modelling framework, is advocated by Woodward (2010).

Mental Causation by Causal Modelling

Suppose that we are dealing with two strong Kimian events (that are not omissions) such that one event occurs later than the other. Suppose that we have a causal model that accurately represents the counterfactuals that are true about the two events; let '$X = 1$' represent the occurrence of the earlier event in the model and '$Y = 1$' the occurrence of the later event, where X and Y are binary variables. Suppose, lastly, that variable Y counterfactually depends on variable X in the model. In such a situation, $X = 1$ causes $Y = 1$ by our simple sufficient condition for causation in the causal modelling framework. (Unlike the sufficient condition that required holding off-path variables fixed, the simple sufficient condition does not introduce any problematic model-relativity, because the counterfactual that underlies the counterfactual dependence of Y on X is true in any model that accurately represents the counterfactuals that are true about the corresponding events.) That such a situation obtains, I suggest, is also a defeasible sufficient condition for its being the case that $X = 1$ is explanatorily relevant to $Y = 1$. Typically, counterfactual dependence is indicative not only of causation but also of explanatory relevance.[45] My throwing the dart, for instance, is not merely a cause of the balloon's bursting; it is also a cause that explains its effect.

In some cases, however, other factors defeat counterfactual dependence as a sufficient condition for explanatory relevance (though not as a sufficient condition for causation). I will not attempt to give an exhaustive list of such factors, but one of them is excessive temporal distance in the absence of a thing or feature that persists. My bumping into Albert, for instance, is among the causes of Berta's death, because her death, like her birth, counterfactually depends on it. But the bumping is too far removed in time. And it does not create a thing or feature that persists until the death, unlike, say, the actions of an artist whose paintings both cause and explain the viewers' delight despite the fact that the artist died long ago.

Another factor that defeats counterfactual dependence as a sufficient condition for causation, I suggest, is the failure to satisfy the condition of dependence while off-path variables are held fixed. Thus, in the electrocution case as it is represented in the model EL, the opacity-instance causes the electrocution owing to the counterfactual dependence of the electrocution-variable on the variable for the ladder's opacity. But the opacity-instance does not explain the electrocution if model EL is used, because the

---

[45] See Swanson 2010 and note 16 of Chapter 2. Ney (2012) holds that we ordinarily classify something as causation on the basis of counterfactual dependence, but denies that this is in conflict with 'thick' notions of causation such as transfer accounts. In light of the double-prevention cases discussed in Section 1.6, however, this denial is hard to defend.

electrocution-variable no longer depends on the opacity-variable if the variable for the ladder's conductivity is held fixed at its actual value.

Whether the condition of dependence while holding off-path variables fixed is satisfied depends on the causal model that is being considered. Although relativity to a model is implausible for conditions on causation, it is not a problem for conditions on explanatory relevance, for explanation is sensitive to context, and the context is in turn partly constituted by the causal model that is being considered.[46] Thus, when we do not consider the ladder's conductivity and model the electrocution example by the causal model EL', say, which represents only the ladder's opacity and the electrocution, the opacity-instance qualifies as both a cause of the electrocution and a cause that explains the effect. (I concede that it is difficult to get into the mindset of not considering the conductivity once one has considered it, as we have. This is a common phenomenon for certain kinds of context-shift, however.) When we consider the ladder's conductivity as well as its opacity in the original model EL, the opacity-instance is still a cause of the electrocution, but opacity's claim to explanatory relevance is defeated by the failure of the electrocution variable to depend on the opacity variable when the conductivity variable is held fixed at its actual value. By contrast, if model EL is considered, the conductivity-instance is not simply a cause, but one that is explanatorily relevant, because conductivity's claim to explanatory relevance, which is due to the counterfactual dependence of the electrocution variable on the conductivity variable, is not defeated by the failure of the off-path condition.[47]

Mental causes remain explanatorily relevant if the condition of dependence while holding off-path variables fixed is used as a criterion of explanatory relevance. For we saw that their physical effects counterfactually depend on them, and still depend on them when the off-path variables are held fixed. Thus, using the causal modelling framework to formulate conditions for causation as well as conditions for explanatory relevance allows us

---

[46] For the context to be thus constituted, one need not consider a causal model *per se* (that is, under the mode of presentation of variables, equations, etc.) as long as one represents the relevant counterfactual structure.

[47] The model EL''' yields a *prima facie* difficulty for the suggestion that the condition of dependence while holding off-path variables fixed is a condition on (model-relative) causal explanation. In EL''', both conductivity and opacity are represented and both satisfy the condition of dependence while holding off-path variables fixed. If EL''' represents the context, the opacity should count as an explanatorily relevant cause of the electrocution despite the fact that the conductivity is also in play. One way to respond is to say that a context in which both the opacity and the conductivity are relevant and their counterfactual relationship is assessed accurately is most likely also a context where the overlapping realizers of opacity and conductivity are salient, so the model that should be used is EL, not EL'''.

Mental Causation by Causal Modelling 141

to accommodate mental causes and their explanatory relevance, while also offering an attractive solution to the problem of overlapping realizers.

3.6 Objections and Replies

Let us return to our model for mental causation, MC. We have seen that, if we choose MC as a causal model, we can capture how mental events can have physical effects, either by using straightforward counterfactual dependence as a sufficient condition for causation or by using a more complex sufficient condition that invokes the default/deviant distinction or a normality criterion. It might be objected, however, that MC is in some respect inappropriate as a causal model. In this section, I address three such objections: the objection that having a variable for the headache as well as a variable for its realizers violates a constraint on the independence of variables in a model; the objection that the different values for the realizer-variable do not represent versions of the same event; and the objection that the role of the exogenous variable in our model is dubious.

Here is the first objection. Given non-reductive physicalism, the connection between a mental event and its realizers is metaphysically necessary. Specifically, by claims (3)–(6) from Section 3.3, necessarily, variable M is 0 if and only if variable P is 0, because, necessarily, there is no headache just in case no realizer of headaches is instantiated. Similarly, it is necessary that M is not 0 if and only if P is not 0, because, necessarily, there is a headache just in case a realizer of headaches is instantiated. It is sometimes claimed by causal modelling theorists that there should be no metaphysically necessary connections between the values of different variables.[48] If we do not impose this constraint, they hold, we get spurious cases of causation. In our model, for instance, by (9) and (10), M would have been 0 if P had been 0, and P would have been 0 if M had been 0. Given that the actual values of our variables are all 1, it follows that M counterfactually depends on P and that P counterfactually depends on M. But it seems that we should not say that $P = 1$ causes $M = 1$ or that $M = 1$ causes $P = 1$. In other words, it seems that we should not say that the instance of the actual realizer of my headache, the c-fibre firing, causes my headache or that the headache causes the c-fibre firing.

If we deny any causal relation between the property-instances represented by M and P, we need to impose some kind of restriction. One possible restriction is a ban on causal models where some values of different variables are related by metaphysical necessity (call such variables *metaphysically*

---

[48] See, for instance, Hitchcock 2007a: 502 and Halpern and Hitchcock 2010, §4.3.

dependent). But there are two alternatives. When the principle about causation in terms of counterfactual dependence was introduced outside of the causal modelling context in Section 1.4, it was restricted to cases where the putative effect occurs after the putative cause. We can impose the same restriction on the corresponding principle about counterfactual dependence in a model. The other alternative is to restrict the principle about counterfactual dependence in a model to putative cause and effect variables that are metaphysically independent. (Both alternatives could be implemented similarly if one endorsed one of the qualifications that were discussed in Section 3.4.)

Imposing either of these alternative restrictions on the sufficient condition for causation allows us to represent the structure of our case more perspicuously than using models that have been purged of metaphysically dependent variables would. We could in principle ban either M or P from our model and preserve the counterfactual dependence of P^* on P and on M, respectively, but the new models would be much impoverished.[49] So we should restrict the sufficient condition for causation rather than ban models with metaphysically dependent variables.[50]

Faced with the choice between the restriction of the principle about causation to metaphysically independent variables and the restriction that the putative cause variable represent an event that occurs earlier than the putative effect variable, we should choose the temporal restriction. Given non-reductive physicalism, the temporal restriction entails the restriction to (putative) cause and effect variables that are not metaphysically dependent. At least it does if, as in Section 1.5, we confine ourselves to instances of properties that are temporally intrinsic, for there cannot be a metaphysically necessary connection between properties that are temporally intrinsic and instantiated at different times. Thus, the temporal restriction achieves what we want in the case of non-reductive physicalism. It has the advantage of also dealing nicely with the dualist case. If dualism is true, variables M and P are no longer metaphysically dependent, since dualists take it to be metaphysically possible for the mental event to occur without any of its bases, and metaphysically possible for any such base to occur without the mental event. Still, as we saw in Section 3.3, dualists can endorse all the counterfactuals that are true in our model MC if

---

[49] Hitchcock demands that an appropriate causal model 'include enough variables to capture the essential structure of the situation being modeled' (2007a: 503). For further discussion of variable choice, see Woodward 2016.

[50] Another restriction on variables that one could demand would specify admissible and inadmissible total settings of the endogenous variables in a given model (see Halpern and Pearl 2005: 869–870); one could thus declare metaphysically impossible combinations of values inadmissible. This would not help with the present problem, however, because the settings that manifest the counterfactual dependence between M and P are metaphysically possible.

they adopt super-nomological dualism. In particular, they can endorse counterfactuals (9) and (10), which express the counterfactual dependence of P on M, and vice versa. The mental property and its base are instantiated at the same time, so restricting the sufficient condition for causation to (variables that represent) events that occur one after the other avoids commitment to a simultaneous causal relation between the instances of the mental property and the instances of its base.[51] (The same result could be achieved by banning variables that represent simultaneous events from models instead of restricting our sufficient condition for causation, but as Max Kistler (2013: 73) points out, such a ban would have the disadvantage of disallowing models where the variable for a later event depends on the variables for two earlier events which are simultaneous yet mutually counterfactually and causally independent.)

The second objection to using the causal model MC to model mental causation concerns the multi-valued variable P from the model. The model MC uses different non-zero values of P to represent the instantiations of different realizers of the mental property. It might be objected that this violates a constraint on causal modelling, namely the constraint that the various values of non-binary variables represent different versions of the same event and not the occurrence of entirely different events.[52] The different realizers of our mental event are very dissimilar to one another. In Section 3.3, we illustrated the different values of P by assuming that $P = 1$ represents my having firing c-fibres, that $P = 2$ represents my having firing x-fibres, that $P = 3$ represents my having an active semiconductor network of a certain kind in my head, etc. It might be held that there is no single event of which all these different realizer-instantiations are versions. (Our objector might concede that all the realizers of the mental property fall under the description 'being a realizer of such-and-such a mental property', but deny that this description corresponds to a property whose instances are genuine events.)

As we saw in Section 1.3, the individuation of events is a complicated matter. Therefore I will not try to refute the claim that the different values of P do not represent versions of a single event. Instead I will show that we could modify our causal model such that it no longer involves any suspicious non-binary variables. It will turn out that the new model comes at a price that does not justify the benefits, however, so we are better off with the original model.

---

[51] For further discussion of simultaneous causation, see Fenton-Glynn and Kroedel 2015. Kistler (2013) argues against the existence of causal relations in cases where the values of different variables are related by synchronic (classical) association laws.

[52] See Hitchcock 2007a: 499. For further discussion of the relation between variables and events, see Hitchcock 2012a.

144 Mental Causation

Instead of using one non-binary variable to represent all the realizers, we can use a binary variable for each realizer. Thus, we get:

P_1 = 1 if a c-fibre firing occurs, 0 otherwise
P_2 = 1 if an x-fibre firing occurs, 0 otherwise
P_3 = 1 if a certain semiconductor network is active, 0 otherwise
$\vdots$

If we want to mimic the counterfactual relations between the single realizer-variable P and the other variables that held in our old model MC, we can formulate the following equations:

MC^* $U \Leftarrow 1$
$\qquad\quad P_1 \Leftarrow 1$ if U is 0 and M is 1, $M \cdot U$ if is 1, 0 otherwise
$\qquad\quad P_2 \Leftarrow (M \cdot U)/2$ if U is 2, 0 otherwise
$\qquad\quad P_3 \Leftarrow (M \cdot U)/3$ if U is 3, 0 otherwise
$\qquad\quad \vdots$

$\qquad\quad M \Leftarrow \mathrm{Max}\{P_1, P_2, P_3, \ldots\}$
$\qquad\quad P^* \Leftarrow \mathrm{Max}\{P_1, P_2, P_3, \ldots\}$

Figure 3.11 shows the causal graph that corresponds to the equations MC^*.

Although the new model MC^* still verifies counterfactual (15) and thus still establishes that P^* counterfactually depends on M, it has at least two disadvantages. First, it is much more complex than the old model MC. That model has four variables; MC^* has as many variables as there are possible realizers of the mental event, plus another three. Correspondingly, while MC has four equations, MC^* has as many equations as there are possible realizers of the mental property, plus another three. Second, there is massive metaphysical dependence between the variables for the different realizers. Presumably, it is metaphysically impossible for something to be a c-fibre firing and also to be an x-fibre firing, metaphysically impossible for something to be an x-fibre firing and also to be the activity of a semiconductor network, etc. Thus, settings of variables where P_1 and P_2 are both 1, settings where P_2 and P_3 are both 1, etc. are metaphysically impossible. Hence it is metaphysically necessary that P_2 is 0 if P_1 is 1, metaphysically necessary that P_3 is 0 if P_2 is 1, etc. So there is metaphysical dependence between P_1 and P_2, between P_2 and P_3, etc.

We saw above that metaphysically dependent variables are not problematic *per se* and should be tolerated if they are necessary to represent the

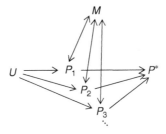

Figure 3.11. The causal graph of MC^*

structure of a case. Nevertheless, we should not multiply them beyond necessity. Our original model MC has just two metaphysically dependent variables; in MC^* they are legion. Moreover, MC^* contains multiple pairs of metaphysically dependent variables irrespective of whether non-reductive physicalism or dualism is assumed, since there is metaphysical dependence among the different realizer-variables. (Given non-reductive physicalism, there is also metaphysical dependence between M and each of the realizer-variables, as was the case in the original model MC.) So whatever the benefit of banning multi-valued variables that fail to represent different versions of the same event, it is outweighed by the added complexity and massive metaphysical dependence between variables that we need to accept if we implement this ban.

The third and final objection claims that complexity considerations in fact tell against our model MC. This model contains an exogenous variable U. It might be held that variable U is dispensable. Moreover, it might be held that U is to blame for the failure of our equations to be acyclic.

We can indeed simplify our model by removing U. This can be done in two obvious ways, depending on the new role that is assigned to P. Both ways, however, yield new problems that are not worth the gain in simplicity.

The first way of removing U delegates the status of being an exogenous variable to P instead. Thus, P is now set independently of the other variables. Given that the actual value of P is 1, we get the following equations:

$$MC \backslash U_{EX} \quad \begin{aligned} P &\Leftarrow 1 \\ M &\Leftarrow \text{Min}\{P, 1\} \\ P^* &\Leftarrow \text{Min}\{P, 1\} \end{aligned}$$

Figure 3.12 shows the causal graph corresponding to $MC \backslash U_{EX}$.

Figure 3.12. The causal graph corresponding to $MC\backslash U_{EX}$

Although the model $MC\backslash U_{EX}$ is simpler than MC, it no longer allows P^* counterfactually to depend on M. Nor does it allow P counterfactually to depend on M. In particular, the counterfactual (i) 'If M had been 0, then P^* would (still) have been 1' is true in $MC\backslash U_{EX}$, as is the counterfactual (ii) 'If M had been 0, then P would (still) have been 1.' In fact, (i) and (ii) are false, however, for they contradict counterfactuals (15) and (10), respectively, which were established in Section 3.3. Thus, some counterfactuals are true in $MC\backslash U_{EX}$ while being in fact false. This makes $MC\backslash U_{EX}$ inappropriate as a causal model for our case.[53]

The second way of removing U from our model continues to treat variable P as endogenous. If we modify the original equation for P minimally to accommodate this change, we get the following equations:

$$MC\backslash U_{END} \quad \begin{aligned} P &\Leftarrow 0 \text{ if } M \text{ is } 0, P \neq 0 \text{ otherwise} \\ M &\Leftarrow \text{Min}\{P, 1\} \\ P^* &\Leftarrow \text{Min}\{P, 1\} \end{aligned}$$

Figure 3.13 shows the causal graph corresponding to $MC\backslash U_{END}$.

It can easily be checked that all the counterfactuals (except of course the counterfactuals involving U) that were true in our original model MC are also true in the model $MC\backslash U_{END}$. So unlike $MC\backslash U_{EX}$, $MC\backslash U_{END}$ is a genuine alternative to MC. It has one drawback, however. The equations from our original model MC had two solutions. The equations $MC\backslash U_{END}$ have as many solutions as there are possible realizers of the mental event.[54] Like metaphysically dependent variables, multiple solutions should be accepted if they cannot be avoided. But like metaphysically dependent variables, they

---

[53] Our sufficient condition for causation allows exogenous variables to be causes. Sometimes causation is defined only for endogenous variables, however (see Halpern 2008, Halpern and Hitchcock 2010). Proponents of such a restrictive definition have an additional reason to reject $MC\backslash U_{EX}$ if they want variable P to be at least a candidate cause. Similarly for the third way of simplifying MC by making M an exogenous variable, which will be discussed in note 55.

[54] This is due to the second case in the equation for P. For definiteness one might want to stipulate that P simply be 1 in this case, but then P would become a *de facto* binary variable, and we could no longer capture multiple realizability.

Figure 3.13. The causal graph corresponding to $MC\backslash U_{END}$

should not be multiplied beyond necessity. The gain in simplicity we get by removing U is not worth having a multitude of solutions instead of just two.[55]

3.7 Interventionism

James Woodward (2003) advocates an interventionist theory of causation. Interventionism is a member of the causal modelling family. Its distinctive feature is that it emphasizes the importance of interventions, that is (roughly), isolated manipulations of variables. Whether interventionism can accommodate mental causation on the assumption of non-reductive physicalism has been a matter of controversy.[56] This section argues that interventionism can accommodate mental causation along the lines suggested in previous sections, although this requires modifications of the original theory.

The framework of the debate over interventionism and mental causation differs somewhat from that of our discussion, as it is primarily about causal relations between variables themselves, and not primarily about causal relations between token events that are represented by specific values of variables. For variables X and Y, the basic idea of Woodward's interventionism is that X causes Y if and only if it is possible to manipulate the value of X for at least some individuals that possess X such that this manipulation changes the value of Y for those individuals, given the satisfaction of certain appropriate conditions (see Woodward 2003: 40). More specifically, Woodward characterizes the relations of being a direct cause and being a contributing cause as follows:

---

[55] A third way of simplifying MC by removing U – though not one that seems particularly obvious – is to make M an exogenous variable, with equations $M \Leftarrow 1$, $P \Leftarrow \text{Min}\{M, 1\}$, and $P^* \Leftarrow \text{Min}\{P, 1\}$. While (10) is true in this model, it still faces problems analogous to those with $MC\backslash U_{EX}$, because (9) is false in it.

[56] See Woodward 2008, Baumgartner 2009, 2010, and Woodward 2015, 2017. Further discussions of the applicability of interventionism to mental causation include Campbell 2007, Shapiro and Sober 2007, Raatikainen 2010, Shapiro 2010, Hoffmann-Kolss 2014, and Weslake 2017.

148   Mental Causation

> (**M**) A necessary and sufficient condition for X to be a (type-level) *direct cause* of Y with respect to a variable set **V** is that there be a possible intervention on X that will change Y [...[57]] when one holds fixed at some value all other variables Z_i in **V**. A necessary and sufficient condition for X to be a (type-level) *contributing cause* of Y with respect to variable set **V** is that (i) there be a directed path from X to Y such that each link in this path is a direct causal relationship; that is, a set of variables $Z_1 \ldots Z_n$ such that X is a direct cause of Z_1, which is in turn a direct cause of Z_2, which is a direct cause of $\ldots Z_n$, which is a direct cause of Y, and that (ii) there be some intervention on X that will change Y when all other variables in **V** that are not on this path are fixed at some value. (Woodward 2003: 59; first emphasis added)

Admittedly, more needs to be said (and is said by Woodward) about what an intervention is. For our purposes, however, we can assimilate interventions to (non-backtracking) counterfactuals. Thus, we can read 'there is a possible intervention on X that will change Y when one holds fixed at some value all other variables Z_i' as 'there is a true (non-backtracking) counterfactual with a possible antecedent according to which the value of Y would have changed if the value of X had changed while the values of the Z_i had been so-and-so'.[58]

Michael Baumgartner (2009, 2010) claims that a mental variable M cannot qualify either as a direct cause or as a contributing cause of a physical variable P^* as characterized in (**M**). He reasons as follows. Given non-reductive physicalism, the relation between a mental event and its realizer is not causal. Hence M is not a direct cause of P. Hence P is not on a causal path from M to P^* (where a *causal path* is a sequence of variables related by direct causation). Hence P is to be held fixed in any interventions that test whether M is a contributing cause of P^*. Being distinct from M, P also has to be held fixed in order to determine whether M is a direct cause of P^*. By non-reductive physicalism, it is impossible to intervene on M while holding P fixed, however. Therefore, M is neither a direct cause nor a contributing cause of P^*.

According to this reasoning, M is not a direct cause of P because, owing to non-reductive physicalism, the relation between M and P is not causal. This is too quick, however. Assume that the variables and their possible values are as in our model *MC*. Then there *is* a possible intervention

---

[57] The omitted phrase concerns the probability distribution of Y, which, given our assumption of determinism, we can ignore for present purposes.

[58] For a detailed discussion of the relation between interventions and counterfactuals, see Woodward 2003: 94–151.

Mental Causation by Causal Modelling

on M that changes the value of P while we hold the remaining variables fixed, namely an intervention that changes the value of M from 1 to 0. Owing to the necessity of the relation between M and P, such an intervention changes the value of P from 1 to 0 even if the values of the remaining variables (that is, U and P^*) are held fixed at their actual values (or at any other values, for that matter). It follows that M *is* a direct cause of P as characterized in (**M**). Assuming that P is a direct cause of P^*, it follows that P is on a causal path from M to P^*. So we need *not* hold P fixed when intervening on M in order to assess whether M is a contributing cause of P^* as characterized in (**M**). Indeed, intervening on M by changing its value from 1 to 0 while holding merely U fixed, P^* changes its value from 1 to 0. Hence M *is* a contributing cause of P^* as characterized in (**M**).

Thus, following the letter of Woodward's characterizations in (**M**), interventionism, far from ruling out mental causation, in fact entails it. But this result comes at the price of predicting too many mental causes. While most theorists (including Woodward himself; see Woodward 2008, 2015) would welcome the result that M is a contributing cause of P^*, few would be happy to call M a direct cause of P. So mental causation still makes trouble for interventionism, although the source of the trouble is not where Baumgartner locates it.

Interventionists could avoid the result that M causes P by restricting causal relations to variables that are not related by metaphysical necessity. More specifically, they could proceed as follows: they could rename 'direct cause' in (**M**) to (say) 'difference-maker', rename 'causal path' to (say) 'difference-making path', define a *direct cause*$_{new}$ of Y as a difference-maker of Y that is not related to Y by metaphysical necessity, and define a *contributing cause*$_{new}$ of Y as a contributing cause of Y as characterized in (**M**) that is not related to Y by metaphysical necessity. Thus, M would not be a direct cause$_{new}$ of P, while being a difference-maker for P; P would be on a difference-making path from M to P^*; and M would be a contributing cause$_{new}$ as well as a contributing cause of P^*. We saw in Section 3.6 that other theories of causal modelling also require a restriction along the lines suggested here in order not to count the mental event as a cause of its realizer. So *prima facie* interventionism seems no worse off than those theories as far as mental causation is concerned.[59]

---

[59] It might seem that there is a further problem, namely that interventionism predicts too few physical causes, because intervening on P while holding M fixed at either 0 or 1 does not change the value of P^*. This result is merely an artefact of our simplifying assumption of claim (2) from Section 3.3, however. If one found this assumption intrinsically plausible, one could allow that we need not

150   Mental Causation

The upshot is that interventionism, like the causal modelling theories of token causation discussed earlier in this chapter, can accommodate mental causation. While interventionism faces certain problems that arise from supervenient mental properties, the problem is that it predicts too much mental causation rather than too little. The problem can be solved, however. In particular, interventionists can forestall the conclusion that mental property-instances cause their realizers to be instantiated if they restrict their conditions on causation to variables that are not related by metaphysical necessity.

3.8 Conclusion

Causal modelling can explain mental causation. Starting from counterfactuals about a mental event, its possible realizers, and a later physical event that are true by the lights of non-reductive physicalism (and supernomological dualism) we can construct a causal model that represents all these counterfactuals. This model is unorthodox in that it fails to have acyclic equations. Nonetheless, it establishes that the variable for the later physical event counterfactually depends on the variable for the mental event. On a simple view, this counterfactual dependence suffices to establish that the mental event causes the later physical event. More sophisticated views that invoke the default/deviant distinction or a normality ordering of worlds still rule the mental event to be a cause of the later physical event. In the causal modelling framework, we can give a precise formulation to the idea that one event depends on another when off-path events are held fixed. One can attempt to use this formulation in a new sufficient condition for causation in order to solve the problem of overlapping realizers, but the resulting sufficient condition is problematic, because it makes causation model-relative. It is promising to use dependence while off-path variables are held fixed as a criterion for explanatory relevance, however, and to solve the problem of overlapping realizers by denying not the efficacy, but the explanatory relevance of one of the supervenient property-instances. Various objections against the specifics of the causal model for mental causation can be met. In particular, it is possible to forestall the conclusion that there is a causal relation between the mental event and its realizer. Interventionism licenses that conclusion,

---

always hold fixed metaphysically dependent variables during interventions. Woodward suggests the latter strategy in response to Baumgartner's criticism; see Woodward 2015: 327–335.

Mental Causation by Causal Modelling　　151

but can solve this difficulty analogously to other causal modelling approaches.

One can take the results of this chapter to show that causal modelling theories can repeat the success of the simpler counterfactual account of explaining mental causation under non-reductive physicalism and super-nomological dualism. Indeed, one can take causal modelling theories to exceed the success of the simpler counterfactual account, since they allow us to spell out a solution to the problem of overlapping realizers. This positive assessment is the attitude I recommend. Alternatively, however, one can take the results to exacerbate the exclusion problem for non-reductive physicalism and super-nomological dualism. One might think that, the more firmly we have established the existence of mental causation given either view about the nature of mind, the more pressing the worry that the physical effects of mental causes are overdetermined becomes. It is time to look at the exclusion problem in more detail.

CHAPTER 4

The Exclusion Problem

4.1 Introduction

The physical world does not manifest any outside influence. A physical event occurs. If we trace its causes, we are likely to find plenty of physical causes. Indeed, it may well be that it is impossible for the physical event not to occur while the laws of physics and the past are as they actually are.[1] How does the physical world leave any room for mental causes that are distinct from physical causes?

There are two issues here. The first issue is that the physical world might not allow any causal influence of the mental whatsoever if the mental is distinct from the physical. Recall Leibniz's argument from the conservation of momentum and kinetic energy from Section 0.2: given these conservation laws, Leibniz held, the mental cannot have physical effects at all. We saw that Leibniz's argument was unsatisfactory as it stands, but the point can be made more generally. Given that the actual physical laws and the actual past necessitate the occurrence of a certain future physical event, it might seem that this event cannot have any additional mental causes.

The first issue can be resolved, at least in principle, by claiming that mental causes of physical effects are never alone in causing these effects, but always act in tandem with physical causes of the same effect. This suggestion, however, gives rise to the second issue. If the physical effects of mental causes always have additional physical causes, it seems to follow that they are overdetermined. Thus, cases of mental causation seem to be similar to firing squads, where the deaths of the victims are overdetermined by the

---

[1] This does not follow from our earlier assumption of determinism alone, which I shall continue to make in this chapter for simplicity. Determinism alone makes it impossible for the actual laws *as a whole* to hold and the actual past to obtain while the future differs. The laws as a whole might contain psychophysical laws as well as physical laws. The claim from the main text does follow, however, if we add our assumption that any actual psychophysical laws are synchronic.

The Exclusion Problem 153

firings of the squad members. It seems implausible, however, that there is this kind of overdetermination whenever there is mental causation.

Both issues would deserve the label 'exclusion problem'.[2] It has been more common to apply the label to the second issue, however, which has also been more prominent in the mental causation debate.[3] In what follows, I shall follow this tradition and use 'exclusion problem' to refer to the second of the issues. It is the exclusion problem in the sense of the second issue that is the main focus of this chapter.

Here is a more rigorous way of presenting the exclusion problem. We can introduce the problem as a set of five claims:[4]

(DISTINCTNESS)	All mental events are distinct from physical events.
(EFFICACY)	Some mental events have physical effects.
(COMPLETENESS)	Every physical event that has a cause at all has a physical cause.
(EXCLUSION)	No effect has more than one cause at a given time, unless it is overdetermined.
(NON-OVERDETERMINATION)	The effects of mental events are not systematically overdetermined.

Each of these five claims seems plausible, yet they are inconsistent or at least in tension with one another.[5] (That the claims fall short of genuine inconsistency is indicated by the sentences starting with 'presumably' in the following reasoning.) Given (EFFICACY), a certain physical event has a mental cause. By (DISTINCTNESS), this mental cause is distinct from the physical causes (if any) of the physical effect. By (COMPLETENESS), the physical effect has a physical cause (for, by (EFFICACY), it has a cause in the first place, namely a mental cause). Presumably, it has a physical cause that is

---

[2] Sometimes the exclusion problem is introduced through the metaphor of causal work – indeed, I have done so myself in Section 0.1. Saying that the physical does all the causal work and leaves nothing for the mental to do remains neutral between the two issues presented here: the causal work metaphor can be read as saying that there is no job opportunity of any kind left for the mental (first issue) or as saying that the mental can do the job of causing physical events only by partaking in some kind of job-sharing with the physical causes of those events (second issue).

[3] In the sense of the second issue, the exclusion problem is due to Malcolm (1968). It has been refined and much discussed by Kim (e.g., 1989, 1998, 2005, 2007). For a recent overview, see Bennett 2007.

[4] I am loosely following Bennett (2008: 281) here. The main difference is that she talks about sufficient causes in her formulation of the exclusion problem while I talk about causes *tout court*. We will discuss sufficient causes in Section 4.5.

[5] For a presentation of the claims of the exclusion problem where they are strictly inconsistent, see Hitchcock 2012b. Such a presentation comes at the price of additional complexity, however.

simultaneous with the mental cause. By (EXCLUSION), the physical effect is overdetermined by its simultaneous physical and mental causes. Presumably, the present case is far from uncommon. Thus, given (EFFICACY), (DISTINCTNESS), (COMPLETENESS), and (EXCLUSION), there is widespread and systematic overdetermination of physical effects by mental and physical causes. By (NON-OVERDETERMINATION), however, there is no such overdetermination; contradiction.

I have just presented the exclusion problem as a set of five principles that are inconsistent or at least in tension with one another. Other presentations are possible along different and independent dimensions. First, one can use slightly different formulations of the principles. Second, one can present the problem not as an inconsistent (or near-inconsistent) set, but as an argument. When the principles are presented as an argument, the negation of one of the principles features as the conclusion of the argument while the remaining principles feature as premises. Typically, the negation of (DISTINCTNESS) or the negation of (EFFICACY) is chosen as the conclusion of the argument, and the whole thing is called the 'exclusion argument' rather than the 'exclusion problem'. Third, one can present the exclusion problem by using fewer principles than I have. Typically, (EXCLUSION) gets omitted or fused with (NON-OVERDETERMINATION) into a single principle.[6]

I have chosen the formulation of the problem as an inconsistent (or near-inconsistent) set of five principles, because on this formulation the logical relation between our principles is straightforward, and, unlike in formulations as arguments, there is no default about which principle to reject. The points from this chapter could also be applied to different formulations, however. For example, we shall encounter objections against (EXCLUSION). Take a presentation of the exclusion problem as an argument for the negation of (DISTINCTNESS) or the negation of (EFFICACY) whose premises comprise the remaining principles except (EXCLUSION). In the context of that presentation, we can read our objections to (EXCLUSION) as objections to a tacit assumption of the argument that is required to make the argument valid.

---

[6] To give some examples of the various possibilities of formulating the exclusion problem: Carey (2011: 251–252) presents the problem as inconsistent set, but with four instead of five principles. Yablo (1992: 247–248) presents the exclusion problem as an argument against the efficacy of the mental with three premises. Lowe (2000: 571–572) and Gibb (2014: 328) present the exclusion problem as an argument against the distinctness of the mental and the physical with three premises that do not include (EXCLUSION). All of these authors use slightly different formulations of the principles. Bennett (2008: 282) also discusses different shapes the exclusion problem can take.

The Exclusion Problem 155

Let us consider the exclusion problem as exemplified by the five (near-) inconsistent claims (DISTINCTNESS), (EFFICACY), (COMPLETENESS), (EXCLUSION), and (NON-OVERDETERMINATION) then. Given the tension between the five claims, everyone, regardless of their views about the nature of mind and their views about causation, has to give up at least one of them.[7] Non-reductive physicalists and dualists hold that all mental properties are distinct from all physical properties. Given the strong Kimian account of events, a difference in constitutive properties entails the distinctness between events, so it follows that all mental events are distinct from all physical events. Thus, non-reductive physicalists and dualists cannot reject (DISTINCTNESS). Rejecting (EFFICACY) means accepting epiphenomenalism, which is far from attractive in its own right. Besides, the arguments from Chapters 2 and 3 have shown that the existence of mental causation follows straightforwardly from non-reductive physicalism and can be accommodated by dualists by making certain assumptions about the status of the psychophysical laws as well. Thus, non-reductive physicalists and dualists who make these assumptions cannot reject (EFFICACY). Rejecting (COMPLETENESS) seems implausible, not just from a general scientific point of view, but also in the case at hand.[8] It is very plausible that the instance of the actual physical realizer or base of our mental property-instance is a cause of the physical effect of the mental property-instance,[9] so our model of mental causation fails to generate a counterexample to (COMPLETENESS). Rejecting (EXCLUSION) or rejecting (NON-OVERDETERMINATION) are the only options left for non-reductive physicalists and dualists then.

The plan for the remainder of this chapter is as follows. The next two sections argue that both the option of rejecting (EXCLUSION) and the option of rejecting (NON-OVERDETERMINATION) are viable for non-reductive physicalists and dualists. Section 4.2 argues that non-reductive physicalists and dualists can reject (EXCLUSION) by making a case for the falsity of certain counterfactuals that are necessary conditions for the overdetermination of physical effects by mental and physical causes. Section 4.3 argues that, even if the argument against (EXCLUSION) should

---

[7] See Bennett 2008: 281. Kim (e.g., 2005) argues that, in the light of the exclusion problem, non-reductive physicalists cannot but deny the efficacy of the mental, which, according to him, amounts to a *reductio* of non-reductive physicalism.

[8] For a discussion of the history of the claim that the physical world is causally complete, see Papineau 2001. For dualist critiques of physical completeness claims, see Lowe 2000, 2003, 2008, BonJour 2010, and Gibb 2015b.

[9] Ignoring, once more, the worries that instances of realizers cannot be causes or effects in principle; see Section 4.4 for further discussion.

156   Mental Causation

fail and non-reductive physicalists and dualist are committed to the overdetermination of the physical effects of mental causes, they can reject
(NON-OVERDETERMINATION) instead. If those physical effects are overdetermined, the argument goes, the cases are very dissimilar to prototypical
cases of overdetermination such as firing squads. Section 4.4 takes up the
issue of whether the instances of realizers can both necessitate instances of
mental events and cause physical events. It shows that the argument for the
causal inertia of realizers is at best inconclusive and that any such inertia
does not spread to the instances of the realized mental properties. Section
4.5 discusses a formulation of the exclusion problem in terms of sufficient
causes. It argues that the problem is more severe if thus formulated, but
that the severity does not carry over to the solution of the original exclusion
problem, because our principle about causation in terms of counterfactual
dependence does not commit us to any potentially problematic claims
about sufficient causes.

4.2   Denying Exclusion

According to (EXCLUSION), no effect has more than one cause at a given
time, unless it is overdetermined. In other words, if an effect has more than
one cause at a given time, then it is overdetermined. What is overdetermination? It seems to be an essential feature of cases of overdetermination
such as the firing squad that the overdetermined event would still have
occurred had either overdetermining event occurred without the other. In
a firing squad of two, for instance, the victim would still have died if the
first squad member had fired while the second had not; likewise the victim
would still have died if the second squad member had fired while the first
squad member had not. Thus, in order for events c and d to overdetermine
event e, the following counterfactuals have to be true:[10]

> (O_1)   If c had occurred without d, then e would still have occurred.
> (O_2)   If d had occurred without c, then e would still have occurred.[11]

---

[10]   If we are dealing with more than two overdetermining events, there are two ways of generalizing (O_1)
and (O_2). We can demand that the overdetermined event would still have occurred if any of the
overdetermining events had not occurred while *all* the other overdetermining events had still
occurred. Alternatively, one can demand that the overdetermined event would still have occurred
if any of the overdetermining events had not occurred while *some* of the other overdetermining
events had still occurred. For further discussion of these generalizations, see Kroedel 2008: 129 n. 14.

[11]   Bennett (2003, 2008) and Mills (1996) endorse the stronger requirement that (O_1) and (O_2) be not
merely true, but non-vacuously true. I will not explore the strategy of pleading vacuity, because it is
not available for dualists. For alleged counterexamples to the truth of (O_1) and (O_2) as a necessary
condition for overdetermination, see Aimar 2011: 474–476, Bennett 2008: 289 n. 13, and Won 2014:

Claims (O_1) and (O_2) are put forward merely as necessary conditions for overdetermination, not as necessary and sufficient conditions.

It may seem that our sufficient condition for causation in terms of counterfactual dependence allows us to give short shrift to (EXCLUSION). Take the case where there is a car crash, and it would not have happened if the driver had not been drunk. If the road had not been icy, the crash would not have happened either. By our sufficient condition for causation, both the driver's being drunk and the road's being icy caused the car crash.[12] But assume that the crash was sensitive both to the driver's being drunk and to the road's being icy in that the crash would not have occurred if either of the driver's being drunk and the road's being icy had occurred without the other. Then (O_1) and (O_2) are false. Given that the truth of (O_1) and (O_2) is necessary for overdetermination, the driver's being drunk and the road's being icy do not overdetermine the car crash. We have a counterexample to (EXCLUSION).

Here is another counterexample to (EXCLUSION) where it is even clearer that (O_1) and (O_2) are false.[13] A defendant faces trial by a jury of two. Both jurors vote to convict, and the defendant goes to jail. At the court, convictions have to be unanimous. Thus, if the first juror had not voted to convict, then the defendant would not have gone to jail. Similarly, if the second juror had not voted to convict, then the defendant would not have gone to jail. By our sufficient condition for causation, the first juror's voting to convict causes the defendant's imprisonment, and so does the second juror's voting to convict. But if either juror had voted to convict while the other had not, the defendant would not have gone to jail either. So again (O_1) and (O_2) are false while we have two simultaneous causes.[14]

These counterexamples against (EXCLUSION) do not dissolve the exclusion problem, however. While (EXCLUSION) was formulated very generally, without reference to mental or physical causes, it was of course intended to be applied to the case of simultaneous mental and physical

---

212–214. For criticism of the claim that the vacuous truth of (O_1) or (O_2) removes overdetermination, see Bernstein 2016.

[12] The example is from Lewis 1986a: 214. As in previous examples, we might have to take a suitable temporal part of, say, the road's being icy in order for our sufficient condition for causation to be applicable.

[13] The example is a simplified version of an example from Kroedel 2008: 127–128.

[14] Friends of (EXCLUSION) might respond by redefining overdetermination such that overdetermination simply is causation by several causes, or perhaps by several simultaneous causes, and no longer requires the truth of (O_1) and (O_2). But this response merely shifts the vulnerability to the counterexamples to (NON-OVERDETERMINATION), which, on the suggested definition of overdetermination, can in turn be given short shrift.

158 Mental Causation

causes of the same effect. We can make this qualification explicit and formulate the claim as follows:

(EXCLUSION*)   No effect has a mental cause and a distinct physical cause that occur at the same time, unless it is overdetermined.

The car crash and jury examples are not counterexamples to (EXCLUSION*), and it is *prima facie* unclear whether we can find analogous cases that involve mental and physical causes. Like (EXCLUSION), (EXCLUSION*) is inconsistent, or at least in tension, with the other four claims from the original presentation of the exclusion problem, so the problem persists.

Non-reductive physicalists and super-nomological dualists can argue against (EXCLUSION*) by showing that, even in the case of mental and physical causes, at least one of the counterfactuals (O_1) and (O_2) is false. Applying (O_1) and (O_2) to our case of mental property M, its actual realizer P, and physical property P^* that is instantiated later than M, we get:

$(O_1{}^*)$ If M had been instantiated without P, then P^* would still have been instantiated. (M & ~P $\square\!\!\!\rightarrow$ P*)

$(O_2{}^*)$ If P had been instantiated without M, then P^* would still have been instantiated. (~M & P $\square\!\!\!\rightarrow$ P*)

Let us consider $(O_2{}^*)$ first. Non-reductive physicalists endorse the strong supervenience of mental properties on physical properties. By this strong supervenience, the instantiation of a realizer necessitates the instantiation of the realized property. In our case, the instantiation of P necessitates the instantiation of M. Thus, P cannot be instantiated without M; hence, the antecedent of $(O_2{}^*)$ is impossible; hence, $(O_2{}^*)$ is vacuously true given non-reductive physicalism, so non-reductive physicalists cannot reject (EXCLUSION*) by rejecting $(O_2{}^*)$.

Like all dualists, super-nomological dualists deny the strong supervenience of mental properties on physical properties. They hold that there are worlds where P is instantiated without M, although this requires a violation of the actual psychophysical laws. Given the modified miracles approach to overall similarity that was presented in Section 2.5 on behalf of super-nomological dualism, it is of the first importance to avoid psychophysical miracles and of the second importance to avoid 'ordinary' miracles. Thus, worlds that do not involve any 'ordinary' miracles in addition to the psychophysical miracle that is requires for P to be instantiated without M are closer to the actual world than any worlds that do. Assuming that the P^*-instance follows lawfully from the previous physical

The Exclusion Problem

state, which includes the P-instance, P^* is still instantiated in the closest worlds where P is instantiated without M. In other words, the closest worlds where the antecedent of $(O_2{}^*)$ is true are just like the actual world except that the instantiation of M is removed by a psychophysical miracle. Hence $(O_2{}^*)$ is non-vacuously true given super-nomological dualism,[15] so super-nomological dualists cannot reject (EXCLUSION*) by rejecting $(O_2{}^*)$ either.

Thus, rejecting (EXCLUSION*) by rejecting $(O_2{}^*)$ does not look promising for non-reductive physicalists and super-nomological dualists. The case of $(O_1{}^*)$ is different, however. Both non-reductive physicalists and super-nomological dualists can make a case against $(O_1{}^*)$. They can argue that, given their respective views, P^* might not have been instantiated if M had been instantiated without P. This result contradicts $(O_1{}^*)$.

Here are the details of the argument against $(O_1{}^*)$. Suppose that we are dealing with our paradigmatic case of putative mental causation, where M is the property of having a headache, P is the property of having firing c-fibres, and P^* is the property of having one's hand moving towards an aspirin. The argument against $(O_1{}^*)$ begins with a counterfactual that has a slightly different antecedent than $(O_1{}^*)$. What would or might have been the case if M had been not only instantiated without P, but accompanied by a physical realizer or base other than P?[16] We already saw in the previous chapter (but ignored the issue for simplicity) that implementing some of the alternative realizers of headaches is likely to be so disruptive that the instantiation of those realizers would no longer make my hand move towards the aspirin. It seems plausible that even the closest possibility of realizing or having a base for headaches other than through firing c-fibres requires some large-scale tampering with my nervous system. Suppose that the closest such possibility is that x-fibres, which are not actually present in humans, be implanted in my brain. It seems plausible that the easiest way of implanting them might not leave all the outgoing connections intact, such that having firing x-fibres no longer makes my hand move towards the aspirin. This seems equally plausible for the non-reductive physicalist case and for the super-nomological dualist case. Thus, we get:

(1) If M had been instantiated with a different physical realizer/base instead of P, then P^* might not have been instantiated. (M & ~P & ∪**P** $\Diamond\!\!\!\longrightarrow$ ~P*)

---

[15] Bennett (2008: 291–292) puts forward a similar argument for the truth of $(O_2{}^*)$ given standard dualism.

[16] Given non-reductive physicalism (though not given dualism), it is of course impossible for M to be instantiated in the absence of P without being accompanied by a realizer other than P.

Further, if I had had a headache without having had firing c-fibres, some other physical realizer or base of headaches would have been instantiated instead:

(2) If M had been instantiated without P, then some other physical realizer/base of M would have been instantiated instead. (M & ~P $\square\!\!\!\longrightarrow$ $\cup$**P**[17])

Claim (2) is true according to non-reductive physicalism, according to which the instantiation of headaches is strictly equivalent to the instantiation of a realizer of headaches.[18] It is also true according to the modified miracles approach that is endorsed by super-nomological dualists. If we face the choice between antecedent-worlds of (2) where some other physical base of headaches is instantiated and antecedent-worlds of (2) where none is, the former worlds come out closer to the actual world according to the modified similarity account, because they do not involve a psychophysical miracle.

Now (1) and (2) logically imply:

(3) If M had been instantiated without P, then P^* might not have been instantiated. (M & ~P $\diamond\!\!\!\longrightarrow$ ~P*)[19]

However, by the definition of the 'might' conditional, (3) is true if and only if $(O_1{}^*)$ is false. So $(O_1{}^*)$ is false.

It might be objected that this result is an artefact of our strong Kimian conception of events, according to which the occurrence of the physical event that underlies the mental event is strictly equivalent to the instantiation of its constitutive property, namely the property of having firing c-fibres, at the relevant time by the relevant subject. According to a weak Kimian conception or a Lewisian conception of events, the event that we

---

[17] In order to facilitate later derivations, the formalization does not include ~P as a conjunct of the consequent. This does not render the formalization unfaithful, for M & ~P $\square\!\!\!\longrightarrow$ $\cup$**P** is logically equivalent to M & ~P $\square\!\!\!\longrightarrow$ $\cup$**P** & ~P.

[18] For further discussion of (2) in the context of non-reductive physicalism, see Loewer 2001b: 319–320, Bennett 2003: 481–482, and references therein.

[19] The inference from (1) and (2) to (3) has the form of an inference from χ & ϕ $\diamond\!\!\!\longrightarrow$ ψ and χ $\square\!\!\!\longrightarrow$ ϕ to χ $\diamond\!\!\!\longrightarrow$ ψ. Given the definition of the 'might' conditional, this inference is valid if and only if the inference from ~[χ & ϕ $\square\!\!\!\longrightarrow$ ~ψ] and χ $\square\!\!\!\longrightarrow$ ϕ to ~[χ $\square\!\!\!\longrightarrow$ ~ψ] is, which is valid if and only if the inference from χ $\square\!\!\!\longrightarrow$ ~ψ and χ $\square\!\!\!\longrightarrow$ ϕ to χ & ϕ $\square\!\!\!\longrightarrow$ ~ψ is, which in turn is valid if and only if the inference from χ $\square\!\!\!\longrightarrow$ ψ and χ $\square\!\!\!\longrightarrow$ ϕ to χ & ϕ $\square\!\!\!\longrightarrow$ ψ is. The premises and conclusion of the last inference are all vacuously true if there is no possible world where χ is true. If there is such a world, premise χ $\square\!\!\!\longrightarrow$ ϕ logically implies χ $\diamond\!\!\!\longrightarrow$ ϕ, which together with the other premise χ $\square\!\!\!\longrightarrow$ ψ logically implies the conclusion χ & ϕ $\square\!\!\!\longrightarrow$ ψ according to Lewis 1973c: 433.

The Exclusion Problem   161

refer to as 'the c-fibre firing' (call it p) can have a different modal profile. In particular, it might be that p would already fail to occur if I had lacked a feature that is more specific than merely having firing c-fibres. It might be, for instance, that p is essentially not merely a c-fibre firing, but a c-fibre firing at a rate between 99 and 101 Hz; then my c-fibres' firing at a rate of 102 Hz instead of the actual rate of, say, 100 Hz would have been enough for p not to occur. If this is the case, p is rather *fragile*; that is, p could not easily have occurred in a different manner (in other words, if a p-like event had occurred in a manner different from p's, it would not have been p, but a distinct event).[20] Similarly for my hand's moving towards the aspirin (call this event p^*). Event p^*, too, might or might not be very fragile. Let us assume that, in fact, my hand moves slowly towards the aspirin with my thumb facing sideways. If p^* is not very fragile, it would still have occurred if my hand had moved fast and with the thumb facing upwards; not so if p^* is very fragile. Now, it seems that the argument against (O_1^*) works only if p is assumed to be not very fragile. If p is very fragile – especially while p^* is not very fragile – then premise (1) no longer seems plausible, for in this case my c-fibres fire only slightly differently in the closest antecedent-worlds of (1), and my hand still moves towards the aspirin.

Friends of counterfactual accounts of causation are not well advised to conceive of events as very fragile, for this might yield too many cases of counterfactual dependence and, consequently, causation (see Lewis 1986d: 196–199). (The strong Kimian conception of events that I have advocated yields fragility along the temporal dimension, which, as we saw in Section 1.3 is undesirable, but worth the overall utility of the strong Kimian account.) But even if we accept for the sake of argument that events may be very fragile – particularly that event p may be very fragile – we can still argue against (O_1^*). More precisely, we can argue against an analogue of (O_1^*) that talks about the (non-)occurrence of token events p and p^* instead of the instantiation of properties P and P^*:

(O_1^{**}) If M had been instantiated while p had not occurred, then p^* would still have occurred. $(M\ \&\ \sim Oc(p) \,\Box\!\!\longrightarrow Oc(p^*))$[21]

---

[20] The terminology is due to Lewis (1986d). Lewis takes events to be very fragile if they could not easily have differed in time and manner.

[21] We could formulate a principle analogous to (O_1^{**}) that talks about the occurrence of a (weak Kimian/Lewisian) event m instead of the instantiation of property M. That would introduce some unnecessary complications, however, for it would make the transition between claims about the mental event and claims about the underlying physical events that correspond to M's realizers/bases much more cumbersome.

The strategy behind the argument against (O_I^{**}) that I will present is that, irrespective of what assumptions we make about the fragility of p and of p^*, (O_I^{**}) is false. We can read the above argument against (O_I^*) as an argument against (O_I^{**}) that assumes event p to be not very fragile: if p is not very fragile, its non-occurrence and replacement with an alternative realizer or base event might have resulted in the failure of p^* to occur. This 'might' claim seems plausible if p^* is itself not very fragile; *a fortiori*, it seems plausible if p^* is very fragile, for in this case it takes even less for p^* not to occur. Thus, the above argument can be read as an argument against (O_I^{**}) that covers two out of four sub-cases, namely the sub-case where p is not very fragile while p^* is very fragile and the sub-case where neither p nor p^* are very fragile.

To cover the remaining two sub-cases, suppose now that p is very fragile. In this case, if p had not occurred, a realizer/base of M might still have been instantiated:

(4) If p had not occurred, a realizer/base of M might have been instantiated. ($\sim$Oc(p) $\Diamond\!\!\!\longrightarrow \cup\mathbf{P}$)

We could even turn (4) into a 'would' counterfactual. If a very fragile p had not occurred, then, it seems, my c-fibres would have fired slightly differently, in which case the different c-fibre-firing property that would have been instantiated would still have been among the realizers/bases of M. For our purposes, however, the weaker 'might' conditional will suffice.

Claim (4) does not talk about the later physical event and thus is true independent of whether or not p^* is very fragile. But the truth of certain counterfactuals about the relation between p, instances of realizers/bases of M, and p^* depends on the fragility (or lack thereof) of p^* as well. Let us therefore treat the two sub-cases about the fragility of p^* separately. Suppose first that p^* is *not* very fragile, while continuing to suppose that p is very fragile. Let us assume that actually my hand moves slowly towards the aspirin with my thumb facing sideways; then the assumption that p^* is not very fragile seems to allow that p^* would still have occurred if my hand had moved quickly towards the aspirin with my thumb facing upwards. It seems that if p^* is not very fragile while p is very fragile, then p^* would still have occurred if some physical realizer/base of M had been instantiated in the absence of p:

(5) If a realizer/base of M had been instantiated in the absence of p, then p^* would still have occurred. ($\sim$Oc(p) & $\cup\mathbf{P}$ $\Box\!\!\!\longrightarrow$ Oc(p^*))

The Exclusion Problem   163

For it seems that if my c-fibres had fired only slightly differently, I would still have reached for an aspirin, although presumably my hand would have moved somewhat differently (a bit faster than it actually did, say); this would still have sufficed for p^* to occur if p^* is not very fragile. Claims (4) and (5) logically imply:

(6) If p had not occurred, then p^* might still have occurred. ($\sim$Oc(p) $\Diamond\!\!\!\longrightarrow$ Oc(p^*))

The inference rule used here is that which licenses the inference from $\chi \Diamond\!\!\!\longrightarrow \phi$ and χ & $\phi \Box\!\!\!\longrightarrow \psi$ to $\chi \Diamond\!\!\!\longrightarrow \psi$, which is logically valid.[22] We saw that it is plausible that the (putative) physical effects of mental property-instances counterfactually depend on the instances of the realizers/bases of those mental property-instances (see Section 2.6). If we apply this result to our case, we get:

(7) If p had not occurred, then p^* would not have occurred. ($\sim$Oc(p) $\Box\!\!\!\longrightarrow \sim$Oc($p^*$))

Claim (7) is inconsistent with (6), however, for by the definition of the 'might' conditional, (7) is equivalent to the negation of (6). So if we assume that p is very fragile (which yields (4)) while p^* is not very fragile (which yields (5)), it follows (via (6)) that p^* does not counterfactually depend on p. Contrapositively, if we want to uphold the claim that p^* counterfactually depends on p, we have to reject either the assumption that p is very fragile or the assumption that p^* is not very fragile. I take it that the plausibility of the claim that p^* counterfactually depends on p outweighs that of either assumption. We can therefore conclude that the sub-case where p is very fragile while p^* is not does not obtain. This leaves us with the sub-case where p and p^* are both very fragile.

Suppose, then, that p and p^* are both very fragile. In this case, it seems, p^* might have failed to occur if a physical realizer/base of M had occurred in the absence of p. For instance, my hand might have moved faster towards the aspirin if my c-fibres had fired at a rate of 102 Hz instead of firing at the actual rate of 100 Hz; in this case, p^* would not have occurred if

---

[22] The inference from (i) $\chi \Diamond\!\!\!\longrightarrow \phi$ and (ii) χ & $\phi \Box\!\!\!\longrightarrow \psi$ to (iii) $\chi \Diamond\!\!\!\longrightarrow \psi$ is valid if the inference from (i) and (ii') χ & $\phi \Diamond\!\!\!\longrightarrow \psi$ to (iii) is valid. For (i) and (ii) logically imply (i) and (ii'): if (i) is true, there is a possible world where both χ and ϕ are true, so (ii') is non-vacuously true if true, in which case (ii') follows from (ii). By the definition of the 'might' conditional, the inference from (i) and (ii') to (iii) is valid if and only if the inference from $\chi \Diamond\!\!\!\longrightarrow \phi$ and $\sim$[χ & $\phi \Box\!\!\!\longrightarrow \sim\psi$] to $\sim$[$\chi \Box\!\!\!\longrightarrow \sim\psi$] is, which is valid if and only if the inference from $\chi \Diamond\!\!\!\longrightarrow \phi$ and $\chi \Box\!\!\!\longrightarrow \sim\psi$ to χ & $\phi \Box\!\!\!\longrightarrow \sim\psi$ is, which in turn is valid if and only if the inference from $\chi \Diamond\!\!\!\longrightarrow \phi$ and $\chi \Box\!\!\!\longrightarrow \psi$ to χ & $\phi \Box\!\!\!\longrightarrow \psi$ is, which is valid according to Lewis 1973c: 433.

164   Mental Causation

p^* is very fragile. So we can reject (5), and there is no obstacle to the joint truth of (7) and (4).

To complete the argument against (O_1^{**}) for the sub-case in which both p and p^* are very fragile, let us leave the counterfactual relation between M's physical realizers/bases and p^* for a moment and consider the relation between p, the physical realizers/bases, and the M-instance itself. What would have been the case if a realizer/base of M had been instantiated in the absence of p? It takes an 'ordinary' miracle to bring about the instantiation of a realizer/base of M while preventing the occurrence of p. According to non-reductive physicalism, it is impossible for M not to be instantiated if a realizer of M is instantiated. According to super-nomological dualism, this is possible, but it requires a psychophysical miracle, which has to be avoided at all costs.[23] Thus, M is still instantiated in the closest worlds where a realizer/base of M is instantiated in the absence of p, and the following is true:

> (8) If some physical realizer/base of M had been instantiated while p had not occurred, then M would still have been instantiated. ($\sim\!Oc(p)$ & $\cup\mathbf{P}\ \Box\!\!\!\longrightarrow M$)

Claims (7), (4), and (8) are inconsistent with (O_1^{**}). To see this, note first that, by the inference rule we used in the derivation of (6) above, (4) and (8) logically imply

> (9) If p had not occurred, then M might still have been instantiated. ($\sim\!Oc(p)\ \Diamond\!\!\!\longrightarrow M$)

By another application of the same rule, (9) and (O_1^{**}) logically imply (6); as we saw, (6) contradicts (7). In sum, (7) (4), (8), and (O_1) are jointly inconsistent. In other words (7), (4), and (8) logically imply that (O_1^{**}) is false.[24]

To summarize the argument against (O_1^{**}): there are four possible cases depending on whether or not event p is very fragile and on whether or not event p^* is very fragile. Given that p^* counterfactually depends on p, we can rule out the case where p is very fragile while p^* is not very fragile. In all other cases, (O_1^{**}) is false. Therefore, (O_1^{**}) is false. If the overdetermination of p^* by p and the M-instance requires the truth of (O_1^{**}), both non-reductive

---

[23] Moreover, on either view, not having M instantiated detracts from match of particular fact with the actual world, where M is instantiated.

[24] Since (7) by itself is consistent with (O_1^{**}) (more on this in the next section), using (7) as a premise in an argument against (O_1^{**}) does not beg the question.

physicalists and super-nomological dualists can reject (EXCLUSION*) and deny that mental causation entails overdetermination.

I have presented a number of arguments that assumed certain events to be very fragile. Friends of our counterfactual principle about causation are ill advised to adopt a fragile conception of events lest they should be committed to too much counterfactual dependence, however (see Lewis 1986d). Thus, in what follows I shall revert to the strong Kimian conception of events, according to which the occurrence of an event is strictly equivalent to the instantiation of its constitutive property by the constitutive object at the constitutive time. If we assume the constitute property not to be too specific, the strong Kimian conception will not yield events that are fragile owing to their constitutive property. (According to the strong Kimian conception, events are still rather fragile owing to their constitutive time, but for simplicity I will continue to ignore this issue.)

Even on a strong Kimian conception of not-so-fragile events, one might have worries about some of the arguments against (EXCLUSION*) that were presented in this section. The argument for (1) works only if realizers/bases of headaches other than c-fibre firings are rather difficult to implement. More generally, in order for the strategy of this section to work even if events are conceived of as not very fragile, it needs to be the case that replacing the actual realizer or base of my headache with an alternative realizer or base would have been sufficiently disruptive to no longer bring it about that my hand moves towards the aspirin. Counterfactuals about what would have been the case if the actual realizer or base had been thus replaced are not the most straightforward claims to evaluate. Their truth is also hostage to empirical fortune, because it is partly an empirical question what the alternative bases or realizers of headaches are and how easy it is to implement them. It would be good for non-reductive physicalists and dualists to have a contingency plan in case the arguments against (EXCLUSION*) turn out to be unworkable.

4.3 Denying Non-Overdetermination

The previous section argued that, modulo some empirical uncertainties, non-reductive physicalists and super-nomological dualists can make a good case against the claim that physical effects must be overdetermined if they have both a physical cause and a simultaneous mental cause. If you are not convinced or too worried about the empirical uncertainties, never mind. In this section I will argue that, even if non-reductive physicalists and super-nomological dualists *are* committed to the overdetermination of those physical effects, they can deny that this kind of overdetermination is objectionable. In other words, even if they accept (EXCLUSION*), they can still deny (NON-OVERDETERMINATION).

Strictly speaking, a failure of the arguments from the previous section need not amount to conceding that the P^*-instance is overdetermined by the M-instance and the P-instance, since the conditions from the $(O_1)/(O_2)$ family were presented only as necessary conditions for overdetermination, not as necessary and sufficient conditions. Indeed, (O_1) and (O_2) are true not only in cases of overdetermination, but also in cases of pre-emption. Recall the example of Billy and Suzy, who each throw a rock at a bottle at the same time. Billy's rock arrives there first and shatters the bottle (see Section 1.4). If Billy had not thrown and Suzy had, then the bottle would still have shattered; likewise if Suzy had not thrown and Billy had.

The difference between the cases seems to be that Billy's throw has a better claim to causing the bottle's shattering than Suzy's throw has – indeed, Suzy's throw seems to have no such claim at all – while the firings of the two squad members have an equally good claim to causing the victim's death. It may seem promising to conjoin the condition that the putative overdeterminers have an equally good or bad claim to being a cause to the claim that (O_1) and (O_2) be true in order to formulate a necessary and sufficient condition for overdetermination (see Lewis 1986d: 193–200).

I will not, however, assume this or any other specific characterization of overdetermination. After all, 'overdetermination' is a technical term, so, to a certain extent, theorists are free to stipulate how they understand it.[25] Non-reductive physicalists and super-nomological dualists might insist on a comparatively demanding notion of overdetermination that requires much besides the truth of (O_1^*) and (O_2^*) and thus insist on the falsity of (NON-OVERDETERMINATION), but by itself this would not win the day. As I will explain in more detail below, the rationale behind the (EXCLUSION*)-cum-(NON-OVERDETERMINATION) part of the exclusion problem is that cases where physical effects have simultaneous mental and physical causes would be similar to prototypical cases of overdetermination such as deaths by firing squads. Such cases can be specified without appeal to any specific characterization of overdetermination. Thus, the condition that the physical effects of mental causes are overdetermined is

---

[25] For instance, Bennett holds that overdetermination requires that both overdetermining events be 'causally sufficient' for the overdetermined event (2008: 288). For a discussion of various alternative proposals, see Carey 2011.

merely an intermediary step in the presentation of the exclusion problem, which could be omitted in principle.[26] Since there is nothing to be gained for non-reductive physicalists and super-nomological dualists by insisting on any specific characterization of overdetermination, I shall concede not merely the truth of the claims from the $(O_1)/(O_2)$ family for the sake of argument, but also the truth of any other conditions required by a reasonable characterization of overdetermination.[27]

Assume, then, that the M-instance and the P-instance overdetermine the P^*-instance and that (O_1^*) and (O_2^*) are true. What would be objectionable about this? The standard answer is that it would make cases of mental causation like firing squad cases where two shooters simultaneously fire at their victim, who is simultaneously hit by both bullets, each of which would have sufficed to kill him. Such cases exist, the argument goes, but they have a number of features whose presence in all cases of mental causation would be highly implausible. For instance, deaths by firing squad are rare; mental causation, by contrast, is a common phenomenon. (If it exists, that is, but by our assumption of (EFFICACY) it does.) Even if we set the worry about commonness aside, in firing squad cases the two overdetermining events independently bring about the effect. It would be a strange coincidence if this were the case whenever there is mental causation. In particular, it would be a strange coincidence if a physical effect had a mental cause in addition to its physical cause; that it has a physical cause in the first place does not seem surprising.[28]

Schematically, this line of reasoning can be put as follows:

---

[26] Bennett (2007: 327; 2008: 281 n. 3) agrees.

[27] If these conditions include the condition that both overdetermining events be causes of the overdetermined event, one can ignore worries about their individual efficacy. In any event, such worries do not arise in our case (setting aside the general worries about whether realizer-instances can in principle be causes or effects), owing to the counterfactual dependence of the P^*-instance on both the M-instance and the P-instance. For further discussion of the efficacy of individual overdetermining events, see Schaffer 2003.

If the conditions on overdetermination include Lewis's requirement that both overdeterminers have an equally good (or bad) claim to be a cause of the overdetermined event, one might think that the exclusion problem dissolves because mental events have a worse claim to be causes of physical events than physical events have. This reasoning, however, only solves the exclusion problem at the expense of a highly unattractive assumption, namely the assumption that mental events have a worse claim to having physical effects.

[28] If the two firings in firing squad cases have a common cause, such as someone's command, they might still be considered independent in the sense of involving two distinct causal processes (see Bennett 2008: 287) and in the sense of not standing in a relation of synchronic dependence. It is sometimes claimed (e.g., by Zhong (2011: 132 n. 4)) that in the context of mental causation appeals to overdetermination would be 'ad hoc'. Presumably, such appeals are taken to be *ad hoc* by virtue of overdetermination's having certain objectionable features such as the ones described.

168 Mental Causation

(i)   If x is an F, then x is like a prototypical F.
(ii) Prototypical Fs are Gs.
(iii) x is not a G.

(iv) x is not an F.

Premise (i) is ambiguous, however. Similarity comes in different aspects. 'Being like a prototypical F' can mean being like a prototypical F *with respect to being an F*, or it can mean being like a prototypical F *with respect to being a prototypical F*. Take an x that is an F, but not a prototypical F. Then on the first reading of 'being like a prototypical F', (i) is true, but (iv) does not follow from (i)–(iii). On the second reading, (i) is false, because our x is not a prototypical F. On either reading, the argument is unsound.

In the case of mental causation, it is claimed that, if mental causation involves overdetermination, cases of mental causation are like firing squad cases, which in turn are prototypical cases of overdetermination. On one reading of this claim, it is true, but all that is said is that cases of mental causation are cases of overdetermination. It does not follow that mental causation has any of the potentially problematic features that firing squads have, such as being rare. (Don't prototypical things have to be common for the kind of thing they are prototypical for? Or at least more common for the kind of thing they are prototypical for than very atypical members of this kind? No. Perhaps award-winning Alsatians are prototypical mammals, but this is perfectly consistent with their being vastly outnumbered by whales.) On the other reading of the claim that cases of mental causation are like firing squad cases, what is said is that cases of mental causation share the prototypical features of overdetermination that firing squad cases have. This claim, however, can be denied without contradiction.

Thus, it is consistent with mental causation's involving overdetermination that cases of mental causation have little in common with prototypical cases of overdetermination such as firing squad cases. Consistency, of course, is not the same as plausibility. But more can be said for the claim that cases of mental causation are rather dissimilar to prototypical cases of overdetermination.

On the account of mental causation presented here, there is a synchronic dependence relation between the physical cause and the mental cause of the physical effect. According to super-nomological dualism, the two causes are related by psychophysical laws, which could not have failed so

The Exclusion Problem

easily as ordinary laws of nature. According to non-reductive physicalism, the two causes are related by metaphysical necessity. In prototypical cases of overdetermination like the firing squad, no such synchronic dependence relation holds between the two overdeterminers (which might, of course, still have a common cause).

The synchronic dependence relation also explains, or at least contributes to explaining, why the physical effect in question has a mental cause in addition to the physical cause; thus, it is no coincidence that the effect is overdetermined. This explanation has two parts. One part is an explanation of why the mental event occurs. The other is an explanation of why that mental event causes the physical effect.[29] Take the instances of our properties M, P, and P^*. Given that the instantiation of P implies the instantiation of M at least with super-nomological necessity, we can straightforwardly explain why M is instantiated from P's being instantiated. That the M-instance causes the P^*-instance does not follow quite so straightforwardly from the relation between M and P, even if we take into account that P causes P^* by counterfactual dependence. Given this counterfactual dependence, we have the following claim:

(10) If P had not been instantiated, then P^* would not have been instantiated. ($\sim P \;\square\!\!\rightarrow\; \sim P^*$)

According to non-reductive physicalism, it is metaphysically necessary that M is instantiated if P is instantiated. Contrapositively, we have the following:

(11) Necessarily, if M is not instantiated, then P is not instantiated. ($\square[\sim M \supset \sim P]$)

According to super-nomological dualism, (11) is false, but the synchronic relation between the P-instance and the M-instance still yields the following:

(12) If M had not been instantiated, then P would not have been instantiated. ($\sim M \;\square\!\!\rightarrow\; \sim P$)

Neither the conjunction of (10) and (11) nor the conjunction of (10) and (12) entails that the P^*-instance counterfactually depends on the M-instance (see Section 2.2). Still, we can regard claims (10), (11), and (12) as contributing to an explanation of why the M-instance causes the P^*-instance. The claims are close cognates of the premises we have used

---

[29] Sharpe (2015) also holds that the worry should be addressed by giving these two explanations.

to argue for this causal claim in Chapter 2. We can also combine them with further premises to get a watertight argument for this claim.[30] Together with the explanation of M's instantiation as such, this should sufficiently attenuate the coincidence worry about the overdetermination of the P^*-instance by the P-instance and the M-instance.[31]

The most important dissimilarity between cases of mental causation and cases of overdetermination is that, according to the account I have presented, the physical effect counterfactually depends on its mental cause and also counterfactually depends on the instance of the actual physical realizer/base of the mental cause. Thus, if M had not been instantiated, then P^* would not have been instantiated; nor would P^* have been instantiated if P had not been instantiated. This is compatible with the assumed truth of (O_1^*) and (O_2^*). Dualists have to assume that (O_1^*) and (O_2^*) are non-vacuously true if true. In this case, all that is required is, first, that the closest worlds where M is instantiated without P (where P^* is instantiated by (O_1^*)) be further from actuality than the closest worlds where P is not instantiated (where the P^*-instance does not occur, by its counterfactual dependence on the P-instance), and, second, that the closest worlds where P is instantiated without M (where P^* is instantiated by (O_2^*)) be likewise further from actuality than the closest worlds where M does not occur (where the P^*-instance does not occur, by its counterfactual dependence on the M-instance).[32] Non-reductive physicalists will take claim (O_2^*) to be vacuously true. Its vacuous truth is even more straightforward to square with the counterfactual dependence of the P^*-instance on the M-instance, for in this case there are no worlds where P is instantiated in the absence of M to consider. Figure 4.1 illustrates the point for the dualist case. In the figure, ~P is true inside the bottom left parabola, and ~M is true in the area that largely coincides with the ~P-area, but diverges from it where

---

[30] We can, for instance, recover premise (18) ($\sim\cup\mathbf{P}_M \square\!\!\rightarrow \sim P^*$) from the argument for the causation of the P^*-instance by the M-instance from Section 2.5 as follows. Assume that (i) no alternative realizer/base of M would have been instantiated if P had not been instantiated ($\sim P \square\!\!\rightarrow \sim\cup\mathbf{P}_M$). It is trivially true that (ii) necessarily, if no realizer of M had been instantiated, then P would not have been instantiated ($\square[\sim\cup\mathbf{P}_M \supset \sim P]$). From (i), (ii), and (10) we get (18). Premise (17) ($\sim M \square\!\!\rightarrow \sim\cup\mathbf{P}_M$) follows from (12) and the assumption that if neither M nor P had been instantiated, then no realizer of M would have been instantiated ($\sim M$ & $\sim P \square\!\!\rightarrow \sim\cup\mathbf{P}_M$).

[31] For further discussion of the coincidence worry, see Carey 2011. See also Sider 2003.

[32] As is witnessed by so-called reverse Sobel sequences, there can be a tension between a counterfactual ϕ & $\psi \square\!\!\rightarrow \chi$ and a counterfactual $\phi \square\!\!\rightarrow \sim\chi$ if they are asserted in this order (see von Fintel 2001 and Gillies 2007). Following Moss (2012), I think this tension is best explained as a pragmatic phenomenon, and at any rate it does not seem to arise in our case: it seems fine to say, for instance, that P^* would have been instantiated if P had been instantiated in the absence of M, while also saying that P^* would not have been instantiated if M had not been instantiated.

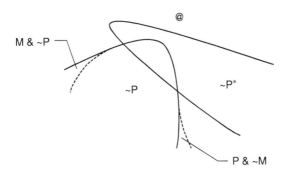

Figure 4.1. Overdetermination with counterfactual dependence

indicated by the dashed lines. The figure shows a situation in which (O_1^*) and (O_2^*) are non-vacuously true while the P^*-instance also counterfactually depends on both the M-instance and the P-instance.

While mental causation involves both counterfactual dependence and overdetermination if we assume (EXCLUSION*), in prototypical cases of overdetermination such as the firing squad, the overdetermined event does not counterfactually depend on each of the overdetermining events. If one of the shooters had not fired, the victim would still have died because the other shooter would still have fired. The counterfactual dependence of the physical effect on both its mental and its physical cause marks out cases of mental causation as very atypical cases of overdetermination. Therefore it should not come as a surprise that mental causation can involve overdetermination in an unobjectionable way, such that (NON-OVERDETERMINATION) can be rejected.[33]

I have argued that the exclusion problem can be solved even if we grant that the physical effects of mental causes are overdetermined, because the resulting cases of overdetermination are very dissimilar to prototypical cases of overdetermination such as the firing squad. It might be objected that such a solution misses the point of the exclusion problem. The point,

---

[33] It might seem that cases of mental causation by counterfactual dependence are dissimilar to prototypical cases of overdetermination like firing squad cases in a further respect. Firing squad cases, it seems, involve separate transfers of energy from each of the shooters to the victim, but cases of mental causation by counterfactual dependence need not involve such transfers; in particular, they need not involve a separate transfer of energy from the mental cause to the physical effect. The claim that firing squad cases involve separate transfers of energy is less straightforward than it seems, however, for various stages in the process involve double prevention, for instance, the shooters' muscle contractions as they pull the trigger and the guns' operations (see Schaffer 2000a, 2004a, and Sections 1.6 and 2.6).

the objection goes, is that it is unintelligible how physical effects can have distinct mental causes if they already have physical causes.[34] To put the point more positively, the challenge posed by the exclusion problem is to explain how distinct mental events can make a causal contribution to the physical world in light of the fact that physical effects already have physical causes.[35] According to the objection, this challenge is not met if it is merely pointed out that cases of mental causation are dissimilar to prototypical cases of overdetermination.

A version of this objection is due to Sara Bernstein.[36] Bernstein argues that the problem that arises from the overdetermination of physical effects by mental and physical causes is not that the resulting cases are like prototypical cases of overdetermination. Rather, she holds, the problem is that we cannot give a precise explanation of the individual contribution of the mental cause. In particular, according to her objection, non-reductive physicalists have a hard time answering the following two questions: first, the question of where the extra causal power of the mental 'comes from', that is, the source of the extra causal contribution of the mental; second, the question of where the extra causation by the mental event 'goes', that is, how exactly it contributes to the outcome.[37] The corresponding questions are much more straightforward to answer about prototypical cases of overdetermination, Bernstein holds. Given a firing squad of two, for example,[38] it can neatly be explained where the extra causation 'comes from': it is there because there is a second shooter. It can also be neatly explained where the extra causation 'goes': the victim's heart is hit with twice the force, owing to the presence of the second bullet. Thus, according to Bernstein, dissimilarity to prototypical cases of overdetermination is a problem rather than an advantage for theories of mental causation, because it makes it harder for them to explain where mental causation 'comes from' and where it 'goes'.

My account of mental causation has no difficulty in explaining the causal contribution of the mental, however. According to the account, mental events have physical effects because certain physical events

---

[34] See Kim (1998: 53), Morris (2015), and Bernstein (2016). For critical discussion, see Árnadóttir and Crane 2013.

[35] Thus, the present challenge has similarities both with the first issue and with the second issue from Section 4.1.

[36] See Bernstein 2016. Bernstein puts her objection forward in the context of transference theories of causation, but it can equally well be made without this presupposition.

[37] See Bernstein 2016: 30–31. The scare quotes are hers.

[38] I'm substituting our example for Bernstein's here; she uses the case of two rocks that shatter a window at the same time.

counterfactually depend on mental events. This counterfactual dependence is in turn explained by the fact that a given physical event would not have occurred if no realizer or base of a given mental property-instance had been instantiated, together with the intimate modal relation between the mental property-instance and its realizers or bases. Thus, we can give a perfectly satisfying explanation of where the mental causes 'come from'. To be sure, the source of the mental cause is not an extra object, unlike the source of the extra causation in the firing squad case, where the extra causation is due to the presence of the second shooter. But it would be gratuitous to demand that any explanation of where the contribution of an overdetermining cause 'comes from' mirror the explanation in the firing squad case in this respect. For one thing, there are satisfying explanations of where the contribution of an overdetermining cause 'comes from' that do not involve a distinct object but merely a distinct feature of a single object. A bee's attraction to a flower might be overdetermined by the smell and the colour of the flower. Explaining the contribution of, say, the smell does not require invoking an extra object similar to the second shooter in the firing squad case. For another, explaining the contribution of the mental cause by explaining the counterfactual dependence of the physical effect on it seems perfectly satisfying without invoking a distinct object (which, in our context, could only be a Cartesian soul or something of that kind).

Where does the causation by the mental event 'go'? The account of mental causation I have defended suggests an answer similar to the answer to the first question: the mental event brings about the physical event by counterfactual dependence. This counterfactual dependence can in turn be explained by certain facts about the counterfactual relation between the realizers or bases on the one hand and the physical event on the other, plus the intimate modal relation between the mental event and the realizers or bases. Again, this explanation is somewhat disanalogous to the explanation of where the extra causation 'goes' in the firing squad case. There, the extra cause modifies the effect, which involves the victim's heart being hit with twice the force compared to a case where only one shooter fires.

As was the case with the explanation of where the causation by the mental event 'comes from', it is not a problem that the explanation of where it 'goes' does not perfectly mirror the corresponding explanation for the firing squad case. Again, the explanation seems satisfying in spite of this difference. And again, there are unproblematic cases of overdetermination that are like mental causation in that an overdetermining cause does not modify the overdetermined event either. Take, for instance, an overdetermination case that involves idealized neurons. Neurons c and d both fire. Each has an

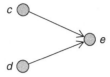

Figure 4.2. A neuron case of overdetermination

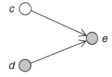

Figure 4.3. If c had not fired . . .

excitatory connection to neuron *e*, which also fires (see Figure 4.2). The firings of *c* and *d* overdetermine the firing of *e*. We can make perfect sense of where the causation of, say, *c* 'goes'. We can do so, at least in part, because of the counterfactuals that are true: if only *c* had fired, then *e* would still have fired; if only *d* had fired, then *e* would still have fired; if neither *c* nor *d* had fired, *e* would not have fired; etc. Still, in the idealized neuron scenario, if *c* had not fired, then *e* would not merely still have fired, but would have fired in exactly the same way that it actually did (see Figure 4.3). We can make perfect sense of where the causation by *c* goes, but *c* does not modify the overdetermined event in the way that one shooter's firing modifies the way in which the victim dies.

Admittedly, mental causation on my account differs both from the firing squad and from the neuron example in that the overdetermining mental and physical causes are difficult to disentangle. Given non-reductive physicalism, it is metaphysically impossible for the physical cause to occur without the mental cause. Given super-nomological dualism, such a situation is possible, but it is more remote from actuality than a violation of the ordinary laws of nature. One might worry that the intimate modal relation between the mental cause and its realizer or base threatens the causal contribution of the mental *qua* mental and makes it parasitic on the contribution of its realizer.[39] But this worry can be allayed. As we saw in Section 2.4, the mental cause is not parasitic on the physical cause in the sense that the physical cause is a causal intermediary. The set of

---

[39] Bernstein (2016: 31–32) expresses a similar worry.

realizers or bases of the mental cause is a logical intermediary when the counterfactual dependence of the physical effect on the mental cause is derived, but this is not detrimental to the genuine efficacy of the mental cause. Further, as we saw in Section 2.2, the counterfactual dependence of the physical effect on the mental cause also shows that the mental cause is efficacious *qua* mental, because, given the strong Kimian conception of events, the counterfactual dependence is due to a general feature of the mental event, namely its constitutive mental property.

In summary, the account of mental causation that I have defended can meet further objections even when we grant that the physical effects of mental causes are overdetermined. It can explain where the contribution of the mental cause 'comes from' and where it 'goes', and it can uphold that the mental cause is efficacious *qua* mental.

The upshot of this section is that non-reductive physicalists and super-nomological dualists may grant that mental causation involves overdetermination without running into trouble. They can deny that cases of mental causation are in any interesting sense like prototypical cases of overdetermination, such as firing squad cases. Unlike the firing squad, cases of mental causation involve an intimate synchronic relation between the simultaneous causes, which also partially explains why the mental event is a cause of the later physical event. Unlike the firing squad, in cases of mental causation the effect counterfactually depends both on the mental cause and on the physical cause. Non-reductive physicalists and super-nomological dualists can also meet objections that locate the source of the problem not in the similarity of mental causation to firing squad cases, but in the difficulty in explaining the causal contribution of the mental cause or of the mental cause *qua* mental. In sum, there would be nothing objectionable about physical effects' being overdetermined by mental and physical causes.

I should perhaps repeat that there might be no need to establish these claims in the first place. If the argument from the previous section succeeds, non-reductive physicalists and dualists have no need to admit that physical effects of mental causes are overdetermined by their mental and physical causes. But should they turn out to be thus overdetermined after all, no harm would befall non-reductive physicalists and super-nomological dualists.

4.4 The Efficacy of Realizers

In the previous sections, I have made some assumptions about the actual realizer P of our mental property M in the non-reductive physicalist case. I have assumed that P necessitates M and that the P-instance causes the P^*-instance because the P^*-instance counterfactually depends on the M-instance. Indeed, I have tacitly assumed that the P-instance is the single physical cause of the P^*-instance that is simultaneous and, as it were, coordinated with the M-instance. If there are alternative physical causes of this kind, the arguments I have presented need to be augmented, for, as it stands, they leave it open that our physical effect, the P^*-instance, is overdetermined by the M-instance and a physical cause other than the P-instance. They also leave it open that *that* instance of overdetermination is particularly objectionable.

Are the assumptions from the previous sections justified? We took property P to be the property of having firing c-fibres and property M to be the property of having a headache. Consider the first assumption. Does having firing c-fibres necessitate having a headache? On the face of it, the answers seems to be 'Yes', at least by the lights of non-reductive physicalism. But what about a case where the c-fibres are disconnected from the rest of the nervous system (see Bennett 2003: 485, 2008: 291)? And what about a case where the laws of physics are radically different, such that (say) the electrical impulses that actually travel down the c-fibres in an orderly fashion randomly pop up and disappear? It might seem that, in either case, there would be no headache.[40] Let us grant that there would indeed be no headache in either case. Then we can no longer say that having firing c-fibres by itself necessitates having a headache. But, it seems, having a headache still is necessitated by a conjunctive property that has having firing c-fibres as a conjunct, the other conjuncts being that the laws of physics are such-and-such and that suitable background conditions obtain (such as the c-fibres' being appropriately connected to the rest of the nervous system). Call this conjunctive property a *total realizer, P_{total}*, of headaches. Call the c-fibre firing itself, that is, the total realizer minus the other conjuncts, a *core realizer, P_{core}*, of headaches.[41] (Non-reductive physicalists might claim that it was the total realizer that they had in mind all along when they talked about the c-fibre firing. Nonetheless, there is also a more narrow sense of 'c-fibre firing', so the distinction between total and core realizers is useful irrespective of the antecedent meaning of 'c-fibre firing'.)

---

[40] It is not clear whether realizer functionalists such as Lewis (1966) would agree that no pain is instantiated when the disconnected c-fibres fire.

[41] The terminology – strictly speaking, the terminology of properties that are 'core realizations' vs properties that are 'total realizations' – is due to Shoemaker (1981: 97). Bennett (2003, 2008) makes a similar distinction but does not use the same terminology. She holds that the additional properties that are required for what we have called the core realizer to necessitate the mental property are exactly those that are required for the core realizer to bring about the physical effect. Her suggestion is criticized by Aimar (2011) and Keaton and Polger (2014).

The Exclusion Problem 177

If there is a total realizer and a distinct (but included) core realizer, we must reassess the arguments against (EXCLUSION*) and (NON-OVERDETERMINATION) from the previous two sections. Whether the instance of the actual total realizer P_{total} of the mental property M still qualifies as a cause of the later physical property-instance P^* will be discussed in a moment. The instance of the actual core realizer P_{core} of M certainly has a good claim to being a cause of the P^*-instance. Not least because it seems that the P^*-instance counterfactually depends on the P_{core}-instance: if the c-fibre firing – that is, the c-fibre firing in the narrow sense, not including laws or background conditions – had not occurred, then my hand would not have moved towards the aspirin.

The argument against (EXCLUSION*) – at any rate, the argument against (O_1^*) from (1) and (2) – is still plausible if we read 'realizer' as 'core realizer' throughout. The argument against (NON-OVERDETERMINATION) also still works in this case. While P_{core} no longer necessitates M, there is still an intimate synchronic relation between the P_{core}-instance and the M-instance that is absent in proto-typical cases of overdetermination, for P_{core} is a constitutive part of a related property (namely P_{total}) that necessitates M. And if the P^*-instance is overdetermined by the M-instance and the P_{core}-instance, there is still counterfactual dependence between the individual over-determining events and the overdetermined event, which also makes the case very dissimilar to prototypical cases of overdetermination such as the firing squad.

Thus, having a causally efficacious core realizer by itself does not revive the exclusion problem. What if the instance of the total realizer as well as the instance of the core realizer is causally efficacious? The previous two sections tacitly assumed the actual realizer to be the actual total realizer of the mental property, because we assumed the realizer to necessitate the mental property. If the arguments from those sections are sound, the P^*-instance is not overdetermined by the P_{total}-instance and the M-instance, or at least not overdetermined in any objectionable way. We just saw that, *mutatis mutandis*, the same holds for P_{core} and M. What about the pair P_{total} and P_{core}? Perhaps the instances of P_{total} and P_{core} overdetermine the P^*-instance. But, as is the case with M and P_{total}, there is an intimate synchronic relationship between P_{total} and P_{core}, for P_{total} has P_{core} as a conjunct and thus necessitates it. If a necessary connection between the overdetermining property-instances is enough to dispel worries about the case's involving a particularly objectionable kind of overdetermination

178 Mental Causation

with respect to M and P_{total}, it should also dispel any such worries in the case of P_{total} and P_{core}.[42]

While it seems plausible that the instance of the actual core realizer is a cause of the later physical event, there are reasons for doubting that the instance of the actual total realizer is in fact capable of causing the later physical event. The possibility of the total realizer's thus being causally inert has advantages and disadvantages for non-reductive physicalists. On the one hand, it attenuates problems that arise from the possible over-determination of the physical effect: the fewer potential overdeterminers, the better. On the other hand, there is a danger that the mental property inherits the causal inertia of the total realizer. In what follows, I shall argue that the reasons for thinking that the instance of the total realizer is causally inert are at best inconclusive and that, even if it is thus inert, it does not follow that the instance of the mental property is likewise inert.

One might doubt that the instance of the actual total realizer causes the later physical event if one doubts that the later physical event counter-factually depends on the instance of the total realizer. The total realizer P_{total} is a conjunctive property some of whose conjuncts are about the laws of physics. Assume that one of the conjuncts of P_{total} is the property of being such that the laws of electricity are such-and-such. That conjunct fails to be instantiated at a world w which is like the actual world in particular fact until some time in the distant future, when a small violation of the laws of electricity occurs; hence, in w, P_{total} is not instantiated at the time at which P_{total} is instantiated in the actual world. Moreover, by the miracles approach, w comes out closer to the actual world than any other worlds where P_{total} is not instantiated (provided no big miracle occurs in those worlds), for w has more perfect match of particular fact with the actual world than those worlds. But P^* is still instantiated at w, because w does not differ from the actual world in particular fact until well after P^* is instantiated. Thus, 'If P_{total} had not been instantiated, then P^* would not have been instantiated' is false, and the P^*-instance does not counter-factually depend on the P_{total}-instance.

---

[42] Bennett (2003) is worried about the possible overdetermination of the physical effect by the instances of what I have called P_{total} and P_{core} too, but her own account of overdetermination should in fact dispel the worries even more straightforwardly. Bennett holds that what is required for overdetermination is not merely the truth of the claims from the $(O_1)/(O_2)$ family, but their non-vacuous truth. Owing to the necessitation of P_{core} by P_{total}, the counterfactual 'If P_{total} had been instantiated without P_{core}, then P^* would still have been instantiated' comes out vacuously true, so, by Bennett's standards, the P^*-instance is not overdetermined by the P_{total}-instance and the P_{core}-instance in the first place. See also Sider 2003.

It does not follow, however, that the P_{total}-instance does not cause the P^*-instance, for we did not assume counterfactual dependence to be necessary for causation. Moreover, the argument against the counterfactual dependence of the P^*-instance on the P_{total}-instance can be questioned. The argument assumes that the conjunct of P_{total} that is about laws of physics is about those laws' holding everywhere and at any time. But if the purpose of the nomic conjunct is to ensure that the realizer necessitates the mental property, it suffices for it to require that the laws of physics are such-and-such more locally, that is, in and perhaps around the space–time region where the core realizer is instantiated. The local failure of the laws of physics would still suffice to prevent the total realizer from being instantiated, but perhaps it likewise suffices to prevent the later physical event from occurring. If the laws of electricity had been different while and where my c-fibres fired, perhaps my hand would not have moved towards the aspirin after all.

Setting the issue of counterfactual dependence aside, one might deny that the P_{total}-instance causes the P^*-instance if one thought that instances of P_{total} are *per se* incapable of causing anything. Thus, one might think that P_{total}, just like the property of shattering-in-one-minute (see Section 1.5), fails to be a causal property. Why should one think so? One of the conjuncts of P_{total} is the property that the laws of physics are such-and-such. It might seem that instances of this kind of property can never cause or be caused by anything.[43] It might seem, further, that being a non-causal property is closed under conjunction:

(CLOSURE-&) If the property of being F is non-causal, then the property of being F and G is non-causal for any G.[44]

Given that the nomic conjunct of P_{total} is non-causal, it follows from (CLOSURE-&) that P_{total} itself is non-causal.

If (CLOSURE-&) is true, the causal inertia of the nomic conjunct of P_{total} spreads to P_{total} itself. Douglas Keaton thinks that it spreads even further. He holds that being a non-causal property is closed not merely under conjunction, but under disjunction as well (Keaton 2012: 253):

---

[43] McLaughlin (2009) holds this with respect to Shoemaker's 'causal laws' (2007: 6). Christensen and Kallestrup (2012) build on McLaughlin's argument; they focus on the issue of whether realizers can be effects (see Section 2.4).

[44] Keaton (2012: 251) endorses the principle that a conjunctive property is causal just in case each of its conjunct properties is causal. This principle entails (but is not entailed by) (CLOSURE-&). McLaughlin (2009) seems to assume something like (CLOSURE-&) too.

(closure-V) If the property of being F is non-causal, then the property of being F or G is non-causal for any G.

Given (closure-V) and given that P_{total} is non-causal, the disjunctive property that contains P_{total} and all other possible total realizers of M as disjuncts is non-causal too. By the strong supervenience of mental properties on physical properties, the instantiation of that disjunctive property is strictly equivalent to the instantiation of M. One might or might not be inclined to identify properties whose instantiations are strictly equivalent,[45] but at any rate it seems that a property that is thus strictly equivalent to a non-causal property fails to be causal itself:

(closure-$\equiv$) If the property of being F is non-causal and necessarily F is instantiated just in case property G is, then G is non-causal.

Given (closure-$\equiv$) and given that the disjunctive property that contains P_{total} and all other possible total realizers of M as disjuncts is non-causal, M comes out non-causal too.

In sum, assuming that the nomic conjunct of P_{total} is non-causal, one can use the principles (closure-&), (closure-V), and (closure-$\equiv$) to argue that M is non-causal too.

It is easy to show that there must be something wrong with that argument. All we need to show this is the existence of a property F such that both F and its complement, that is, the property of being not-F, are non-causal. Such a property, it seems, is not hard to find.[46] A property that everything necessarily instantiates, such as the property of being self-identical, is a good candidate, for it seems that neither instances of this property nor instances of the complementary property of failing to be self-identical (which, of course, do not exist, because the complementary property cannot ever be instantiated by anything) can cause anything. Alternatively, we can take a property that is randomly distributed over all

---

[45] See Kim 1992 and Keaton 2012: 252–253 for discussion.

[46] Such a property would be very easy to find if being a non-causal property were closed under negation. This additional closure principle would yield a lot of causation by omission, however, which some might find objectionable. Here is how the commitment to causation by omission would come about. Assume that the property of being not-F is not causal. By the envisaged closure of being non-causal under negation, it follows that the property of being not-not-F is not causal. By (closure-$\equiv$), it follows that the property of being F is not causal (because the properties of being F and of being not-not-F are necessarily co-instantiated). In sum, if the property of being not-F is not causal, then the property of being F is not causal. Contrapositively, if the property of being F is causal, so is the property of being not-F.

The Exclusion Problem

actual and possible individuals. Such a property and its complement have a good claim to being non-causal. Suppose, then, that both the property of being F and the property of being not-F are non-causal. Let G be any causal property. By (CLOSURE-&), the property of being both G and F is non-causal; likewise for the property of being both G and not-F. By (CLOSURE-V), the property of being either both G and F or both G and not-F is non-causal too. Necessarily, something instantiates the property of being either both G and F or both G and not-F just in case it instantiates the property of being G. So by (CLOSURE-≡), the property of being G is non-causal (substitute 'the property of being either both G and F or both G and not-F' for 'the property of being F' in (CLOSURE-≡)). But we assumed G to be causal: contradiction.

Thus, the argument that purports to show that M is non-causal fails. Assuming that it is the same feature that is supposedly responsible for the nomic conjunct's being non-causal and for P_{total}'s being non-causal, we can locate the failure of the argument more precisely if we know more about why exactly the nomic conjunct of P_{total} is supposed to be non-causal. Perhaps the source of the nomic conjunct's being non-causal is that the property of being such that the laws of physics are such-and-such is extrinsic. It seems plausible that extrinsicality is closed under conjunction and strict equivalence.[47] It also seems plausible that extrinsicality is closed under complementation: if the property of being F is extrinsic, so is the property of being not-F (see Lewis 1983: 199). These features of extrinsicality allow us to construct a counterexample to the closure of extrinsicality under disjunction. Take the properties of being accompanied, of being unaccompanied, and of being square. The property of being accompanied is extrinsic. By the closure of extrinsicality under complementation, so is the property of being unaccompanied. By the closure of extrinsicality under conjunction, the property of being square and accompanied is extrinsic, as is the property of being square and unaccompanied. If extrinsicality were closed under disjunction, the property of being either both square and accompanied or both square and unaccompanied would be extrinsic, but by the closure of extrinsicality under strict equivalence, if this property were extrinsic, so would the equivalent property of being square, which is not extrinsic.[48] So extrinsicality cannot be closed under disjunction. If extrinsicality is the source of the nomic

---

[47] At least the closure of extrinsicality under strict equivalence seems plausible on the orthodox view that intrinsicality and extrinsicality are non-hyperintensional. Hyperintensional accounts of intrinsicality and extrinsicality such as Bader's (2013) may reject that kind of closure.

[48] The example is from Lewis (1983: 200), whose assumption of the closure of extrinsicality under conjunction is tacit; he also tacitly assumes that properties that are strictly equivalent are identical.

conjunct's being non-causal, the argument for the total realizer's being non-causal fails because (CLOSURE-V) fails. (Notice that, if extrinsicality is behind being non-causal in that argument, the counter-argument is strengthened, for given the closure of extrinsicality under complementation, it is straightforward to find a property such that both the property and its complement are extrinsic and, thus, non-causal.)

We need not, however, concede in the first place that total realizers are non-causal properties because of the supposed extrinsicality of the nomic properties they contain as conjuncts. For one thing, the nomic properties need not be extrinsic at all. If the laws of nature can vary independently of whether the bearer of our nomic property is alone in the universe or not, the nomic properties might come out intrinsic (see Langton and Lewis 1998: 339). Even if they come out extrinsic, they might still be causal. Extrinsicality is a matter of degree. The property of being a sibling, say, is more extrinsic than the property of being a brother (see Lewis 1983: 197). In Section 1.5, we merely required that a property be *sufficiently* intrinsic (and temporally intrinsic) in order to be causal. Even if they are on the extrinsic side of the spectrum, nomic properties might meet this requirement. (Analogously, someone might be rather short, yet sufficiently tall to do a certain task.)

The total realizers contain properties about background conditions as conjuncts besides the core realizers and the nomic conjuncts. The properties about background conditions are likely to qualify as extrinsic too and thus are another potential source of the total realizers' being non-causal. Like the nomic conjuncts, however, the mere extrinsicality of the properties about background conditions does not imply that they are too extrinsic to be causal, for they might still be *sufficiently* intrinsic.

So far we have considered the distinction of core vs total realizers in the context of non-reductive physicalism. Is an analogous distinction needed in the case of super-nomological dualism? According to super-nomological dualism, the relation between the bases of mental properties and the mental properties themselves is a matter of psychophysical laws. In other words, the instantiation of a physical base together with the psychophysical laws necessitates the instantiation of the mental property. It seems that, like the necessitation of the mental property by its realizers according to non-reductive physicalism, this necessitation holds only if the physical base is a conjunctive property that includes properties pertaining to background conditions and properties pertaining to 'ordinary' laws of nature as conjuncts, besides a physical base property in the narrow sense. Indeed, it seems that, for a given mental property, this base property in the narrow sense is identical to what non-reductive physicalists take to be the core

The Exclusion Problem

realizer of the mental property, and it seems that the conjunctive property is identical to what non-reductive physicalists take to be the total realizer of the mental property. Thus, super-nomological dualists should make the same kind of distinction as non-reductive physicalists and apply it to the very same physical properties. Super-nomological dualists could call the non-reductive physicalists' total realizers *total bases* of mental properties and the non-reductive physicalists' core realizers *core bases*.

The issues ramify for super-nomological dualists just as they did for non-reductive physicalists. The solutions are analogous too. The instance of the core base of the mental property causes the later physical effect by counterfactual dependence. So does the instance of the mental property. Thus, if the later physical effect is overdetermined, the case is very dissimilar to prototypical cases of overdetermination. It is also dissimilar to prototypical cases of overdetermination by virtue of the intimate synchronic relation between the instance of the core base of the mental property and the instance of the mental property itself. While the instantiation of the core base no longer implies the instantiation of the mental property with super-nomological necessity, the core base is a constitutive part of another property (namely the total base) that does imply the instantiation of the mental property. The question of whether the instance of the total base is capable of causing anything receives the same answer as the question of whether the total realizer is capable of causing anything, for we are dealing with one and the same property. The question of whether the mental property somehow inherits the (putative) causal inertia of the total base is even more likely to be answered in the negative, however. For super-nomological dualists cannot follow the step of the argument for the causal inertia of realizers for the non-reductive physicalist case that assumed the instantiation of the mental property to be strictly equivalent to the instantiation of the disjunction of its total realizers.[49]

The upshot of this section is that if non-reductive physicalists make a distinction between total realizers, which necessitate the mental properties they realize, and core realizers, which do not, this distinction does not affect the solution to the exclusion problem. In particular, if the instance of a core realizer overdetermines a later physical event together with the instance of a mental property, the case we get is still very dissimilar to prototypical cases of overdetermination such as firing squad cases. The

---

[49] A proponent of the argument for the super-nomological dualist case could add a nomic conjunct about the actual psychophysical laws' being such-and-such to every disjunct. That would yield the strict equivalence between the mental property and the disjunction of its bases-cum-psychophysical-laws. This manoeuvre might seem to turn the disjuncts into rather arbitrary properties, however. At any rate, the counter-argument for the non-reductive physicalist case stands undefeated.

184   Mental Causation

total realizer might or might not turn out to be a non-causal property, but if it does, this does not affect the efficacy of the mental property. Similarly for super-nomological dualists who distinguish between core bases and total bases of mental properties.

It is worth repeating a point from Section 2.4. The argument for mental causation from Chapter 2 that showed the P^*-instance to be caused by the M-instance is completely independent of whether or not total realizers/ bases are causal properties. The argument used the disjunction of M's (total) realizers merely as a logical intermediary, not as a causal one. Thus, it does not require instances of total realizers to be capable of causing anything. And the property that is involved in the effect, P^*, need not realize anything in the first place, so the causal relation between the M-instance and the P^*-instance can be established independently of whether total realizers/bases turn out to be causal.

4.5   Sufficient Causes

In Section 4.1, I formulated the exclusion problem in terms of causation without qualifying the kind of causation that is supposed to be in play. Thus, (EFFICACY) says that some mental events cause physical events; (COMPLETENESS) says that every physical effect has a physical cause; and (EXCLUSION) says that no effect has more than one cause at a given time, unless it is overdetermined. Often the exclusion problem is formulated not in terms of causation *simpliciter*, but in terms of *sufficient* causation. Thus reformulated, the principle corresponding to (EFFICACY) says that some mental events are *sufficient* causes of physical events; the principle corresponding to (COMPLETENESS) says that every physical effect has a *sufficient* physical cause; and the principle corresponding to (EXCLU-SION) says that no effect has more than one *sufficient* cause at a given time, unless it is overdetermined.[50] Friends of formulations of the exclusion problem in terms of sufficient causes would also, I take it, be inclined to replace (EXCLUSION) with a version of the more specific principle (EXCLUSION*), which says that no effect has a mental and a distinct

---

[50] Formulations of the exclusion problem are found, for instance, in Kim 2005, Bennett 2007, Moore 2012, Carey 2013, and Morris 2015. Sometimes only some of the principles are formulated in terms of sufficient causation and others in terms of causation *simpliciter*. For instance, Bennett formulates the principles corresponding to (COMPLETENESS) and (EXCLUSION) in terms of sufficient causes, but formulates the principle corresponding to (EFFICACY) in terms of causation *simpliciter*. For the claims in Bennett's exclusion problem to be inconsistent, however, the principle corresponding to (EFFICACY) must be read as talking about sufficient causation too. Perhaps hybrid formulations of the problem are possible that still make the principles inconsistent, but I shall confine myself to formulations that talk about sufficient causes throughout.

The Exclusion Problem 185

physical cause at the same time, unless it is overdetermined. Reformulated in terms of sufficient causes, the principle says that no effect has a *sufficient* mental cause and a distinct *sufficient* physical cause that occur at the same time, unless it is overdetermined. In sum, we get the following new version of the exclusion problem in terms of sufficient causes (the principles (DISTINCTNESS) and (NON-OVERDETERMINATION) do not talk about causation, so they retain their original formulations):

(DISTINCTNESS)	All mental events are distinct from physical events.
(EFFICACY-S)	Some mental events are sufficient causes of physical effects.
(COMPLETENESS-S)	Every physical event that has a cause at all has a sufficient physical cause.
(EXCLUSION*-S)	No effect has a sufficient mental cause and a distinct sufficient physical cause that occur at the same time, unless it is overdetermined.
(NON-OVERDETERMINATION)	The effects of mental events are not systematically overdetermined.

Like the principles from the original presentation of the exclusion problem, (DISTINCTNESS), (EFFICACY-S), (COMPLETENESS-S), (EXCLU-SION*-S), and (NON-OVERDETERMINATION) are inconsistent, or at least in tension with one another.

This section investigates how the exclusion problem fares if it is formulated by these five principles. We shall see that the nature of the problem depends on what exactly we understand by sufficient causation. Generally, the exclusion problem will turn out to be harder to solve than the problem formulated in terms of causation *simpliciter*. The difficulties do not spread to the original exclusion problem and our solution, however, for we shall see that, on our solution, the original exclusion problem does not entail the version of the problem in terms of sufficient causes.

There are two salient ways of understanding sufficient causation. First, we can understand a sufficient cause as one that transfers a physical quantity on its effect. Second, we can understand a sufficient cause as one that is modally sufficient, in a sense to be spelled out, for its effects. In what follows, I will discuss these different ways of understanding sufficient causes in turn. The discussion of sufficient causation as transference will allow us to build on results from previous chapters.

Let us first consider sufficient causes as characterized in terms of transference. On the face of it, it might seem tempting to flesh out such a characterization by saying that event c is a sufficient cause of event e if and only if c transfers a physical quantity to e. But there is an immediate complication. Recall our observation from Section 1.6, according to which there can be transference without causation, as in the case of a rock that is first heated over a fire and then thrown at a bottle, which shatters. The fire transfers a physical quantity (namely heat) on the bottle, but does not qualify as a cause of the shattering; *a fortiori*, the fire does not qualify as a *sufficient* cause of the shattering. So transference cannot be a sufficient condition for being a sufficient cause and hence transference cannot be a necessary and sufficient condition, as our initial characterization has it. We can, however, still formulate at least a partial characterization of sufficient causes in terms of transference by formulating a necessary condition for sufficient causation in terms of transference, that is, by saying that event c is a sufficient cause of event e only if c transfers a physical quantity on e. For our purposes, this partial characterization will suffice.

(In what follows, I shall confine myself to discussing sufficient causation as partially characterized in terms of the transference of a physical quantity. *Mutatis mutandis*, the arguments would also apply if we partially characterized sufficient causation in terms of the transference of powers instead.)

Suppose that (DISTINCTNESS), (EFFICACY-S), and (COMPLETENESS-S) are all true. Thus, there is a mental event that transfers a physical quantity on a later physical event. There is also a physical event distinct from, but simultaneous with, the mental event that also transfers a physical quantity on the later physical event; presumably, the first physical event is the realizer or base event of the mental event. Would such a situation be acceptable? It seems hard to make sense of the idea that the mental event transfers an additional amount of the physical quantity on the later physical event, or an additional kind of quantity. Perhaps non-reductive physicalists could try to explain such a double transference by claiming that mental causes and the simultaneous physical causes transfer the same (token) dose of the quantity in question (see Bennett 2008: 294). The mass of a statue and the mass of the lump of clay that constitutes the statue do not add up; rather, the statue and the lump seem to have the same (token) mass. Similarly, non-reductive physicalists might claim, when a physical cause and a distinct mental cause transfer a quantity to a physical effect, this does not require that the mental cause transfer a distinct (token) dose of that quantity. Whether we think of this response as a denial of the (EXCLUSION*-S) principle or the (NON-OVERDETERMINATION) principle does not matter for the dialectic; what does matter is that the resulting situation where the mental cause and the physical cause transfer the same (token) dose of the physical quantity to the physical effect is claimed not to be metaphysically problematic.

I will leave it open how plausible this claim is, but things certainly get worse for mental causation with sufficient causation as transference. Whatever its merits given non-reductive physicalism, the 'two transfers, one dose' response is not open to dualists, super-nomological or otherwise. By dualists' lights the relation between the mental cause and the physical cause is less intimate than the relation between a mental property-instance and its realizer-instance is according to non-reductive physicalism, because the instance of the base of the mental property no longer necessitates the instance of the mental property. Given that the connection between the mental property-instance and its physical base is contingent, it is hard to see how dualists could still claim that the mental cause and the physical cause transfer one and the same (token) dose of a physical quantity on the effect. (Compare: if, *per impossibile*, the existence of the lump of clay no longer necessitated the existence of the statue, could one still claim that their masses did not add up?)

Further, given the characterization of sufficient causation as transfer, non-reductive physicalists and dualists have a hard time accommodating certain cases which, it seems, have as good a claim as any to be cases of mental causation. In particular, they have a hard time accommodating the causation of bodily movements by mental events via muscle contraction. We saw in Section 2.6 that muscle contractions work by double prevention: calcium release at the neuromuscular junction causes the muscle to contract by preventing the obstruction of the binding sites of myosin and actin, which, unless prevented, prevents the muscle contracting. No transfer takes place between the calcium release and the muscle contraction. Thus, the calcium release is not a sufficient cause of the contraction. Moreover, there can be no chain of events that are connected by sufficient causation that contains the link between the calcium release and the contraction as a (non-redundant) link. But mental events can only be sufficient causes of bodily movements through such a chain. Therefore, mental events cannot be sufficient causes of bodily movements. Strictly speaking, this result is not a denial of (EFFICACY-S), because mental events might still be sufficient causes of physical events further upstream on the causal chain, but it comes close enough to epiphenomenalism to be unacceptable.[51]

---

[51] For further discussion, see Russo 2016.

Mental Causation

A parallel argument shows that the instances of realizers or bases of mental properties, such as my c-fibre firing, cannot be sufficient causes of bodily movements either, for they, too, could only achieve this via a chain of sufficient causes that contains the link between the calcium release and the contraction as a (non-redundant) link. On the one hand, the result that realizers or bases are not sufficient causes of bodily movements attenuates the difficulties of explaining how physical effects such as those movements can have both a sufficient physical cause and a sufficient mental cause: as far as these difficulties are concerned, the fewer sufficient causes, the better. But this is not much of a consolation, for by itself the result that realizers or bases cannot be sufficient causes of bodily movements is very implausible. So is the parallel result that mental events cannot be sufficient causes of bodily movements. Overall, the situation looks bleak if sufficient causation requires transfer.

Fortunately, the trouble does not carry over to the counterfactual account of mental causation that I have defended. For we saw that double-prevention cases such as muscle contractions not only show that there is no transfer in what seem to be genuine cases of causation, but also show that there are cases of counterfactual dependence (and hence of causation) without transfer. Thus, mental causation on my account does not entail sufficient causation in a sense that requires the transfer of a physical quantity. Nor does my account entail that the physical causes of bodily movements are sufficient causes of these movements in a sense that requires transfer. Since neither the mental cause of a physical effect nor the physical cause of this effect needs to transfer anything on the effect, there is also no problem of explaining how *both* the mental cause and the physical cause could transfer a physical quantity on the effect.

Let us now consider sufficient causes that are characterized not in terms of the transfer of a physical quantity, but in terms of modal sufficiency. The idea behind this characterization is that the occurrence of sufficient causes implies the occurrence of their effects, at least in a suitable range of circumstances. In what range of circumstances? Certainly not in all possible circumstances, for otherwise there is never causation between distinct events that are sufficiently (temporally) intrinsic, for it is always possible for such distinct events to occur separately. How about restricting the relevant circumstances to nomologically possible ones? In other words, how about characterizing sufficient causes as events whose occurrence implies the occurrence of their effects with nomological necessity?[52]

---

[52] If some events imply other, *simultaneous* events with nomological necessity, this characterization would yield spurious cases of simultaneous causation. Even worse, we will get cases of backward

The Exclusion Problem

On such a characterization, only very big events would qualify as sufficient causes. For unless the causes are made very big, it is always nomologically possible for something to interfere and prevent the effect. Take, for instance, my throwing a dart at a balloon, which causes the balloon to burst. It might seem that my throwing is a sufficient cause of the balloon's bursting. But it does not, in conjunction with our laws of nature, entail that the balloon bursts. Something might interfere. And the possible interference is not limited to the actions of bystanders. Suppose that it takes a bit more than a second for my dart to reach the balloon. Then a strong laser beam sent at the time of my throw from one light-second away could have destroyed the dart and prevented the balloon from bursting. Actually, no such thing happens, but to make sure that no such thing happens in any worlds where our laws of nature hold and the sufficient cause of the bursting occurs, we need to make the sufficient cause big enough to include all the space–time points that are a potential source of interference. Given that such interference propagates at or below the speed of light, we would need to make the sufficient cause big enough to include a cross-section of the effect's past light cone that includes my throw (see Loewer 2007: 253–254). Such a cross-section is big indeed. It needs to include everything that is going on at the time of my throw as far as a light-second away from it – that is, everything that is going on within a radius of 300,000 kilometres.

It seems implausible that only very big events can be sufficient causes. We therefore need a characterization of them that does not require sufficient causes to imply their effects with nomological necessity, but still somehow deals with potential interfering factors. It seems promising to use counterfactuals for that purpose, by characterizing a sufficient cause as an event such that, had it occurred, the effect would have occurred. The advantage of using counterfactuals is that they take care of the potential interfering factors. If none of them are actually present, then, it seems, none of them are present in the closest worlds where the cause occurs. Notice that, while the present suggestion also uses counterfactuals, it is very different from our sufficient condition for causation in terms of counterfactual dependence. That sufficient condition uses counterfactuals of the form 'If this event had *not* occurred, then that event would *not* have occurred', while sufficient causation, according to the suggestion, is spelled

---

causation whenever there is backward nomological necessitation. Therefore it seems sensible to restrict the characterization to pairs of events where one occurs later than the other, as we did in previous chapters.

out by using counterfactuals of the form 'If this event *had* occurred, then that event *would have* occurred.'

The present suggestion is in need of refinement. Given that the putative sufficient cause and its effect both occur, it is trivially true that the effect would have occurred had the cause occurred, given Lewis's truth-conditions for counterfactuals. At least this is trivially true if we assume that the actual world is closer to itself than any other world is (see Lewis 1973b: 26–31). Given this assumption, the actual world, where the antecedent of our counterfactual is true, is the closest antecedent-world. In the actual world, the consequent of our counterfactual is also true, so the counterfactual is true. In order to avoid this triviality, we should demand not that the effect would have occurred if the cause had occurred, but that the effect would also have occurred if the cause had occurred in different circumstances.

What are the relevant different circumstances? It is tempting to say that the relevant different circumstances are sufficiently similar to the actual circumstances and that they should not involve interfering factors, but that is somewhat vague, and there is a danger of circularity if 'interfering factors' are in turn defined in terms of sufficient causes. A more promising suggestion is that the relevant circumstances are those where there are no other factors in play whatsoever, interfering or otherwise. In other words, the suggestion is that if the sufficient cause had been the only event occurring at the time at which it actually occurred, then the effect would have occurred as well.[53]

Again, this suggestion needs refinement, for few causes would have brought about their effects all by themselves. For instance, if I had thrown the dart, but there had been no gravitational field, then I might have missed the balloon. If I had thrown the dart, but there had been no balloon, then the balloon's bursting would not have occurred. We could build the various factors that are required for the effect's occurrence into the cause, but then causes again become too big and cumbersome. A more elegant alternative is to characterize sufficient causes in terms of membership of a set of simultaneous events that is sufficient to bring about the effect in the sense that, if all the members of the set had occurred and no other contemporaneous events, then the effect would still have occurred. (In the following, I will use the notion of a set of events' being *sufficient* for an event in this sense.) The

---

[53] This suggestion, together with the further refinement discussed below, is due to Paul and Hall 2013: 14–16.

members of the set besides the sufficient cause can represent background conditions, such as the presence of a gravitational field and of the balloon.

Membership in a set of events that is sufficient for the effect is not quite what we need yet. Often such sets can be enlarged with further events while retaining the collective sufficiency for the effect. For instance, if my throw, the gravitational field, etc. are sufficient for the balloon to burst, presumably the president's drinking tea, my throw, the gravitational field, etc. are also sufficient for the balloon to burst. But it seems odd to say that the president's drinking tea is a sufficient cause of the balloon's bursting.[54] In the example, the difference between the enlarged set and the original set is that the enlarged set minus the president's drinking tea is still sufficient for the balloon to burst, while the original set minus my throw is no longer sufficient for the balloon to burst. This suggests that what matters for being a sufficient cause is not membership in a set of events that are collectively sufficient for the effect, but membership in a set that is just big enough to be sufficient for the effect.[55] Let us define a set of events that occur at the same time as *minimally sufficient* for an event e if and only if, first, e would have occurred if all the members of the set had occurred, but no other contemporaneous events, and, second, it is not the case that e would have occurred if only some, but not all of the members of the set had occurred, but no other contemporaneous events (see Paul and Hall 2013: 16). In other words, a set of events is minimally sufficient for e if and only if it is sufficient for e, but no proper subset of it is sufficient for e. We can now state the modal characterization of sufficient causes: a *sufficient cause* of an event e is an event that is a member of a set of actually occurring events that is minimally sufficient for e (Paul and Hall 2013: 16). This characterization states necessary and sufficient conditions for sufficient causes. For our purposes, it will again be enough to work with a necessary condition. Thus, in what follows I will merely make use of the claim that *if* an event c is a sufficient cause of e, then c is a member of a set of actually occurring events that is minimally sufficient for e.[56]

---

[54] By the failure of counterfactuals to obey the rule of strengthening the antecedent (see Section 1.4), the sufficiency of the larger set does not follow logically from the sufficiency of the original set, but nonetheless there are many cases where both sets are sufficient.

[55] The suggestion is similar in spirit to Mackie's (1965) idea that causes are INUS conditions, that is, conditions that are insufficient but necessary parts of unnecessary but sufficient conditions.

[56] Taking membership in a minimally sufficient set of events to be a sufficient condition for being a sufficient cause would have the implausible result that the background conditions from the set are sufficient causes. By merely assuming the corresponding necessary condition for being a sufficient cause, we are not committing ourselves to this result.

What does the exclusion problem look like if sufficient causation is understood like this? Let us first consider claim (EFFICACY-S), which says that some mental events are sufficient causes of physical effects. We can easily find a set of simultaneous events that contains my headache and that is sufficient for my hand to move towards the aspirin. We can find a set of events, that is, that contains my headache and that is such that my hand would have moved had all members in the set occurred, but no other events at the time in question. This set contains my headache, my c-fibre firing and events that represent various background conditions, such as the presence and integrity of the rest of my body. The question is whether this set is also *minimally* sufficient for my hand's movement. In particular, the question is whether the events in the set minus the headache would still have brought about my hand's movement if no other events had occurred at the time in question.

The answer depends on whether non-reductive physicalism or dualism is true. Consider dualism first. Given dualism, it is metaphysically possible for the c-fibre firing to occur without the headache. If the c-fibre firing had occurred without the headache, but together with the actual background conditions, my hand would still have moved. Thus, the set {c-fibre firing, background conditions} is sufficient for my hand's movement, so the set {c-fibre firing, headache, background conditions}, while also sufficient for my hand's movement, is not minimally sufficient for it. Hence my headache is not a sufficient cause of my hand's movement. More generally, given dualism, mental events cannot be sufficient causes of physical events: (EFFICACY-S) is false, and epiphenomenalism about sufficient causes is true.

Now consider non-reductive physicalism. For simplicity, I will assume my headache to be an instance of a total realizer of headaches, that is, an event whose occurrence necessitates the occurrence of the headache. Given non-reductive physicalism, it is still the case that the set {c-fibre firing, headache, background conditions} is sufficient for my hand's movement. Is there still a danger that the set is not minimally sufficient because its proper subset, {c-fibre firing, background conditions}, is already sufficient?

One might think that there is, for the following reason. It is impossible for the c-fibre firing to occur without the headache. *A fortiori* it is impossible for the c-fibre firing to occur and the background conditions to obtain without the headache. *A fortiori* it is impossible for the c-fibre firing to occur and the background conditions to obtain without the occurrence of *any other* contemporaneous events. Thus, when we consider the counterfactual 'If the c-fibre firing had occurred and the background conditions had obtained, but no other contemporaneous events had occurred, then

The Exclusion Problem

my hand would still have moved', we are considering a counterfactual with an impossible antecedent. This counterfactual is (vacuously) true, one might continue to reason; therefore the set {c-fibre firing, background conditions} is sufficient for my hand's movement; therefore the set {c-fibre firing, headache, background conditions} is not minimally sufficient; therefore the headache is not a sufficient cause of my hand's movement.

This way of reasoning leaves few sufficient causes, because it leaves few minimally sufficient sets of events. Consider the following parallel argument: I throw a dart at a balloon, but this time I throw the dart particularly vigorously. The balloon bursts. It seems that my throwing the dart vigorously has a good claim to being a sufficient cause of the balloon's bursting, but so does my throwing the dart *simpliciter* (it does not take a particularly vigorous thrown to burst the balloon).[57] But, the reasoning goes, my throwing the dart *simpliciter* cannot be a sufficient cause of the balloon's bursting. For suitable background conditions, the set {my throwing, my throwing vigorously, background conditions} is sufficient for the balloon to burst. It is impossible for me to throw the dart vigorously without throwing it. *A fortiori* it is impossible for me to throw the dart vigorously and for the background conditions to obtain without the occurrence of *any other* contemporaneous events, such as my throwing the dart *simpliciter*. Thus, it is vacuously true that if I had thrown the dart vigorously, the background conditions had obtained, but *no other* contemporaneous events had occurred, then the balloon would have burst. Therefore, the set {my throwing vigorously, background conditions} is sufficient for the balloon's bursting; therefore, the original set, {my throwing, my throwing vigorously, background conditions}, is not minimally sufficient; therefore, my throwing *simpliciter* is not a sufficient cause of the balloon's bursting.

One might conclude that neither my throwing *simpliciter* nor my headache are sufficient causes. Generalizing from the headache example, non-reductive physicalists then have to deny (EXCLUSION-S) and accept epiphenomenalism about sufficient mental causes, just as dualists had to. But non-reductive physicalists do not have to give in so easily. A natural response to the above arguments, which supposedly show that neither my headache nor my throwing the dart *simpliciter* are sufficient causes, is to

---

[57] I am not engaging in the use of any 'proportionality' constraint on causation here (see Yablo 1992); my argument merely requires that my throwing the dart *simpliciter* should count as a sufficient cause of the balloon's bursting. For recent discussions of proportionality in the context of mental causation, see Weslake 2013, Harbecke 2014, and McDonnell 2017.

insist on a reading of sufficiency and minimal sufficiency that does not have this consequence.

Here is the reading we should advocate on behalf of non-reductive physicalists who want to claim that there are sufficient mental causes. We should, first, demand that the phrase 'no other contemporaneous events' in the definition of sufficiency and minimal sufficiency not be read as 'no other contemporaneous *whatsoever*', which is the reading used in the above arguments. Rather, we should demand that 'no other contemporaneous events' be read as 'no other contemporaneous events *other than those necessitated by the events in the set in question*'. Unless we use the latter reading, virtually any set of events counts as sufficient for virtually any event owing to the vacuous truth of the relevant counterfactual, which would leave us with few *minimally* sufficient sets of events.

Second, we should not infer lack of minimal sufficiency from the sufficiency of sets that are subsets in name only. For instance, even if we read 'no other contemporaneous events' in the way just suggested, the set {c-fibre firing, background conditions} is still already sufficient for my hand's movements, for if all members of the set had occurred, but no other contemporaneous events other than those necessitated by the events in the set, then my hand would still have moved. But if all members of the set had occurred, but no other contemporaneous events other than those necessitated by the events in the set, then my headache would still have occurred. So the sufficiency of the set {c-fibre firing, background conditions} does not show that the headache is dispensable in bringing about the movement of my hand. If one takes the sufficiency of the set {c-fibre firing, background conditions} to show that the occurrence of *some, but not all* events in the set {headache, c-fibre firing, background conditions} suffices for the movement of my hand, one is again relying on the vacuous truth of the relevant counterfactual, because a situation where the c-fibre firing occurs and the background conditions obtain but not all members of {headache, c-fibre firing, background conditions} occur is impossible.

In order to accommodate these insights, I suggest adopting the following modified definition of minimal sufficiency: a set of events that occur at the same time is *minimally sufficient* for an event e if and only if, first, e would have occurred if all the members of the set had occurred, but no other contemporaneous events *other than those necessitated by the events in the set in question* and, second, it is not the case *or merely vacuously true* that e would have occurred if only some, but not all of the members of the set had occurred, but no other contemporaneous events *other than those necessitated by the events in the subset in question*.

The Exclusion Problem 195

Given the new definition of minimal sufficiency, it is possible for the headache to be a member of a set that is minimally sufficient for the hand's movement, because it is possible for {headache, c-fibre firing, background conditions} to be such a set. At least this is possible in principle and not forestalled by the necessary connection between the c-fibre firing and the headache. The headache can satisfy our necessary condition for being a sufficient cause by being a member of this set.[58] Similarly, the c-fibre firing can satisfy the necessary condition for being a sufficient cause of the hand's movement by virtue of being a member of the set {c-fibre firing, background conditions}, which is also minimally sufficient for the hand's movement. Given the new definition of minimal sufficiency, the sufficiency of the set {c-fibre firing, background conditions} does *not* undermine the minimal sufficiency of the set {headache, c-fibre firing, background conditions}.

Assume that the headache and the c-fibre firing are indeed both sufficient causes of the hand's movement. Would this yield overdetermination? If so, would the overdetermination be problematic? On the face of it, it seems that one could still deny that overdetermination follows. One could deny, that is, that (EXCLUSION*-s) is true.[59] For nothing that has been argued in the meantime diminishes the plausibility of the argument against claims (O_1^*) and (O_1^{**}) from Section 4.2. These claims, recall, stated a necessary condition for the hand's movement's being overdetermined by the headache and the c-fibre firing, namely the condition that the hand would still have moved if the headache had occurred without the c-fibre firing.

Perhaps the situation is different and a denial of (O_1^*) and (O_1^{**}) is more problematic if we are assuming that the hand's movement has two distinct sufficient causes and not merely two distinct causes, however. Karen Bennett holds that denying (O_1^*) or (O_1^{**}) threatens the causal sufficiency of the mental cause for the physical effect (see Bennett 2003: 481, 2008: 289). Her argument, adapted to our example, is as follows: if (O_1^*) or (O_1^{**}) is false, it is not the case that my hand would still have moved if the headache had

---

[58] Likewise for a number of other events that are constituted by supervenient properties. But this yields no problematic overgeneration of sufficient causes, because we are merely dealing with a necessary condition for sufficient causation.

[59] Lowe (1999, 2000, 2008) discusses a case of the following kind: a physical event p_1 is a sufficient cause of a simultaneous mental event m, which in turn is a sufficient cause of a later physical event p_2, such that, by the transitivity of sufficient causation, p_1 is also a sufficient cause of p_2. This case would constitute a counterexample to (EXCLUSION*-s), because p_1 and m are two simultaneous sufficient causes of p_2, but do not seem to overdetermine p_2. I am sceptical about this way of arguing against (EXCLUSION*-s), however, because of worries about the transitivity of causation and about simultaneous causation that were discussed in earlier chapters.

occurred without the c-fibre-firing. Thus, the headache needs the help of the c-fibre firing to bring about my hand's movement. But if the headache needs the help of the c-fibre firing in order to bring about the hand's movement, it is not itself sufficient for it. So a denial of $(O_1{}^*)$ or $(O_1{}^{**})$ is incompatible with the headache's being a sufficient cause of my hand's movement.

Bennett's argument succeeds only if sufficient causes have to bring about their effects all by themselves. As we saw earlier in this section, however, this notion of sufficient causes is unworkable, because only very big events bring about other events all by themselves. If, as we are currently assuming, a sufficient cause has to be a member of a set of events that is minimally sufficient for the effect, then Bennett's argument no longer applies, for nothing prevents the c-fibre firing from also being a member of the relevant set of events that is minimally sufficient for the hand's movement, like the set {headache, c-fibre firing, background conditions}.[60] In fact, if the c-fibre firing is a member of a minimally sufficient set that also includes the headache, it is the truth of $(O_1{}^*)$ and $(O_1{}^{**})$ that threatens the causal sufficiency of the headache for the hand's movement, not their falsity. For the truth of these counterfactuals at least comes close to saying that the set {headache, c-fibre firing, background conditions} is not minimally sufficient because the subset {headache, background conditions} already is sufficient.[61] Perhaps the lesson to be learned is merely that we have started with the wrong set and that we should take {headache, background conditions} as minimally sufficient for the hand's movement. But in any event Bennett's argument does not prevent us from endorsing an argument against (EXCLUSION*-s) that is based on the denial of $(O_1{}^*)$ or $(O_1{}^{**})$.[62]

---

[60] Mills (1996: 106) endorses a different necessary condition for an event's being 'causally sufficient' for another event. Applied to our case, Mills's condition says that if the headache had not occurred, *then if it had*, my hand would have moved. This condition is consistent with the falsity of $(O_1{}^*)$ and $(O_1{}^{**})$, however, since the headache-worlds that are closest to the no-headache-worlds that are closest to the actual world need not coincide with the no-c-fibre-firing-but-headache-worlds that are closest to the actual world. The condition invoked by Mills is also discussed in Yablo 1992.

[61] Since the occurrence of the headache merely necessitates the instantiation of some realizer or other of headaches, but does not necessitate the instantiation of a specific realizer, the set {headache, background conditions} is not a subset-in-name-only of {headache, c-fibre firing, background conditions} (unlike the set {c-fibre firing, background conditions}).

[62] Bennett's argument does not threaten the causation *simpliciter* of the hand's movement by virtue of the counterfactual dependence of the hand's movement on both the headache and the c-fibre firing, for this counterfactual dependence is clearly not undermined by the falsity of $(O_1{}^*)$ or $(O_1{}^{**})$. Nor does her argument have to rule out the causal sufficiency of the headache if one takes it to be a necessary condition for event c's being a sufficient cause of event e that the material conditional 'If c occurs, then e occurs' is true in a range of worlds that are sufficiently similar to the actual world. For if the c-fibre firing could not easily have failed to occur (perhaps because it is not very fragile), then the closest worlds where the headache occurs in the absence of the c-fibre firing (in some of which my hand does not move if $(O_1{}^*)$/$(O_1{}^{**})$ is false) are rather dissimilar to the actual world. It is at least

The Exclusion Problem   197

Should such an argument against (EXCLUSION*-S) fail, one could follow the fall-back strategy we used in Section 4.3 and deny (NON-OVERDETERMINATION) instead. It is inessential to this strategy how the overdetermination of physical effects by mental and physical causes (which is assumed for the sake of the argument) comes about. Thus, the fall-back strategy can also be followed if the overdetermination is assumed be due to the fact that both the mental cause and the physical cause are sufficient causes of the physical effect in the sense of each being a member of a set of events that is minimally sufficient for the effect. For irrespective of how the overdetermination is assumed to come about, the case of mental causation is very dissimilar to prototypical cases of overdetermination like the firing squad. In particular, irrespective of the kind of causal relation that is assumed, the metaphysical connection between the two causes is much more intimate owing to the metaphysically necessary (or, in the case of super-nomological dualism, at least nomologically necessary) connection between the headache and the c-fibre firing than it is in cases like the firing squad. Moreover, nothing we have learned in this section tells against the counterfactual dependence of the physical effect on both the mental and the physical cause. This counterfactual dependence remains a major aspect in which cases of mental causation are dissimilar to prototypical cases of overdetermination.

Thus, if we formulate a necessary condition for sufficient causation in terms of minimal sufficiency and if both the headache and the c-fibre firing can be sufficient causes of the hand's movement, then the exclusion problem can be solved by denying either (EXCLUSION*-S) or (NON-OVERDETERMINATION). Unfortunately, it turns out that neither the headache nor the c-fibre firing is a sufficient cause of the hand's movement, so this route to solving the exclusion problem is blocked. The reason does not lie in the modal connection between the two causes, which we discussed in the context of the original formulation of minimal sufficiency above, but, as with sufficient causation as transfer, lies with the inability of our account of sufficient causes to deal with cases of double prevention. To see why double prevention makes trouble for sufficient causes as members of minimally sufficient sets of events, consider the example of double prevention involving idealized neurons from Section 1.6 (see Figure 1.1). In the

---

an open question whether these worlds are within the range of worlds where the occurrence of the headache needs to materially imply my hand's movement in order for the former to be a sufficient cause of the latter.

example, the firing of c causes the firing of e. But there is no set of events that is minimally sufficient for the firing of e and that includes c. The sets {the firing of c, the firing of b, the firing of a} and {the firing of c, the firing of a} are sufficient for the firing of e, but they are not minimally sufficient, because the set {the firing of a} is sufficient too: if the only event to occur at the relevant time had been the firing of a, then e would still have fired.[63] Thus, the firing of c is not a sufficient cause of the firing of e.

As was the case for sufficient causation as transfer, the fact that muscle contractions operate by double prevention threatens the status of mental and physical causes of bodily movements if sufficient causation is spelled out in terms of minimal sufficiency. Since the calcium release at the neuromuscular junction causes the muscle contraction by double prevention, the calcium release is not a member of a set of events that is minimally sufficient for the contraction and hence is not a sufficient cause of the contraction. Consequently, as was the case with sufficient causation as transfer, there can be no chain of events connected by sufficient causation that contains the link between the calcium release and the contraction as a (non-redundant) link. But, again, it seems that both the headache and the c-fibre firing could only be sufficient causes of a muscle contraction by being a link in such chain. Perhaps this last claim is a bit less obvious than it was in the case of sufficient causation as transfer, but it certainly seems plausible enough to shift the burden of proof to advocates of causal sufficiency. Thus, we are again left with a situation that is tantamount to epiphenomenalism and that also leaves fewer physical causes of bodily movements than seem to exist.

Fortunately, the problems of sufficient causation as minimal sufficiency, like the problems of sufficient causation as transfer, do not carry over to the account of mental causation by counterfactual dependence that I have defended. For the sufficiency of counterfactual dependence for causation yields the correct verdict that cases of double prevention, in muscle contraction or elsewhere, are cases of causation.

I have argued that the exclusion problem, when it is formulated in terms of sufficient causes, is no problem for the counterfactual account of causation, because causation by counterfactual dependence entails neither that a transfer takes place nor that the cause is a member of a set of events that is minimally sufficient for the effect. So far, I have focused on brain

---

[63] See Paul and Hall 2013: 190–194. Strictly speaking, all the sets would have to include background conditions such as the presence of neuron e. These background conditions are omitted for simplicity.

The Exclusion Problem 199

events such as my c-fibre firing as potential sources of trouble for mental causes. One might worry that physical events other than brain events exclude mental causes or that certain physical events exclude mental causes without being a sufficient cause in either of the two senses we have discussed. Before concluding this section, I shall briefly address such worries.

Let us first revisit the causation of bodily movements by double prevention. Owing to the mechanism of muscle contraction, events in the brain do not transfer anything on muscles, but merely release energy that has been transferred from a different source.[64] What about the events that do transfer the energy that is released when muscles contract? Might they exclude the existence of further causes? That seems unlikely. Energy is transferred to the myosin filaments by adenosine triphosphate (ATP) molecules that are present in the muscle fibre. The ATP 'cocks' the myosin filaments, providing them with energy that is released when the myosin moves the actin filaments forward during muscle contraction.[65] The earlier presence of the ATP molecules in the muscle fibre certainly does not rule out any further causes of the later muscle contraction that are simultaneous with the earlier presence of ATP.[66] On the contrary, the earlier presence of ATP clearly allows further causes of the muscle contraction as much as the tenseness of the myosin filaments does. More specifically, the earlier presence of ATP allows additional causes of the muscle contraction by counterfactual dependence. According to the counterfactual account I have presented, mental causes can operate by counterfactual dependence, so they are not threatened by the transfer source in muscle contractions.

A second potential threat comes from the large event whose occurrence implies the occurrence of the effect with nomological necessity. We discarded the suggestion that only events that imply the effect with nomological necessity should count as sufficient causes. We did so for good reason, because otherwise events that are smaller than a cross-section of an effect's past light cone could not be sufficient causes of the effect. One might worry, however, that irrespective of whether we characterize sufficient causation in terms of nomological necessitation, the big events that do nomologically necessitate other events do not leave room for any other

---

[64] At least the brain events do not transfer anything relevant, although in fact the calcium might transfer, say, a little bit of momentum to the tropomyosin. As in Section 1.6, I am idealizing slightly.

[65] See Guyton and Hall 2006: 76–79. ATP is in turn supplied by several processes, among them glycolysis (Guyton and Hall 2006: 76–79).

[66] By 'the ATP molecules' I mean those ATP molecules that are actually involved in the later 'cocking' of the myosin filaments.

causes of the latter events. If a big event and the laws of nature necessitate another event, can the necessitated event still have other causes? It can. We have implicitly assumed so all along. For we have assumed that determinism is true. If determinism is true, every time-slice of the universe is necessitated by the laws of nature and any other time-slice of the universe. *A fortiori*, every event is necessitated by the laws of nature and any (non-contemporaneous) time-slice of the universe. A time-slice of the universe is basically a very big event. But that all events are necessitated by the laws of nature and these very big events does not prevent the necessitated events from having ordinary causes, by counterfactual dependence or otherwise. In particular, an event may be necessitated by the laws of nature together with a time-slice of the universe while also having an ordinary cause that is simultaneous with this time-slice.[67] If there can be causation of effects by ordinary events under determinism, then there can be causation of effects by ordinary events even if these effects are necessitated by the laws of nature and events that are bigger than the ordinary causes.

It might be objected that, in ordinary cases, the ordinary cause is a part of the bigger event that nomologically necessitates the effect. For instance, my throwing the dart is a part of a cross-section of the past light cone of the balloon's bursting that nomologically necessitates that the balloon bursts. Putative mental causes, the objection continues, are not parts of those bigger nomologically necessitating events, however, and are therefore threatened in their efficacy by the bigger events.

As it stands, the objection misses the point, because nothing I have said rules out that the bigger events have mental events as parts.[68] But presumably what is meant is this: if a certain event is necessitated by another *physical* event (perhaps as big as a physical time-slice of the universe) and the laws of *physics*, then it cannot have a distinct mental cause. This new formulation of the objection brings us back to the first problem from the beginning of this chapter: if something is determined by the physical, how can it have additional mental causes? The answer should not come as a surprise: physical events can have mental causes by counterfactual dependence. Nothing prevents mental events from making a difference to physical events, even if these physical events are necessitated by physical laws and events. Indeed, for the reasons given in Chapter 2, this difference-making relation is almost unavoidable for non-reductive physicalists, and dualists can easily have it too by adopting

---

[67] For simplicity I'm talking here as though all events are instantaneous, which of course they are not. But the points can easily be generalized by taking into account all the time-slices that a given event overlaps.

[68] Although if the psychophysical laws are synchronic, they are idle in this necessitation; see note 1.

The Exclusion Problem 201

super-nomological dualism. What we cannot have, of course, is that mental events make a difference to a given physical event (except perhaps vacuously) if we hold fixed the physical past and the physical laws. But, as we saw in Chapter 3, this is not the right way to think about the situation. For we can also prevent *physical* events from making a difference to other physical events by holding further physical events fixed (suitable intermediate events, for instance). If we assess the difference-making claims correctly, mental events can be *bona fide* causes of physical events.

The upshot of this section is that the exclusion problem is generally more severe if it is formulated in terms of sufficient causation rather than in terms of causation *simpliciter*. We can spell out sufficient causation in terms of transfer of a physical quantity or in terms of minimal sufficiency. Either way, mental causation is in jeopardy; somewhat surprisingly, the causation of bodily movements by events in the brain is also in jeopardy. But the problems do not carry over to the account of mental causation by counterfactual dependence. Thus, the exclusion problem for other notions of causation yields indirect support to the account of mental causation that I have defended.[69]

4.6 Conclusion

At the heart of the exclusion problem are two claims: the claim that physical effects of physical causes can have distinct mental causes only if the mental and physical causes overdetermine the physical effects; and the claim that there is no widespread overdetermination of physical effects. We have seen that non-reductive physicalists and super-nomological dualists can respond in two ways. They can deny that mental causation entails overdetermination, or they can deny that the kind of overdetermination that would ensue would be problematic. We have also seen that non-reductive physicalists can deny that the nature of physical realizers has any detrimental consequences for the efficacy of the mental properties they realize. Similarly, super-nomological dualists can deny that the nature of physical bases has any such detrimental consequences for the efficacy of mental properties. When formulated in terms of sufficient causes rather than in terms of causation *simpliciter*, the exclusion problem is generally more severe, but none of this severity spills over to the account of mental causation by counterfactual dependence.

---

[69] For further discussion of the relation between different theories of causation and accounts of mental causation, see Bennett 2008: 293; Lycan 2009: 557–558; Hitchcock 2012b.

CHAPTER 5

Conclusion

What is going on in our minds has physical effects because it makes a difference to what is going on in the physical world. Generally, difference-making, or counterfactual dependence, suffices for causation. Both non-reductive physicalists and dualists can show that mental events make a difference to whether or not certain physical events occur. They can do so in the context of classical counterfactual approaches to causation by using the principle that counterfactual dependence is sufficient for causation. Alternatively, they can do so in the context of causal modelling theories by building a model that represents the patterns of difference-making that are true in a given case involving a (putative) mental cause. The model can be subjected to more sophisticated conditions for causation than simple counterfactual dependence, and the conclusion that there is mental causation emerges unscathed.

By appealing to the fact that the mind makes a difference, non-reductive physicalists and dualists can solve not merely the interaction problem but also the exclusion problem. If mental events are difference-making causes of physical effects, it does not follow that those effects are overdetermined by their mental causes and distinct physical causes, or at any rate it does not follow that cases of mental causation are similar to standard cases of overdetermination, such as firing squads, in any interesting respect.

In order to show that mental events make a difference to whether or not physical events occur, dualists have to assume that there are laws that relate mental and physical properties and that these laws could not have failed so easily as ordinary laws of nature. The resulting position, super-nomological dualism, is somewhat unorthodox and, as far as I know, has not been advocated before, but from a dualist perspective it seems worthwhile to adopt this position in order to be able to explain mental causation.

Non-reductive physicalists do not have to make any extra assumptions in order to secure the efficacy of the mental. As long as they assume that mental properties strongly supervene on physical properties, the result that

Conclusion 203

mental events have physical effects follows. Some non-reductive physical-ists have advocated positions stronger than the formulation in terms of strong supervenience that I have given here (see, e.g., Yablo 1992, Horgan 1993). Perhaps such a stronger formulation of non-reductive physicalism has other advantages, but if the arguments I have presented are sound, it is not needed for the purposes of making room for mental causation.

Thus, all prominent theories about the nature of mind can explain mental causation. (I have not mentioned *reductive* physicalists in a while, but it is clear that they can do so too.) This has repercussions for the philosophy of mind in general. Issues of mental causation have loomed large in the debate over the nature of mind. Worries that a certain theory might be committed to epiphenomenalism have been among the main reasons for rejecting that theory. In particular, the interaction problem has provided a main reason why people have rejected dualism, and the exclusion problem has provided a main reason why people have rejected non-reductive physicalism along with dualism. By showing that all the prominent theories about the nature of mind can accommodate mental causation, the account of mental causation by difference-making changes the dialectical situation. Issues of mental causation are taken out of the equation. Questions about the nature of mind will ultimately have to be decided on different grounds.

APPENDIX I

Counterfactuals and Spheres

The dualist argument for the counterfactual dependence of the P^*-instance on the M-instance from Section 2.5 goes as follows:

(16) If none of M's bases had been instantiated, then M would not have been instantiated. ($\sim\cup\mathbf{P}_M \,\square\!\!\!\rightarrow \sim M$)

(17) If M had not been instantiated, then none of M's bases would have been instantiated. ($\sim M \,\square\!\!\!\rightarrow \sim\cup\mathbf{P}_M$)

(18) If none of M's bases had been instantiated, then P^* would not have been instantiated. ($\sim\cup\mathbf{P}_M \,\square\!\!\!\rightarrow \sim P^*$)

---

(19) If M had not been instantiated, then P^* would not have been instantiated. ($\sim M \,\square\!\!\!\rightarrow \sim P^*$)

The non-vacuous truth of the premises, (16)–(18), yields the existence of a sphere $\mathbf{S}$ in which M is instantiated just in case a base of M is instantiated and which contains a world w where neither M nor a base of M nor P^* is instantiated (see Figure A.1, which repeats the earlier Figure 2.5).[1] It follows from the existence of such a sphere that (19) is true.

To see why (19) follows, and to see how exactly we get to the situation represented in Figure A.1 in the first place, let us proceed in three steps.

First, given that (16) and (17) are non-vacuously true, there is a sphere in which M is instantiated just in case a base of M is instantiated and that contains a world where neither M nor a base of M is instantiated. Proof: By the non-vacuous truth of (16), there is a world v where neither a base of M nor M is instantiated that it closer to the actual world than all worlds where M is instantiated in the absence of a base. By the non-vacuous truth of (17), there is a world u where neither M nor a base of M is instantiated that is closer to the actual world than all worlds where a base of M is instantiated in the absence

---

[1] Throughout this appendix, phrases of the form 'a sphere in which . . . if and only if . . .' should be read such that 'a sphere in which' takes wide scope over the biconditional.

Appendix I: Counterfactuals and Spheres

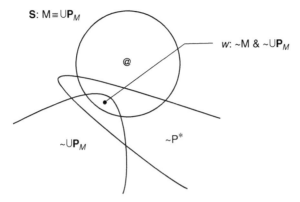

Figure A.1. (16) ($\sim\cup\mathbf{P}_M \square\!\!\rightarrow \sim M$), (17) ($\sim M \square\!\!\rightarrow \sim\cup\mathbf{P}_M$), (18) ($\sim\cup\mathbf{P}_M \square\!\!\rightarrow \sim P^*$) true

of M. Worlds v and u might be equally close to the actual world, or one might be closer to the actual world than the other.[2] If v and u are equally close, let **S** be a sphere that contains both worlds at the very edge; that is, let **S** be a sphere that contains no worlds that are less close to the actual world than v and u are. If one of v and u is closer to the actual world than the other, let **S** contain whichever world is closer at the very edge. Sphere **S** does not contain a world where M is instantiated in the absence of a base of M, for the worlds at its edge are closer to the actual world than any such worlds. Similarly, **S** does not contain a world where a base of M is instantiated in the absence of M. Thus, it is true in **S** that M is instantiated just in case a base of M is instantiated. By our choice of **S**, it contains a world where neither M nor a base of M is instantiated.

Second, given that (18) is non-vacuously true, any sphere that has the characteristics of **S**, that is, any sphere that contains a world where neither M nor a base of M is instantiated and in which it is true that M is instantiated just in case a base of M is instantiated, contains a world where neither a base of M nor P^* is instantiated that is closer to the actual world than any worlds where P^* is instantiated while no base of M is instantiated. Proof: Let **S** be a sphere in which it is true that M is instantiated just in case a base of M is instantiated. Let w be a world in **S** at which neither M nor a base of M is instantiated. Suppose that **S** does not contain a world where neither a base of M nor P^* is instantiated that is closer to the actual world than any worlds where P^* is instantiated while no base of M is instantiated. Suppose, in other

---

[2] It does *not* follow from the possibility that one of u and v is closer to the actual world than the other that the closest antecedent-worlds of (16) and (17) – if such there be – fail to coincide.

words, that no world in **S** where neither a base of M nor P^* is instantiated is closer to the actual world than any worlds where P^* is instantiated while no base of M is instantiated. There are two cases to consider. Sphere **S** might not contain a world where neither a base of M nor P^* is instantiated at all. Then w must be a world where P^* is instantiated while no base of M is instantiated. Any worlds where neither a base of M nor P^* is instantiated are outside of **S** and hence less close to the actual world than w, which renders (18) false, in contradiction to its (non-vacuous) truth. In the other case, **S** does contain worlds where neither a base of M nor P^* is instantiated, but none of these worlds is closer to the actual world than any worlds where P^* is instantiated while no base of M is instantiated. In this case, too, (18) comes out false, contrary to our assumption of its truth. For there are no antecedent-cum-consequent-worlds of (18) that are closer to the actual world than the antecedent-cum-consequent-worlds of (18) in **S** are. Since all the antecedent-cum-consequent-worlds of (18) in **S** fail to be closer to the actual world than any worlds where the antecedent of (18) is true while its consequent is false, (18) comes out false.

Third, let w be a world where neither a base of M nor P^* is instantiated that is closer to the actual world than any worlds where P^* is instantiated while no base of M is instantiated. Let w be contained in a sphere in which it is true that M is instantiated just in case a base of M is instantiated. Then at w neither M nor P^* is instantiated, and w is closer to the actual world than any worlds where P^* is instantiated while M is not, such that (19) is non-vacuously true. Proof: Again, let **S** be a sphere in which it is true that M is instantiated just in case a base of M is instantiated. Let w be a world in **S** where neither a base of M nor P^* is instantiated that is closer to the actual world than any worlds where P^* is instantiated while no base of M is instantiated. By the equivalence of M's instantiation with the instantiation of a base of M within **S**, w is a world where neither M nor P^* is instantiated. Further, by the equivalence, all worlds in **S** where P^* is instantiated while M is not instantiated are worlds where P^* is instantiated while no base of M is instantiated. By assumption, w is closer to the actual world than worlds of the latter kind. Therefore, w is also closer to the actual world than any worlds where P^* is instantiated while M is not instantiated. (If **S** does not contain any worlds where P^* is instantiated while M is not instantiated, then all such worlds are less close to actuality than w by virtue of being outside of **S**.)

In sum, and returning to Figure A.1, from the non-vacuous truth of (16), (17), and (18) we get the existence of a sphere **S** in which M is instantiated just in case a base of M is instantiated which contains a world w where neither M nor a base of M (nor P^*) is instantiated. It follows from the existence of such a sphere that (19) is non-vacuously true.

APPENDIX 2

Valid and Invalid Inference Rules for Counterfactuals

Valid	Invalid
$\phi \boxed{\rightarrow} \chi, \phi \,\&\, \chi \boxed{\rightarrow} \psi \vDash \phi \boxed{\rightarrow} \psi$	$\phi \boxed{\rightarrow} \chi, \chi \boxed{\rightarrow} \psi \vDash \phi \boxed{\rightarrow} \psi$
$\phi \boxed{\rightarrow} \chi, \Box[\chi \supset \psi] \vDash \phi \boxed{\rightarrow} \psi$	$\Box[\phi \supset \chi], \chi \boxed{\rightarrow} \psi \vDash \phi \boxed{\rightarrow} \psi$
$\phi \boxed{\rightarrow} \psi, \phi \Diamond\!\!\rightarrow \chi \vDash \phi \,\&\, \chi \boxed{\rightarrow} \psi$	$\phi \boxed{\rightarrow} \psi \vDash \phi \,\&\, \chi \boxed{\rightarrow} \psi$
$\Box[\phi \equiv \chi], \chi \boxed{\rightarrow} \psi \vDash \phi \boxed{\rightarrow} \psi$	
$\phi \boxed{\rightarrow} \chi, \chi \boxed{\rightarrow} \phi, \chi \boxed{\rightarrow} \psi \vDash \phi \boxed{\rightarrow} \psi$	
$\chi \Diamond\!\!\rightarrow \phi, \chi \,\&\, \phi \boxed{\rightarrow} \psi \vDash \chi \Diamond\!\!\rightarrow \psi$	
$\chi \boxed{\rightarrow} \phi, \chi \,\&\, \phi \Diamond\!\!\rightarrow \psi \vDash \chi \Diamond\!\!\rightarrow \psi$	
$\Box[\phi \supset \psi] \vDash \phi \boxed{\rightarrow} \psi$	

(Further valid and invalid inference rules involving counterfactuals can be found in Lewis 1973b: 31–36 and 1973c.)

207

References

Aimar, S. 2011. Counterfactuals, Overdetermination and Mental Causation. *Proceedings of the Aristotelian Society* 111: 469–477.

Armstrong, D.M. 1983. *What Is a Law of Nature?* Cambridge: Cambridge University Press.

Árnadóttir, S.T. and T. Crane. 2013. There is no Exclusion Problem. In S.C. Gibb, E.J. Lowe, and R. Ingthorsson, eds, *Mental Causation and Ontology*. New York: Oxford University Press, 248–266.

Aronson, J.L. 1971. On the Grammar of 'Cause'. *Synthese* 22: 414–430.

Averill, E.W. and B. Keating. 1981. Does Interactionism Violate a Law of Classical Physics? *Mind* 90: 102–107.

Bader, R.M. 2013. Towards a Hyperintensional Theory of Intrinsicality. *Journal of Philosophy* 110: 525–563.

Bailey, A.M., J. Rasmussen, and L. Horn. 2011. No Pairing Problem. *Philosophical Studies* 154: 349–360.

Baker, L.R. 1993. Metaphysics and Mental Causation. In J. Heil and A. Mele, eds, *Mental Causation*. Oxford: Clarendon Press, 75–95.

Baker, L.R. 2009. Nonreductive Materialism. In B.P. McLaughlin, A. Beckermann, and S. Walter, eds, *The Oxford Handbook of Philosophy of Mind*. Oxford: Oxford University Press, 109–127.

Baumgartner, M. 2009. Interventionist Causal Exclusion and Non-Reductive Physicalism. *International Studies in the Philosophy of Science* 23: 161–178.

Baumgartner, M. 2010. Interventionism and Epiphenomenalism. *Canadian Journal of Philosophy* 40: 359–384.

Beebee, H. 2017. Epiphenomenalism for Functionalists. In H. Beebee, C. Hitchcock, and H. Price, eds, *Making a Difference*. Oxford: Oxford University Press, 286–306.

Bennett, J. 2003. *A Philosophical Guide to Conditionals*. Oxford: Clarendon Press.

Bennett, K. 2003. Why the Exclusion Problem Seems Intractable, and How, Just Maybe, to Tract It. *Noûs* 37: 471–497.

Bennett, K. 2007. Mental Causation. *Philosophy Compass* 2: 316–337.

Bennett, K. 2008. Exclusion Again. In J. Hohwy and J. Kallestrup, eds, *Being Reduced*. Oxford: Oxford University Press, 280–305.

Bernstein, S. 2016. Overdetermination Underdetermined. *Erkenntnis* 81: 17–40.

Bhaskar, R. 1975. *A Realist Theory of Science*. Leeds: Leeds Books.

Block, N. 1978. Troubles with Functionalism. *Minnesota Studies in the Philosophy of Science* 9: 261–325.

BonJour, L. 2010. Against Materialism. In J. Hohwy and J. Kallestrup, eds, *The Waning of Materialism: New Essays on Reduction, Explanation, and Causation.* Oxford: Oxford University Press, 3–23.

Bourget, D. and D.J. Chalmers. 2014. What Do Philosophers Believe? *Philosophical Studies* 170: 465–500.

Brand, M. 1977. Identity Conditions for Events. *American Philosophical Quarterly* 14: 329–337.

Briggs, R. 2012. Interventionist Counterfactuals. *Philosophical Studies* 160: 139–166.

Burge, T. 1993. Mind-Body Causation and Explanatory Practice. In J. Heil and A. Mele, eds, *Mental Causation.* Oxford: Clarendon Press, 97–120.

Campbell, J. 2007. An Interventionist Approach to Causation in Psychology. In A. Gopnik and L. Schulz, eds, *Causal Learning.* Oxford: Oxford University Press, 58–66.

Campbell, K. 1990. *Abstract Particulars.* Oxford: Blackwell.

Carey, B. 2011. Overdetermination and the Exclusion Problem. *Australasian Journal of Philosophy* 89: 251–262.

Carroll, J.W. 1988. General Causation. In *PSA 1988: Proceedings of the Biennial Meeting of the Philosophy of Science Association, Vol. 1: Contributed Papers.* East Lansing, MI: Philosophy of Science Association, 311–317.

Carroll, J.W. 1991. Property-Level Causation? *Philosophical Studies* 63: 245–270.

Cartwright, N. 1989. *Nature's Capacities and Their Measurement.* Oxford: Oxford University Press.

Caston, V. 1997. Epiphenomenalisms, Ancient and Modern. *Philosophical Review* 106: 309–363.

Chalmers, D.J. 1996. *The Conscious Mind.* New York: Oxford University Press.

Christensen, J. and J. Kallestrup. 2012. Counterfactuals and Downward Causation: A Reply to Zhong. *Analysis* 72: 513–517.

Clifford, W.K. 1874. Body and Mind. *Fortnightly Review* 16: 714–736.

Collins, J. 2000. Preemptive Prevention. *Journal of Philosophy* 97: 223–234.

Crane, T. and D.H. Mellor. 1990. There Is No Question of Physicalism. *Mind* 99: 185–206.

Crook, S. and C. Gillett. 2001. Why Physics Alone Cannot Define the 'Physical': Materialism, Metaphysics, and the Formulation of Physicalism. *Canadian Journal of Philosophy* 31: 333–359.

Cross, C.B. 2006. Conditional Logic and the Significance of Tooley's Example. *Analysis* 66: 325–335.

Dancy, J. 1993. *Moral Reasons.* Oxford: Blackwell.

Davidson, D. 1969. The Individuation of Events. In N. Rescher, ed., *Essays in Honor of Carl G. Hempel.* Dordrecht: Reidel, 216–234.

Davidson, D. 1970. Mental Events. In L. Foster and J. Swanson, eds, *Experience and Theory.* New York: Humanities Press, 79–101.

References

Davidson, D. 1985. Reply to Quine on Events. In E. LePore and B. McLaughlin, eds, *Actions and Events: Perspectives on the Philosophy of Donald Davidson.* Oxford: Blackwell, 172–176.

Descartes, R. 1984–1991. *The Philosophical Writings of Descartes,* ed. and trans. J. Cottingham, R. Stoothoff, D. Murdoch, and A. Kenny, 3 vols. Cambridge: Cambridge University Press.

Descartes, R. 1996. *Oeuvres de Descartes,* ed. C. Adam and P. Tannery, 11 vols. Paris: Vrin.

Dowe, P. 2000. *Physical Causation.* Cambridge: Cambridge University Press.

Dunn, J. 2011. Fried Eggs, Thermodynamics, and the Special Sciences. *British Journal for the Philosophy of Science* 62: 71–98.

Ehring, D. 2003. Part-Whole Physicalism and Mental Causation. *Synthese* 136: 359–388.

Ehring, D. 2011. *Tropes: Properties, Objects, and Mental Causation.* Oxford: Oxford University Press.

Elga, A. 2001. Statistical Mechanics and the Asymmetry of Counterfactual Dependence. *Philosophy of Science* 68: S313–S324.

Ellis, B. 2001. *Scientific Essentialism.* Cambridge: Cambridge University Press.

Esfeld, M. 2007. Mental Causation and the Metaphysics of Causation. *Erkenntnis* 67: 207–220.

Fair, D. 1979. Causation and the Flow of Energy. *Erkenntnis* 14: 219–250.

Feigl, H. 1958. The 'Mental' and the 'Physical'. In H. Feigl, M. Scriven, and G. Maxwell, eds, *Concepts, Theories, and the Mind-Body Problem.* Minneapolis, MN: University of Minnesota Press, 370–497.

Fenton-Glynn, L. and T. Kroedel. 2015. Relativity, Quantum Entanglement, Counterfactuals, and Causation. *British Journal for the Philosophy of Science* 66: 45–67.

Fodor, J.A. 1989. Making Mind Matter More. *Philosophical Topics* 17:59–79.

Galles, D. and J. Pearl. 1998. An Axiomatic Characterization of Causal Counterfactuals. *Foundations of Science* 3: 151–182.

Garber, D. 1983a. Mind, Body and the Laws of Nature in Descartes and Leibniz. *Midwest Studies in Philosophy* 8: 105–133.

Garber, D. 1983b. Understanding Interaction: What Descartes Should Have Told Elisabeth. *Southern Journal of Philosophy* 21: 15–32.

Gebharter, A. 2017. Causal Exclusion and Causal Bayes Nets. *Philosophy and Phenomenological Research* 95: 353–375.

Gibb, S.C. 2004. The Problem of Mental Causation and the Nature of Properties. *Australasian Journal of Philosophy* 82: 464–476.

Gibb, S.C. 2010. Closure Principles and the Laws of Conservation of Energy and Momentum. *Dialectica* 64: 363–384.

Gibb, S.C. 2013. Mental Causation and Double Prevention. In S.C. Gibb, E. J. Lowe, and R. Ingthorsson, eds, *Mental Causation and Ontology.* Oxford: Oxford University Press, 193–214.

Gibb, S.C. 2014. Recent Work: Mental Causation. *Analysis* 74: 327–338.

Gibb, S.C. 2015a. Physical Determinability. *Humana.Mente* 29: 69–90.

Gibb, S.C. 2015b. The Causal Closure Principle. *Philosophical Quarterly* 65: 626–647.

Gibbons, J. 2006. Mental Causation Without Downward Causation. *Philosophical Review* 115: 79–103.

Gillies, A.S. 2007. Counterfactual Scorekeeping. *Linguistics and Philosophy* 30: 329–360.

Ginley, D.S., Hosono, H., and D.C. Paine (eds) 2010. *Handbook of Transparent Conductors*. New York: Springer.

Gorham, G., 2013. The Theological Foundations of Hobbesian Physics: A Defense of Corporeal God. *British Journal for the History of Philosophy* 21: 240–261.

Guyton, A.C. and J.E. Hall. 2006. *Textbook of Medical Physiology*, 11th edn. Philadelphia, PA: Elsevier Saunders.

Hájek, A. (ms.). Most Counterfactuals Are False. URL: http://philpapers.org/rec/hjemca.

Hall, Ned. 2004a. The Intrinsic Character of Causation. *Oxford Studies in Metaphysics* 1: 255–300.

Hall, N. 2004b. Two Concepts of Causation. In J. Collins, N. Hall, and L.A. Paul, eds, *Causation and Counterfactuals*. Cambridge, MA: MIT Press, 225–276.

Hall, N. 2007. Structural Equations and Causation. *Philosophical Studies* 132: 109–136.

Halpern, J.Y. 2000. Axiomatizing Causal Reasoning. *Journal of Artificial Intelligence Research* 12: 317–337.

Halpern, J.Y. 2008. Defaults and Normality in Causal Structures. In G. Brewka and J. Lang, eds, *Principles of Knowledge Representation and Reasoning: Proceedings of the Eleventh International Conference (KR 2008)*. Menlo Park, CA: AAAI Press, 198–208.

Halpern, J.Y. 2013. From Causal Models to Counterfactual Structures. *Review of Symbolic Logic* 6: 305–322.

Halpern, J.Y. and C. Hitchcock. 2010. Actual Causation and the Art of Modeling. In R. Dechter, H. Geffner, and J.Y. Halpern, eds, *Heuristics, Probability and Causality: A Tribute to Judea Pearl*. London: College Publications, 383–406.

Halpern, J.Y. and C. Hitchcock. 2015. Graded Causation and Defaults. *British Journal for the Philosophy of Science* 66: 413–457.

Halpern, J.Y. and J. Pearl. 2005. Causes and Explanations: A Structural-Model Approach. Part I: Causes. *British Journal for Philosophy of Science* 56: 843–887.

Harbecke, J. 2014. Counterfactual Causation and Mental Causation. *Philosophia* 42: 363–385.

Harré, R. and E.H. Madden. 1975. *Causal Powers: A Theory of Natural Necessity*. Oxford: Blackwell.

Hart, W.D. 1988. *The Engines of the Soul*. Cambridge: Cambridge University Press.

Hawthorne, J. 2004. Why Humeans Are Out of Their Minds. *Noûs* 38: 351–358.

Hawthorne, J. 2005. Chance and Counterfactuals. *Philosophy and Phenomenological Research* 70: 396–405.

Heil, J. 1992. *The Nature of True Minds*. Cambridge: Cambridge University Press.

Heil, J. 2003. *From an Ontological Point of View*. Oxford: Clarendon Press.

Heil, J. 2012. *The Universe As We Find It*. Oxford: Oxford University Press.

Heil, J. and D. Robb. 2003. Mental Properties. *American Philosophical Quarterly* 40: 175–196.

Hiddleston, E. 2005. A Causal Theory of Counterfactuals. *Noûs* 39: 632–657.

Hitchcock, C. 1995. Salmon on Explanatory Relevance. *Philosophy of Science* 62: 304–320.

Hitchcock, C. 2001. The Intransitivity of Causation Revealed in Equations and Graphs. *Journal of Philosophy* 98: 273–299.

Hitchcock, C. 2003. Of Humean Bondage. *British Journal for the Philosophy of Science* 54: 1–25.

Hitchcock, C. 2004a. Do All and Only Causes Raise the Probabilities of Effects? In J. Collins, N. Hall, and L.A. Paul, eds, *Causation and Counterfactuals*. Cambridge, MA: MIT Press, 403–417.

Hitchcock, C. 2004b. Routes, Processes, and Chance-Lowering Causes. In P. Dowe and P. Noordhof, eds, *Cause and Chance: Causation in an Indeterministic World*. London: Routledge, 139–151.

Hitchcock, C. 2007a. Prevention, Preemption, and the Principle of Sufficient Reason. *Philosophical Review* 116: 495–532.

Hitchcock, C. 2007b. What's Wrong with Neuron Diagrams? In J.K. Campbell, M. O'Rourke, and H. Silverstein, eds, *Causation and Explanation*. Cambridge, MA: MIT Press, 69–92.

Hitchcock, C. 2012a. Events and Times: A Case Study in Means-Ends Metaphysics. *Philosophical Studies* 160: 79–96.

Hitchcock, C. 2012b. Theories of Causation and the Causal Exclusion Argument. *Journal of Consciousness Studies* 19: 40–56.

Hoffmann-Kolss, V. 2014. Interventionism and Higher-level Causation. *International Studies in the Philosophy of Science* 28: 49–64.

Honderich, T. 1982. The Argument for Anomalous Monism. *Analysis* 42: 59–64.

Horgan, T. 1989. Mental Quausation. *Philosophical Perspectives* 3: 47–76.

Horgan, T. 1993. From Supervenience to Superdupervenience: Meeting the Demands of a Material World. *Mind* 102: 555–586.

Hornsby, J. 2015. Causality and the Mental. *Humana.Mente* 29: 125–140.

Huber, F. 2013. Structural Equations and Beyond. *Review of Symbolic Logic* 6: 709–732.

Hüttemann, A. 2013. A Disposition-Based Process Theory of Causation. In S. Mumford and M. Tugby, eds, *Metaphysics and Science*. Oxford: Oxford University Press, 101–122.

Huxley, T. 1874. On the Hypothesis that Animals Are Automata, and Its History. *Fortnightly Review* 95: 555–580.

Ismael, J. 2016. How Do Causes Depend on Us? The Many Faces of Perspectivalism. *Synthese* 193: 245–267.

Jackson, F. 1998. *From Metaphysics to Ethics*. Oxford: Clarendon Press.

References

Jackson, F. and P. Pettit. 1990. Causation in the Philosophy of Mind. *Philosophy and Phenomenological Research* 50: 195–214.

Jenkins, C.S. and D. Nolan. 2008. Backwards Explanation. *Philosophical Studies* 140: 103–115.

Kallestrup, J. 2006. The Causal Exclusion Argument. *Philosophical Studies* 131: 459–485.

Keaton, D. 2012. Kim's Supervenience Argument and the Nature of Total Realizers. *European Journal of Philosophy* 20: 243–259.

Keaton, D. and T.W. Polger. 2014. Exclusion, Still Not Tracted. *Philosophical Studies* 171: 135–148.

Keil, G. 2001. How Do We Ever Get Up? On the Proximate Causation of Actions and Events. *Grazer Philosophische Studien* 61: 43–62.

Kim, J. 1973. Causes and Counterfactuals. *Journal of Philosophy* 70: 570–572.

Kim, J. 1976. Events as Property Exemplifications. In M. Brand and D. Walton, eds, *Action Theory*. Dordrecht: Reidel, 159–177.

Kim, J. 1984. Concepts of Supervenience. *Philosophy and Phenomenological Research* 45: 153–176.

Kim, J. 1989. Mechanism, Purpose, and Explanatory Exclusion. *Philosophical Perspectives* 3: 77–108.

Kim, J. 1992. Multiple Realization and the Metaphysics of Reduction. *Philosophy and Phenomenological Research* 52: 1–26.

Kim, J. 1993. *Supervenience and Mind*. Cambridge: Cambridge University Press.

Kim, J. 1998. *Mind in a Physical World*. Cambridge, MA: MIT Press.

Kim, J. 2005. *Physicalism, or Something Near Enough*. Princeton, NJ: Princeton University Press.

Kim, J. 2007. Causation and Mental Causation. In B.P. McLaughlin and J.D. Cohen, eds, *Contemporary Debates in Philosophy of Mind*. Oxford: Blackwell, 227–242.

Kistler, M. 2013. The Interventionist Account of Causation and Non-Causal Association Laws. *Erkenntnis* 78: 65–84.

Kment, B. 2006a. Counterfactuals and Explanation. *Mind* 115: 261–310.

Kment, B. 2006b. Counterfactuals and the Analysis of Necessity. *Philosophical Perspectives* 20: 237–302.

Kment, B. 2010. Causation: Determination and Difference-Making. *Noûs* 44: 80–111.

Kment, B. 2014. *Modality and Explanatory Reasoning*. Oxford: Oxford University Press.

Koksvik, O. 2007. Conservation of Energy Is Relevant to Physicalism. *Dialectica* 61: 573–582.

Kripke, S.A. 1980. *Naming and Necessity*. Oxford: Blackwell.

Kroedel, T. 2008. Mental Causation as Multiple Causation. *Philosophical Studies* 139: 125–143.

Kroedel, T. 2015a. A Simple Argument for Downward Causation. *Synthese* 192: 841–858.

Kroedel, T. 2015b. Dualist Mental Causation and the Exclusion Problem. *Noûs* 49: 357–375.

Kroedel. T. 2018. A New Future Similarity Objection. *Philosophical Studies* 175: 1477–1493.

Kroedel, T. and F. Huber. 2013. Counterfactual Dependence and Arrow. *Noûs* 47: 453–466.

Kvart, I. 2001. Lewis's 'Causation as Influence'. *Australasian Journal of Philosophy* 79: 409–421.

La Mettrie, J.O. 1912. *Man a Machine*, ed. G.C. Bussey. Chicago, IL: Open Court.

Langton, R. and D. Lewis. 1998. Defining 'Intrinsic'. *Philosophy and Phenomenological Research* 58: 333–345.

Leibniz, G.W. 1898. *The Monadology and Other Philosophical Writings*, trans. R. Latta. Oxford: Oxford University Press.

Leibniz, G.W. 1985. *Theodicy: Essays on the Goodness of God, the Freedom of Man, and the Origin of Evil*, ed. A. Farrer, trans. E.M. Huggard. La Salle, IL: Open Court.

Lemmon, E.J. 1967. Comments on D. Davidson's 'The Logical Form of Action Sentences'. In N. Rescher, ed., *The Logic of Decision and Action*. Pittsburgh, PA: University of Pittsburgh Press, 96–103.

Lepore, E. and B. Loewer. 1987. Mind Matters. *Journal of Philosophy* 84: 630–641.

Lewis, D. 1966. An Argument for the Identity Theory. *Journal of Philosophy* 63: 17–25.

Lewis, D. 1973a. Causation. *Journal of Philosophy* 70: 556–567.

Lewis, D. 1973b. *Counterfactuals*. Oxford: Blackwell.

Lewis, D. 1973c. Counterfactuals and Comparative Possibility. *Journal of Philosophical Logic* 2: 418–446.

Lewis, D. 1979. Counterfactual Dependence and Time's Arrow. *Noûs* 13: 455–476.

Lewis, D. 1980. Mad Pain and Martian Pain. In N. Block, ed., *Readings in the Philosophy of Psychology, Volume I*. Cambridge, MA: Harvard University Press, 216–222.

Lewis, D. 1983. Extrinsic Properties. *Philosophical Studies* 44: 197–200.

Lewis, D. 1986a. Causal Explanation. In *Philosophical Papers, Volume II*. New York: Oxford University Press.

Lewis, D. 1986b. Events. In *Philosophical Papers, Volume II*. New York: Oxford University Press.

Lewis, D. 1986c. *On the Plurality of Worlds*. Oxford: Blackwell.

Lewis, D. 1986d. Postscripts to 'Causation'. In *Philosophical Papers, Volume II*. New York: Oxford University Press.

Lewis, D. 1986e. Postscripts to 'Counterfactual Dependence and Time's Arrow'. In *Philosophical Papers, Volume II*. New York: Oxford University Press.

Lewis, D. 1994a. Humean Supervenience Debugged. *Mind* 103: 473–490.

Lewis, D. 1994b. Reduction of Mind. In S. Guttenplan, ed., *A Companion to the Philosophy of Mind*. Oxford: Blackwell, 412–431.

Lewis, D. 2000. Evil for Freedom's Sake? In *Papers in Ethics and Social Philosophy*. Cambridge: Cambridge University Press.

References

Lewis, D. 2004. Causation as Influence. In J. Collins, N. Hall, and L.A. Paul, eds, *Causation and Counterfactuals*. Cambridge, MA: MIT Press, 75–106.

List, C. and P. Menzies. 2009. Nonreductive Physicalism and the Limits of the Exclusion Principle. *Journal of Philosophy* 106: 475–502.

Loewer, B. 2001a. From Physics to Physicalism. In C. Gillett and B. Loewer, eds, *Physicalism and Its Discontents*. Cambridge: Cambridge University Press, 37–56.

Loewer, B. 2001b. Review of J. Kim, *Mind in a Physical World*. *Journal of Philosophy* 98: 315–324.

Loewer, B. 2007. Mental Causation, or Something Near Enough. In B.P. McLaughlin and J.D. Cohen, eds, *Contemporary Debates in Philosophy of Mind*. Oxford: Blackwell, 243–264.

Lombrozo, T. 2010. Causal-Explanatory Pluralism: How Intentions, Functions, and Mechanisms Influence Causal Ascriptions. *Cognitive Psychology* 61: 303–332.

Lowe, E.J. 1996. *Subjects of Experience*. Cambridge: Cambridge University Press.

Lowe, E.J. 1999. Self, Agency and Mental Causation. *Journal of Consciousness Studies* 6: 225–239.

Lowe, E.J. 2000. Causal Closure Principles and Emergentism. *Philosophy* 75: 571–585.

Lowe, E.J. 2003. Physical Causal Closure and the Invisibility of Mental Causation. In S. Walter and H.-D. Heckmann, eds, *Physicalism and Mental Causation*. Exeter: Imprint Academic, 137–154.

Lowe, E.J. 2008. *Personal Agency: The Metaphysics of Mind and Action*. Oxford: Oxford University Press.

Lowe, E.J. 2013. Substance Causation, Powers, and Human Agency. In S.C. Gibb, E.J. Lowe, and R. Ingthorsson, eds, *Mental Causation and Ontology*. Oxford: Oxford University Press, 153–172.

Lycan, W.G. 2009. Giving Dualism Its Due. *Australasian Journal of Philosophy* 87: 551–563.

MacDonald, C. and G. MacDonald. 1986. Mental Causes and Explanation of Action. *Philosophical Quarterly* 36: 145–158.

MacDonald, C. and G. MacDonald. 2006. The Metaphysics of Mental Causation. *Journal of Philosophy* 103: 539–576.

Mackie, J.L. 1965. Causes and Conditions. *American Philosophical Quarterly* 2: 245–264.

Malcolm, N. 1968. The Conceivability of Mechanism. *Philosophical Review* 77: 45–72.

Malebranche, N. 1997. *Dialogues on Metaphysics and on Religion*, ed. N. Jolley, trans. D. Scott. Cambridge: Cambridge University Press.

Martin, C.B. 2008. *The Mind in Nature*. Oxford: Oxford University Press.

Maudlin, T. 2007. A Modest Proposal Concerning Laws, Counterfactuals, and Explanations. In *The Metaphysics Within Physics*. Oxford: Clarendon Press.

Mayr, E. 2017. Powers and Downward Causation. In M. Paolini Paoletti and F. Orilia, eds, *Philosophical and Scientific Perspectives on Downward Causation*. New York: Routledge, 76–91.

McDermott, M. 1995. Redundant Causation. *British Journal for the Philosophy of Science* 46: 523–544.

McDonnell, N. 2017. Causal Exclusion and the Limits of Proportionality. *Philosophical Studies* 174: 1459–1474.

McGrath, S. 2005. Causation By Omission: A Dilemma. *Philosophical Studies* 123: 125–148.

McLaughlin, B.P. 1995. Varieties of Supervenience. In E.E. Savellos and U. Yalcin, eds, *Supervenience: New Essays*. Cambridge: Cambridge University Press, 16–59.

McLaughlin, B.P. 2009. Review of S. Shoemaker, *Physical Realization*. *Notre Dame Philosophical Reviews*. URL: https://ndpr.nd.edu/news/24086-physical-realization/.

Melnyk, A. 2003. *A Physicalist Manifesto: Thoroughly Modern Materialism*. Cambridge: Cambridge University Press.

Menzies, P. 1988. Against Causal Reductionism. *Mind* 97: 551–574.

Menzies, P. 2004. Difference-Making in Context. In J. Collins, N. Hall, and L.A. Paul, eds, *Causation and Counterfactuals*. Cambridge, MA: MIT Press, 139–180.

Mills, E. 1996. Interactionism and Overdetermination. *American Philosophical Quarterly* 33: 105–117.

Molnar, G. 2003. *Powers: A Study in Metaphysics*. Oxford: Oxford University Press.

Montero, B. 2006. What Does the Conservation of Energy Have to Do with Physicalism? *Dialectica* 60: 383–396.

Moore, D. 2012. Causal Exclusion and Dependent Overdetermination. *Erkenntnis* 76: 319–335.

Moore, M.S. 2009. *Causation and Responsibility*. Oxford: Oxford University Press.

Morreau, M. 2010. It Simply Does Not Add up: Trouble with Overall Similarity. *Journal of Philosophy* 107: 469–490.

Morris, K. 2015. Against Disanalogy-Style Responses to the Exclusion Problem. *Philosophia* 43: 435–453.

Moss, S. 2012. On the Pragmatics of Counterfactuals. *Noûs* 46: 561–586.

Mumford, S. and R.L. Anjum. 2009. Double Prevention and Powers. *Journal of Critical Realism* 8: 277–293.

Mumford, S. and R.L. Anjum. 2011. *Getting Causes from Powers*. Oxford: Oxford University Press.

Nadler, S. 1997. Occasionalism and the Mind-Body Problem. In M.A. Stewart, ed., *Studies in Seventeenth-Century European Philosophy*. Oxford: Clarendon Press, 75–96.

Newen, A. and R. Čuplinskas. 2002. Mental Causation: A Real Phenomenon in a Physicalistic World Without Epiphenomenalism or Overdetermination. *Grazer Philosophische Studien* 65: 139–167.

Ney, A. 2012. The Causal Contribution of Mental Events. In S. Gozzano and C.S. Hill, eds, *New Perspectives on Type Identity: The Mental and the Physical*. Cambridge: Cambridge University Press, 230–250.

Noordhof, P. 1998. Do Tropes Resolve the Problem of Mental Causation? *Philosophical Quarterly* 48: 221–226.

Papineau, D. 2001. The Rise of Physicalism. In C. Gillett and B. Loewer, eds, *Physicalism and Its Discontents*. Cambridge: Cambridge University Press, 3–36.

Paprzycka, K. 2014. Lowe's Argument Against the Psychoneural Token Identity Thesis. *Pacific Philosophical Quarterly* 95: 372–396.

Pauen, M. 2002. Is Type Identity Incompatible with Multiple Realization? *Grazer Philosophische Studien* 65: 37–49.

Paul, L.A. 2000. Aspect Causation. *Journal of Philosophy* 97: 235–256.

Paul, L.A. and N. Hall. 2013. *Causation: A User's Guide*. Oxford: Oxford University Press.

Pearl, J. 2000. *Causality: Models, Reasoning and Inference*. New York: Cambridge University Press.

Perler, D. 1996. *Repräsentation bei Descartes*. Frankfurt: Klostermann.

Pernu, T.K. 2016. Causal Exclusion and Downward Counterfactuals. *Erkenntnis* 81: 1031–1049.

Place, U.T. 1956. Is Consciousness a Brain Process? *British Journal of Psychology* 47: 44–50.

Polger, T.W. 2004. *Natural Minds*. Cambridge, MA: MIT Press.

Price, H. and R. Corry (eds) 2007. *Causation, Physics, and the Constitution of Reality: Russell's Republic Revisited*. Oxford: Oxford University Press.

Princess Elisabeth of Bohemia and R. Descartes. 2007. *The Correspondence Between Princess Elisabeth of Bohemia and René Descartes*, ed. and trans. L. Shapiro. Chicago, IL: University of Chicago Press.

Putnam, H. 1967. Psychological Predicates. In W.H. Capitan and D.D. Merrill, eds, *Art, Mind, and Religion*. Pittsburgh, PA: University of Pittsburgh Press, 37–48.

Quine, W.V.O. 1970. *Philosophy of Logic*. Englewood Cliffs, NJ: Prentice Hall.

Quine, W.V.O. 1974. *The Roots of Reference*. La Salle, IL: Open Court.

Raatikainen, P. 2010. Causation, Exclusion, and the Special Sciences. *Erkenntnis* 73: 349–363.

Robb, D. 1997. The Properties of Mental Causation. *Philosophical Quarterly* 47: 178–194.

Robb, D. 2001. Reply to Noordhof on Mental Causation. *Philosophical Quarterly* 51: 90–94.

Robb, D. 2013. The Identity Theory as a Solution to the Exclusion Problem. In S.C. Gibb, E.J. Lowe, and R.D. Ingthorsson, eds, *Mental Causation and Ontology*. Oxford: Oxford University Press, 215–232.

Robb, D. 2015. Mental Causation and Intelligibility. *Humana.Mente* 29: 213–226.

Russell, B. 1912. On the Notion of Cause. *Proceedings of the Aristotelian Society* 13: 1–26.

Russo, A. 2016. Kim's Dilemma: Why Mental Causation Is Not Productive. *Synthese* 193: 2185–2203.

Rutherford, D. 1993. Natures, Laws, and Miracles: The Roots of Leibniz's Critique of Occasionalism. In S. Nadler, ed., *Causation in Early Modern Philosophy*. University Park, PA: Pennsylvania State University Press, 135–158.

Salmon, W. 1994. Causality Without Counterfactuals. *Philosophy of Science* 61: 297–312.

Sartorio, C. 2005. Causes as Difference-Makers. *Philosophical Studies* 123: 71–96.

Sartorio, C. 2006. Disjunctive Causes. *Journal of Philosophy* 103: 521–538.

Sartorio, C. 2007. Causation and Responsibility. *Philosophy Compass* 2: 749–765.

Sartorio, C. 2010. The Prince of Wales Problem for Counterfactual Theories of Causation. In A. Hazlett, ed., *New Waves in Metaphysics*. New York: Palgrave Macmillan, 259–276.

Sartorio, C. 2016. *Causation and Free Will*. Oxford: Oxford University Press.

Schaffer, J. 2000a. Causation by Disconnection. *Philosophy of Science* 67: 285–300.

Schaffer, J. 2000b. Trumping Preemption. *Journal of Philosophy* 97: 165–181.

Schaffer, J. 2003. Overdetermining Causes. *Philosophical Studies* 114: 23–45.

Schaffer, J. 2004a. Causes Need Not Be Physically Connected to Their Effects: The Case for Negative Causation. In C. Hitchcock, ed., *Contemporary Debates in Philosophy of Science*. Oxford: Blackwell, 197–216.

Schaffer, J. 2004b. Of Ghostly and Mechanical Events. *Philosophy and Phenomenological Research* 68: 230–244.

Schaffer, J. 2012. Disconnection and Responsibility. *Legal Theory* 18: 399–435.

Schneider, S. 2012. Non-Reductive Physicalism Cannot Appeal to Token Identity. *Philosophy and Phenomenological Research* 85: 719–728.

Schnieder, B. 2015. The Asymmetry of 'Because'. In S. Lapointe, ed., *Themes from Ontology, Mind, and Logic*. Leiden: Brill Rodopi, 131–164.

Shapiro, L.A. 2010. Lessons from Causal Exclusion. *Philosophy and Phenomenological Research* 81: 594–604.

Shapiro, L.A. and E. Sober. 2007. Epiphenomenalism: The Dos and the Don'ts. In P. Machamer and G. Wolters, eds, *Thinking about Causes: From Greek Philosophy to Modern Physics*. Pittsburgh, PA: University of Pittsburgh Press, 235–264.

Sharpe, K.W. 2015. Causal Overdetermination and Modal Compatibilism. *Philosophia* 43: 1111–1131.

Shoemaker, S. 1981. Some Varieties of Functionalism. *Philosophical Topics* 12: 93–119.

Shoemaker, S. 2001. Realization and Mental Causation. In C. Gillett and B. Loewer, eds, *Physicalism and Its Discontents*. Cambridge: Cambridge University Press, 74–98.

Shoemaker, S. 2007. *Physical Realization*. Oxford: Oxford University Press.

Sider, T. 2003. What's So Bad about Overdetermination? *Philosophy and Phenomenological Research* 67: 719–726.

Sleigh, R.C. Jr 1990. Leibniz on Malebranche on Causality. In J. Cover and M. Kulstad, eds, *Central Themes in Early Modern Philosophy*. Indianapolis, IN: Hackett, 161–194.

References

Slowik, E. 2014. Descartes' Physics. In *The Stanford Encyclopedia of Philosophy* (Summer 2014 edition), ed. E.N. Zalta. URL: http://plato.stanford.edu/archives/sum2014/entries/descartes-physics/.

Smart, J.J.C. 1972. Further Thoughts on the Identity Theory. *The Monist* 56: 177–192.

Spalding, D.A. 1877. The Physical Basis of Mind. *Nature* 16: 261–263.

Spirtes, P., C. Glymour, and R. Scheines. 2000. *Causation, Prediction, and Search*. Cambridge, MA: MIT Press.

Springborg, P. 2012. Hobbes's Challenge to Descartes, Bramhall and Boyle: A Corporeal God. *British Journal for the History of Philosophy* 20: 903–934.

Stalnaker, R. 1968. A Theory of Conditionals. In J.W. Cornman, ed., *Studies in Logical Theory* (American Philosophical Quarterly Monographs, Vol. 2). Oxford: Blackwell, 98–112.

Stephan, A. 2002. Emergentism, Irreducibility, and Downward Causation. *Grazer Philosophische Studien* 65: 77–93.

Swanson, E. 2010. Lessons from the Context Sensitivity of Causal Talk. *Journal of Philosophy* 107: 221–242.

Swanson, E. 2012a. Conditional Excluded Middle without the Limit Assumption. *Philosophy and Phenomenological Research* 85: 301–321.

Swanson, E. 2012b. The Language of Causation. In D. Graff Fara and G. Russell, eds, *The Routledge Companion to the Philosophy of Language*. London: Routledge, 716–728.

Thomson, J.J. 2003. Causation: Omissions. *Philosophy and Phenomenological Research* 66: 81–103.

Tooley, M. 2002. Backward Causation and the Stalnaker–Lewis Approach to Counterfactuals. *Analysis* 62: 191–197.

van Fraassen, B.C. 1980. *The Scientific Image*. Oxford: Clarendon Press.

van Riel, R. 2013. Identity, Asymmetry, and the Relevance of Meanings for Models of Reduction. *British Journal for the Philosophy of Science* 64: 747–761.

Vetter, B. 2015. *Potentiality: From Dispositions to Modality*. Oxford: Oxford University Press.

von Fintel, K. 2001. Counterfactuals in a Dynamic Context. In M. Kenstowicz, ed., *Ken Hale: A Life in Language*. Cambridge, MA: MIT Press, 123–152.

Walter, S. 2010. Taking Realization Seriously: No Cure for Epiphobia. *Philosophical Studies* 151: 207–226.

Wasserman, R. 2006. The Future Similarity Objection Revisited. *Synthese* 150: 57–67.

Weatherson, B. 2001. Intrinsic Properties and Combinatorial Principles. *Philosophy and Phenomenological Research* 63: 365–380.

Weatherson, B. 2007. Humeans Aren't out of Their Minds. *Noûs* 41: 529–535.

Weslake, B. 2013. Proportionality, Contrast and Explanation. *Australasian Journal of Philosophy* 91: 785–797.

Weslake, B. 2017. Difference-Making, Closure and Exclusion. In H. Beebee, C. Hitchcock, and H. Price, eds, *Making a Difference*. Oxford: Oxford University Press, 215–231.

Wilson, J. 2005. Supervenience-Based Formulations of Physicalism. *Noûs* 39: 426–459.

Williams, J.R.G. 2008. Chances, Counterfactuals, and Similarity. *Philosophy and Phenomenological Research* 77: 385–420.

Williamson, T. 2006. Indicative versus Subjunctive Conditionals, Congruential Versus Non-Hyperintensional Contexts. *Philosophical Issues* 16: 310–333.

Williamson, T. Forthcoming. Counterpossibles in Metaphysics. In B. Armour-Garb and F. Kroon, eds, *Philosophical Fictionalism*.

Wolff, J.E. 2016. Using Defaults to Understand Token Causation. *Journal of Philosophy* 113: 5–26.

Won, C. 2014. Overdetermination, Counterfactuals, and Mental Causation. *Philosophical Review* 123: 205–229.

Woodward, J. 2002. What Is a Mechanism? A Counterfactual Account. *Philosophy of Science* 69: S366–S377.

Woodward, J. 2003. *Making Things Happen: A Theory of Causal Explanation.* New York: Oxford University Press.

Woodward, J. 2008. Mental Causation and Neural Mechanisms. In J. Hohwy and J. Kallestrup, eds, *Being Reduced: New Essays on Reduction, Explanation, and Causation.* Oxford: Oxford University Press, 218–262.

Woodward, J. 2010. Causation in Biology: Stability, Specificity, and the Choice of Levels of Explanation. *Biology and Philosophy* 3: 287–318.

Woodward, J. 2012. Causation: Interactions between Philosophical Theories and Psychological Research. *Philosophy of Science* 79: 961–972.

Woodward, J. 2014. Causal Reasoning: Philosophy and Experiment. In T. Lombrozo, J. Knobe, and S. Nichols, eds, *Oxford Studies in Experimental Philosophy.* Oxford: Oxford University Press, 294–324.

Woodward, J. 2015. Interventionism and Causal Exclusion. *Philosophy and Phenomenological Research* 91: 303–347.

Woodward, J. 2016. The Problem of Variable Choice. *Synthese* 193: 1047–1072.

Woodward, J. 2017. Intervening in the Exclusion Argument. In H. Beebee, C. Hitchcock, and H. Price, eds, *Making a Difference.* Oxford: Oxford University Press, 251–268.

Yablo, S. 1992. Mental Causation. *Philosophical Review* 101: 245–280.

Yablo, S. 1997. Wide Causation. *Philosophical Perspectives* 11: 251–281.

Zhong, L. 2011. Can Counterfactuals Solve the Exclusion Problem? *Philosophy and Phenomenological Research* 83: 129–147.

Zhong, L. 2012. Counterfactuals, Regularity and the Autonomy Approach. *Analysis* 72: 75–85.

Zhong, L. 2015. Why the Counterfactualist Should Still Worry about Downward Causation. *Erkenntnis* 80: 159–171.

Index

abstract particulars; *see* tropes

actin filaments; *see* muscle contraction

action at a distance; *see* causation, and spatiotemporal continuity

action, intentional; *see* agency

active causal routes, 134

adenosine triphosphate; *see* ATP

agency, 1, 92, 94

Anjum, Rani Lill, 57–58

Anomalous Monism, 21

Armstrong, David, 88

ATP, 199; *see also* muscle contraction

autonomy approach, 76

background conditions, 16, 191, 192

backtracking; *see* counterfactual conditionals, backtracking evaluations

bases, 81, 82, 87, 155, 159, 160, 162, 164, 165, 173, 182, 188, 204; *see also* realizers; supervenience, nomological

Baumgartner, Michael, 148, 149, 150

Bennett, Karen, 2, 153, 155, 167, 176, 178, 184, 186, 195, 196

Bernstein, Sara, 172

Block, Ned, 11

Burge, Tyler, 75

calcium; *see* muscle contraction

causal graphs, 106, *107*, *109*, *115*, *116*, *120*, *123*, 131, *132*, 133, *136*, *137*, *145*, *146*, *147*
  acyclic vs non-acyclic, 107, 115, 116

causal models, 74, 98, 101, 103, 113, 116, 117, 118, 129, 138, 140
  appropriateness, 74, 134, 136–138, 141–147
  counterfactual dependence in; *see* counterfactual dependence, in causal models
  truth of counterfactual conditionals in; *see* counterfactual conditionals, and causal models

causal paths; *see* paths

causal routes; *see* active causal routes

causation
  and causal models, 105–106, 119, 124, 125, 132, 133–138, 139, 141–143, 146
  and counterfactual dependence, 4, 30–31, 50, 51, 53, 54, 56, 62, 64, 65, 69, 73, 74, 76, 77, 79, 83, 92, 95, 98, 105, 117, 118, 119, 122, 125, 132, 139, 142, 157, 161, 165, 170, 171, 173, 177, 178, 179, 188, 189, 196, 197, 198, 200
  and explanatory relevance; *see* explanatory relevance
  and intrinsic connections, 53–55, *54*,
  and moral responsibility, 55
  and powers, 57–58, 94–95, 186
  and spatiotemporal continuity, 53, 55, 58
  and transference, 3, 49, 50, 51, 53, 56, 57–58, 92, 93, 139, 171, 199; *see also* causation, sufficient
  backward, 189
  contributing; *see* interventionism
  direct; *see* interventionism
  objectivity, 138, 139
  qua; *see* properties, causal relevance of
  relata of, 20, 147, 148
  relevance of properties to; *see* properties, causal relevance of
  simultaneous, 48, 79, 143, 188, 195
  sufficient, 184–201; *see also* causation, and transference; events, sufficient and minimally sufficient sets of
  transitivity; *see* transitivity, of causation

centring; *see* Strong Centring

c-fibres, 14

Chalmers, David, 11, 17, 18

Christensen, Jonas, 78–79, 179

collisions, 8, *9*

conservation laws, 7–9, *9*, 49, 152

conserved quantities, 3, 49, 92; *see also* conservation laws

content, mental, 65

context-sensitivity, 74, 140

222   *Index*

counterfactual conditionals, 4, 31, 61, 88, *89*, 111,
  148, *171*, 189, *205*
  'would' vs 'might', 32, 160, 162
  and causal models, 98, 100, 101, 102, 103, 111,
    113–115, 116, 117, 130–131, 139, 146
  and comparative overall similarity or closeness
    between possible worlds; *see* possible worlds,
    comparative overall similarity
  asymmetry-by-fiat approach, 40–41, 61, 64,
    84, 87
  backtracking evaluations, 39–40, 42–45, 87, 113
  logic of, 33–38, 72, 76, 84, 117, 134, 160, 163,
    204–206, 207
  truth-conditions, 31–33, 61, 102, 190
  vacuous truth, 31, 131, 156, 170, 178, 193, 194,
    201; *see also* counterfactual conditionals,
    truth conditions
counterfactual dependence, 30–31, 105, 139, 161,
  163, 165, *171*, 173, 177, 189, 197, 204; *see also*
  probabilistic dependence
  in causal models, 104, 105–106, 117, 119, 120,
    121, 123, 125, 126, 132, 135, 139, 144, 146
counterfactuals; *see* counterfactual conditionals
counterpossibles, 34; *see also* counterfactual
  conditionals, vacuous truth

Dancy, Jonathan, 66
dark matter, 91
Davidson, Donald, 21,
defaults; *see* variables, default vs deviant values
Descartes, René, 6–7
determinism, 45–46, 102, 117, 152, 200; *see also*
  indeterminism
difference-making, 3, 4, 30, 131; *see also*
  counterfactual dependence
dispositions; *see* causation, and powers
dot-matrix pictures, 15–16, 62
double prevention, 49–58, *51*, *52*, 92, *93*, 94,
  122, 125, 128, 139, 171, 187, 188, 197–198,
  199; *see* also causation, and counterfactual
  dependence; causation, and intrinsic
  connections; causation, and powers;
  causation, and spatiotemporal continuity;
  causation, and transference
dualism, 3, 4, 11, 17, 18, 19, 22, 80, 127, 145, 155, 156,
  170, 187, 192, 203
  about substances, 6, 14; *see also* Descartes, René
  naturalistic, 18, 19, 80, 85, 88
  super-nomological, 88, 90, 91, 96, 118, 158, 159,
    160, 164, 168, 169, 174, 182, 187, 197, 204

early pre-emption; *see* pre-emption, early
Elisabeth, Princess of Bohemia, 6–7
energy, 3, 49, 92; *see also* conserved quantities
  kinetic, 7, *9*, 152; *see also* conservation laws

epiphenomenalism, 10–11, 155, 187, 192, 193, 198, 203
equations, 101–102, 114, 116, 120, 122, 131, 144, 145,
  146; *see also* causal models; counterfactual
  conditionals, and causal models; variables
  acyclic vs non-acyclic, 104, 115, 116, 121, 145
  number of solutions, 115, 116, 117, 146
essentiality of origin, 68
events, 143, 189, 196, 199, 200
  and causal models; *see* variables
  as property-instances, 25–28, 61, 155, 160, 161, 165
  essential properties of, 26–28, 29, 71, 161
  fragility, 161–165, 196
  identity between mental and physical ones,
    21–25; *see also* Anomalous Monism
  identity conditions, 21, 28–30, 61, 71, 160
  sufficient and minimally sufficient sets of,
    189–198
exclusion problem, 2–4, 8, 11, 22, 75, 80, 94,
  151, 203
  different formulations of, 152–154, 158, 184–185
explanatory relevance, 48, 55, 74–75, 138–141

Field, Hartry, 107
firearms, 56
firing squads, 2, 3, 30, 80, 96, 152, 156, 166, 167,
  171, 172, 173, 197; *see also* overdetermination
functionalism, 176

Gibb, Sophie, 8, 94
God; *see* occasionalism
graphs; *see* causal graphs

Hall, Ned, 53, 190, 191, 198
Halpern, Joseph, 125
Hitchcock, Christopher, 49, 98, 101, 119, 121, 125,
  134, 142
Hobbes, Thomas, 10
Honderich, Ted, 22
Hüttemann, Andreas, 58
Huxley, Thomas, 10
hyperintentionality; *see* non-hyperintentionality

identity theory; *see* physicalism,
  reductive
imagination, 91
indeterminism, 45–46
indicative conditionals, 34
interaction problem, 2–4, 21, 80, 203
interventionism, 99, 147–149
INUS conditions, 191; *see also* causation,
  sufficient; events, sufficient and minimally
  sufficient sets of

Kallestrup, Jesper, 78–79, 179
Keaton, Douglas, 179

Index

223

Kim, Jaegwon, 11, 19, 25–28, 91, 92, 93, 95, 155
Kistler, Max, 143
Kment, Boris, 91
Kripke, Saul, 11, 15, 68

La Mettrie, Julien Offray de, 10
late pre-emption; *see* pre-emption, late
laws of nature, 17, 18, 78, 80, 90, 91, 117, 143, 152, 176, 179, 182, 201; *see also* conservation laws
   'best system' theory of, 88
   deterministic, 42; *see also* determinism
   psychophysical, 82, 86, 87, 90, 91, 119, 152, 158, 182
   violations of; *see* miracles
Leibniz, Gottfried Wilhelm, 7–10, 152
Leibniz's law, 21
Lewis, David, 15, 28, 31–32, 44, 47, 56, 59, 88, 98, 99, 161, 166, 181, 190
Limit Assumption, 32
Lipton, Peter, 44
Loewer, Barry, 85, 189
Lowe, Jonathan, 195

Mackie, J.L., 2, 191
Malcolm, Norman, 11
Malebranche, Nicolas, 9
material biconditionals, 37
material conditionals, 34
materialism, 10, 11, 86; *see also* physicalism
McDermott, Michael, 77
McLaughlin, Brian, 179
Menzies, Peter, 68
Mills, Eugene, 196
minimally sufficient sets of events; *see* events, sufficient and minimally sufficient sets of
miracles, 41–45, 84, 85, 86, 87, 90, 158, 164, 174, 178
   big vs small, 41, 44
   psychophysical, 85, 86, 87, 88, 90, 160, 164
modality; *see* necessity and possibility
momentum, 7, 9, 92, 152; *see also* conserved quantities; conservation laws
monism; *see* Anomalous Monism; physicalism
moral particularism, 66
multiple realizability, 11, 15, 17, 20, 146; *see also* realizers
Mumford, Stephen, 57–58
muscle contraction, 92–95, 93, 187–188, 198, 199
myosin; *see* muscle contraction

necessity and possibility
   metaphysical, 15, 34, 82
   nomological, 18, 53, 81, 82, 90, 90, 188–189, 199–201
networks, 121, 124
   self-contained, 121, 122, 123, 124, 128, 132

neuromuscular junction; *see* muscle contraction
neuron diagrams, 50, 51, 54, 128, 173, 174, 197
Ney, Alyssa, 139
non-hyperintensionality, 37, 65, 181
normality, 125–126, 127, 133

occasionalism, 9–10
omissions, 47, 48, 52, 105, 107, 119, 125, 133, 134, 139
overdetermination, 2, 3, 4, 11, 30, 31, 49, 54, 80, 96, 152, 153, 154, 157, 164, 171, 172, 173, 174, 177, 178, 184, 185, 195
   characterizations of, 156–157, 166–167
   efficacy of overdetermining events, 167
   prototypical cases, 166, 167–171, 172, 177, 183, 197

Papineau, David, 8
paths, 73, 74, 75, 109, 121, 124, 132, 134, 136, 148, 149; *see also* networks
   acyclic vs cyclic, 121, 131, 134
Paul, L.A., 190, 191, 198
physicalism, 11, 14, 82, 86; *see also* materialism
   modal arguments against, 11, 20; *see also* zombies
   non-reductive, 3, 11, 15, 16–17, 19, 20, 22, 61, 64, 66, 75, 96, 112, 119, 127, 145, 148, 155, 158, 159, 160, 164, 168, 169, 170, 172, 174, 176, 186, 192, 203
   reductive, 2, 11, 14, 19, 20, 203
pineal gland, 7
possibility; *see* necessity and possibility
possible worlds, 15, 31
   closeness; *see* possible worlds, comparative overall similarity
   comparative overall similarity, 32, 39–46, 61, 84, 89, 126, 158, 204–206
   spheres of, 88–91, 89, 90, 204–206, 205
powers; *see* causation, and powers
pre-emption, 54, 95, 166
   early, 98
   late, 30, 49, 77, 166
   trumping, 30
probabilistic dependence, 46; *see also* counterfactual dependence
properties
   (temporally) intrinsic vs (temporally) extrinsic, 46–47, 48, 142, 181–182, 188
   causal relevance of, 23–25, 67, 174
   causal vs non-causal, 67, 78–79, 179–182, 183; *see also* properties, (temporally) intrinsic vs (temporally) extrinsic
   disjunctive, 47, 65, 179, 180, 181, 183
   moral and aesthetic, 66, 67
   natural, 47

Index

properties (cont.)
  particularized; *see* tropes
proportionality, 193
propositional attitudes, 47, 65
Putnam, Hilary, 11

quantity of motion, 7
quantum entanglement, 55
Quine, W.V.O., 21
realizers, 62–63, 64, 75, 81, 82, 110, 111, 112, 113, 114,
  126, 128, 137, 143, 149, 155, 159, 160, 162, 164,
  165, 173, 188, 196; *see also* bases; multiple
  realizability
  core vs total, 78–79, 176–183, 192

reduction; *see* physicalism, reductive
restricted transitivity, 36, 70; *see also*
  counterfactual conditionals, logic of;
  transitivity, of conditionals
rigid designators, 15
Robb, David, 24–25
Russo, Andrew, 94, 187

Schaffer, Jonathan, 49, 56, 92
Shoemaker, Sydney, 176, 179
social choice theory, 42
souls, 6, 7, 10, 11, 173
speed of light, 189
strengthening the antecedent, 37, 70;
  see also counterfactual conditionals,
  logic of
strict conditionals, 33
Strong Centring, 30, 126, 190
structural equations; *see* equations
sufficient reasons, 9
sufficient sets of events; *see* events, sufficient and
  minimally sufficient sets of
supervenience, 3
  nomological, 17–18, 19, 80–82
  of mental properties; *see* physicalism, non-
  reductive; dualism, naturalistic; dualism,
  super-nomological

of symmetry properties, 15–16, 62
strong, 15–16, 19, 62–63, 64, 66, 82, 112,
  158
Swanson, Eric, 74, 139

token events; *see* events
token identity theory; *see* events, identity
  between mental and physical ones
transference; *see* causation, and transference;
  double prevention
transitivity
  of causation, 77–78, 107, 195
  of conditionals, 34–37, 83, 117; *see also*
  counterfactual conditionals, logic of
tropes, 24–25, 91
tropomyosin; *see* muscle contraction
type causation; *see* causation, relata of
types vs tropes; *see* tropes

variables, 74, 101, 112, 117, 119, 122, 134, 136, 144,
  147; *see also* causal models; causation, relata
  of; equations, structural
  binary vs multi-valued, 101, 105, 106, 110, 112,
  126, 129, 134, 135, 143–145
  default vs deviant values, 121, 122, 123, 124,
  126, 132; *see also* networks, self-contained
  endogenous vs exogenous, 102, 110, 129, 142,
  145, 146, 147
  necessary connections between values, 141–143,
  144, 145; *see also* causal models,
  appropriateness
  networks of; *see* networks
vectors, 7
Vetter, Barbara, 58
vital spirits, 6, 7

Woodward, James, 99, 135, 147–148, 149, 150

Yablo, Stephen, 193

Zhong, Lei, 75–80, *79*
zombies, 11, 20, 90

CPSIA information can be obtained
at www.ICGtesting.com
Printed in the USA
LVHW031835101219
640069LV00013B/657/P